THE BOOK OF
JEREMIAH
I Set Before You the Way

By

Kurt Kennedy, M(BS), D.Min.

Copyright © 2015 Kurt Kennedy

All rights reserved

All scripture references are from the King James Bible

Requests for copies or information should be addressed to:

kennedykt@yahoo.com

ISBN: 978-0692467039

True Word Press

I would like to thank Brother John Knowles who went home with the Lord before this book could be completed. He dedicated many hours to reading and revising this work.

And thank you also to Amador and Candida Pangilinan for proofreading help and insight. I appreciate your help and fellowship in the Lord.

CONTENTS

PREFACE 11

CHAPTER ONE
The Call of Jeremiah 13

CHAPTER TWO
The God Israel Had Forsaken 22

CHAPTER THREE
Return Thou Backsliding Israel 30

CHAPTER FOUR
Judgment from the North 37

CHAPTER FIVE
No Truth, No Pardon 46

CHAPTER SIX
Sound the Alarm 54

CHAPTER SEVEN
The Den of Robbers 61

CHAPTER EIGHT
The Harvest is Past, Summer is Ended And We Are Not Saved..................70

CHAPTER NINE
Glory in the LORD 76

CHAPTER TEN
But the LORD is the True God......................83

CHAPTER ELEVEN
Remember our Covenant................................88

CHAPTER TWELVE
The Prosperity of the Wicked 93

CHAPTER THIRTEEN
A Linen Girdle 98

CHAPTER FOURTEEN
Drought and False Prophets 103

CHAPTER FIFTEEN
A Response to Jeremiah................................110

CHAPTER SIXTEEN
That They Might Know, that My Name is the LORD 117

CHAPTER SEVENTEEN
Remember the Sabbath and Keep it 122

CHAPTER EIGHTEEN
The Potter's House 128

CHAPTER NINETEEN
A Pronouncement of Coming Evil 133

CHAPTER TWENTY
Pashur and Jeremiah's Persecution 138

CHAPTER TWENTY-ONE
Zedekiah's Inquiry 143

CHAPTER TWENTY-TWO
The Curse on Jeconiah 147

CHAPTER TWENTY-THREE
The Righteous Branch 153

CHAPTER TWENTY-FOUR
The Two Baskets of Figs 161

CHAPTER TWENTY-FIVE
Prophetic Pronouncements on Two
World Empires 164

CHAPTER TWENTY-SIX
Jeremiah's Close Call 173

CHAPTER TWENTY-SEVEN
Submit 179

CHAPTER TWENTY-EIGHT
Confronting a False Prophet 184

CHAPTER TWENTY-NINE
Writing Letters 188

CHAPTER THIRTY
In the Latter Days Ye Shall Consider It 196

CHAPTER THIRTY-ONE
A New Covenant 204

CHAPTER THIRTY-TWO
A Promise to Return 217

CHAPTER THIRTY-THREE
Confirmation of the Faithfulness 227

CHAPTER THIRTY-FOUR
Proclaiming Liberty 234

CHAPTER THIRTY-FIVE
The House of Jonadab 240

CHAPTER THIRTY-SIX
A Roll of a Book..................................244

CHAPTER THIRTY-SEVEN
Jeremiah's Imprisonment............................252

CHAPTER THIRTY-EIGHT
Rescued From the Mire..............................257

CHAPTER THIRTY-NINE
The Fall of Jerusalem..............................264

CHAPTER FORTY
Governor Gedalilah.................................272

CHAPTER FORTY-ONE
Murder of Gedalilah................................277

CHAPTER FORTY-TWO
The Rebellion of the Remnant (Part One)......282

CHAPTER FORTY-THREE
The Rebellion of the Remnant (Part Two)......287

CHAPTER FORTY-FOUR
Rebellion of the Remnant (Part Three)...........290

CHAPTER FORTY-FIVE
The Word of God to Baruch........................297

OVERVIEW:
CHAPTERS FORTY-SIX THROUGH FIFTY-ONE
The Judgment on the Gentile 299

CHAPTER FORTY-SIX
Egypt 302

CHAPTER FORTY-SEVEN
The Philistines 307

CHAPTER FORTY-EIGHT
Moab 309

CHAPTER FORTY-NINE
Ammonites, Edom, Damascus, Kedar and Hazor, Elam 317

CHAPTERS FIFTY AND FIFTY-ONE
Judgment on Babylon 325

CHAPTER FIFTY-TWO
Historical fall of Jerusalem 347

CONCLUSION 355

Bibliography 357

PREFACE

The book of Jeremiah is a book of prophecy. Jeremiah is called to "speak" against all the wickedness and apostasy of his nation. Because of this God is bring judgment from other nations against them just as He had done to the Northern Tribes years earlier. The nation that God uses as his rod to punish Judah are the Babylonians who have risen on the scene as the next world power in that region. This is the prevailing event throughout the entire book of Jeremiah. Jeremiah is contemporary with Daniel and Ezekiel. Jeremiah prophecies however are not referring to just the historical events surround the sieges on Jerusalem but also future events of the whole Nation of Israel.

The book of Jeremiah covers the span of the last five kings of Judah (Josiah, Jehoahaz, Jehoiakim, Jehoiachin and Zedekiah). It is during these kings that Babylon comes against Jerusalem in three historical sieges. In the first siege under the reign of Jehoiakim the prophet Daniel is carried away into the palaces of Babylon. The second siege under the reign of Jehoiachin Ezekiel is taken into captivity to the agricultural area of Babylon and the final siege under

King Zedekiah in which the city is destroyed and by a strange turn of events Jeremiah is taken into Egypt. Jeremiah's ministry is unique in that he is called to tell his people that they should yield to the coming Gentile powers invading the land. In other words judgment is unavoidable (II Chron. 36:16).

The book of Jeremiah is not chronological so we will handle each chapter as a "stand alone" chapter unless context demands otherwise.

Lastly Jeremiah is a very passionate man, which can be seen in the book of Laminations and the autobiography portions of Jeremiah as well as Jeremiah's responses to both the LORD and his people. He was raised up under the godly King Josiah, both starting their ministries at a relatively young ages (Josiah 8 years old and Jeremiah but a "child" 1:6).

CHAPTER ONE
The Call of Jeremiah

The words of Jeremiah the son of Hilkiah, of the priests that were in Anathoth in the land of Benjamin: To whom the word of the LORD came in the days of Josiah the son of Amon king of Judah, in the thirteenth year of his reign. It came also in the days of Jehoiakim the son of Josiah king of Judah, unto the end of the eleventh year of Zedekiah the son of Josiah king of Judah, unto the carrying away of Jerusalem captive in the fifth month. Then the word of the LORD came unto me, saying, Before I formed thee in the belly I knew thee; and before thou camest forth out of the womb I sanctified thee, and I ordained thee a prophet unto the nations. Then said I, Ah, Lord GOD! behold, I cannot speak: for I am a child. (Jeremiah 1:1-6)

Jeremiah the Son of Hilkiah (1): Jeremiah's father Hilkiah the priest is the one under the good king Josiah that found the book of the Law (II Kings 22:8).

Anathoth is the home town of Jeremiah in the land of Benjamin. The inhabitance of Jeremiah's hometown plot to kill Jeremiah for his prophesying as a result Jeremiah will pronounce curse from the LORD upon the inhabitance of Anathoth for their treatment of Jeremiah (Jer. 11:21-23). The land of Benjamin is the other tribe that makes up the southern kingdom loyal to the Davidic line.

The Days of Jeremiah - The Historical Background (2-6):

To understand Jeremiah and his writings we need to consider the historical events surrounding his ministry.

Prior to the time of Jeremiah the whole house of Israel was divided into two Kingdoms; Israel to the north *(Northern Kingdom known as Israel)* and Judah to the south *(Southern Kingdom known as Judah)*. This was a direct result of the judgment of God against their idolatry.

The Northern Kingdoms were taken into captivity by the Assyrian armies which conquered all the way to the walls of Jerusalem. God however defeated the Assyrian army in a night. (2 Kings 19: 32-35).

Judah, the Southern Kingdom existed for some time following the fall of the Northern Kingdom. They however were steep in idolatrous practices and apart from King Josiah they all "did evil in the sight of the LORD". God therefore condemned them to be taken captive by the surrounding nation just as the

Northern Tribes has been sometime earlier. It was during this time that God's prophets are preaching, warning the leadership in various ways what judgment is coming and how to escape that coming judgment.

There was a host of prophets and prophetess in Judah at this time. Daniel, Ezekiel as were all contemporaries to Jeremiah. Daniel was deported as a teenager in the first siege against Jerusalem; Ezekiel was taken in the second siege and then Jeremiah.

The Kings of Judah and Influence of the Surrounding Nations During the Time of Jeremiah: Jeremiah was a prophet during the time of the last five Kings of Judah (Gedaliah follows but is placed as governor only for a short time before he is murdered). They are recorded in II Kings chapter 22 – 25 as well as II Chronicles chapter 34 – 36.

<u>**Josiah:**</u> (2 Kings 22:1 – 23:30; 2 Chron. 34:1-35:27) Josiah reigned from about 639 – 609 B.C. Josiah did that which was right in the eyes of the LORD (2 Chron. 34:2 cf. 2 Kings 22:2). After about the 10th year of the reign of Josiah, Jeremiah is called, Josiah would be about 20 at this time. Assyria had been so strong that they had taken the Northern Kingdom captive. The previous kings introduced increasing amounts of Assyrian elements in their worship, namely idolatry. Josiah takes charge as king and God calls him to undertake reforms. God is also raising the strength of

the Babylonians to the south, who are putting pressure on Assyria, giving Judah more freedom from Assyria. With problems between Assyria and Babylon there is more opportunity for Judah to get rid of some of these Assyrian practices. It is also during this time that Hilkiah finds the Book of the Law in the house of the LORD (2 Kings 22:8 cf. 2 Chron. 34:14). Out of the reforms of Josiah came Daniel (taken in the first deportation) and Ezekiel (taken in the second deportation).

It is under this background that Jeremiah is emerging as a prophet. The reforms of Josiah do not take hold. Throughout the book of Jeremiah we have the constant condemnation of the sins of Judah and that God is using the rising power of the Babylonians to be His rod of correction.

Jehoahaz: (II Kings 23:31-34 cf. II Chron. 36:1-4) Son of Josiah king of Judah, he reigned only 3 years before Pharaohnechoh king of Egypt came and took him away to Egypt where he died. Jehoahaz was an evil ruler doing that which was evil in the sight of the LORD (II Kings 23:32).

Jehoiakim: (II Kings 23:34-24:6 cf. II Chron. 36:4-8) At the age of 25 Jehoiakim reigned for 11 years. Original name Eliakim son of Josiah had his name changed to Jehoiakim by Pharaohnechoh. **It was during his reigns that Nebuchadnezzar king of Babylon invades the city (The First Siege)** taking away all the vessels of the temple. Daniel was taken under this siege as well. Jehoiakim was an evil ruler and opposing Jeremiah and his call to reforms on every hand even to the point of burning the prophecies of Jeremiah (36:20-26). Jehoiakim is responsible for widespread idolatry (Jer. 22:13-19). It was during the reign of Jehoiakim that Jeremiah suffers great persecution (26:20-23). Jeremiah warned Jehoiakim that God was rising up Babylon to judge Judah. Jehoiakim however rebels and seeks alliance with Egypt. This however was futile for at the battle of Carchemish Babylon defeats Pharaohnechoh and invades Jerusalem. It is at this time that Nebuchadnezzar places Jehoiachin in office.

Jehoiachin: (II Kings 24:7-16 cf. II Chron. 36:9-10) Jehoiachin reigned only 3 month in Jerusalem before **Nebuchadnezzar lays siege to Jerusalem a second time.** Jehoiachin did evil in the sight of the LORD. Jehoiachin appears as Jeconiah and Coniah (Jer. 22:24, 28; 24:1). It was upon Jehoiachin that God curses the blood line of the Davidic throne (Jer. 22:24-30). During this second siege on Jerusalem the temple items are taken into captivity with the nobles. Ezekiel as well is taken into captivity at this time. During the reign of Evil-merodach king of Babylon Jehoiachin is released from prison and is elevated in the realm of the Babylonians (II Kings 25:27-30).

Zedekiah: (II Kings 24:17 – 25:7 cf. II Chron. 36:10-13) Zedekiah begin to reign during the second siege on Jerusalem following the capture of Jehoiachin. Originally named Mattaniah he had his name changed by Nebuchadnezzar to Zedekiah (II Kings 24;17). Zedekiah was 21 years old when he began to reign and he reigned 11 years in Jerusalem. Zedekiah did that which was evil in the sight of the LORD. Chronicles mentions specifically that Zedekiah did not listen to the words of Jeremiah (II Chron. 36:12). **Zedekiah falls during the third and final siege on Jerusalem** in which the city is destroyed and the temple burned and the people ravished (II Chron. 36:16-19).

Jeremiah prophesies that Babylon is God's rod of judgment and that if they want to live they need to succumb to Babylon and go into captivity, however false prophets in the land are prophesying on the contrary that the yoke of Babylon will not prevail and even that Jehoiachin will be released (Jer. 28-29). Zedekiah listens to the false prophets and rebels against the king of Babylon which leads to the final siege and subsequent fall of Jerusalem. It is during this siege that Zedekiah tries to escape by fleeing the city only to be overtaken at the town of Riblah where he watches his sons be slain before his eyes are taken out and himself deported to Babylon (II Kings 25:4-7).

But the LORD said unto me, Say not, I am a child: for thou shalt go to all that I shall send thee, and whatsoever I command thee thou shalt speak. Be not afraid of their faces: for I am with thee to deliver thee, saith the LORD. Then the LORD put forth his hand, and touched my mouth. And the LORD said unto me, Behold, I have put my words in thy mouth. See, I have this day set thee over the nations and over the kingdoms, to root out, and to pull down, and to destroy, and to throw down, to build, and to plant. Moreover the word of the LORD came unto me, saying, Jeremiah, what seest thou? And I said, I see a rod of an almond tree. Then said the LORD unto me, Thou hast well seen: for I will hasten my word to perform it. And the word of the LORD came unto me the second time, saying, What seest thou? And I said, I see a seething pot; and the face thereof is toward the north. Then the LORD said unto me, Out of the north an evil shall break forth upon all the inhabitants of the land. For, lo, I will call all the families of the kingdoms of the north, saith the LORD; and they shall come, and they shall set every one his throne at the entering of the gates of Jerusalem, and against all the walls thereof round about, and against all the cities of Judah. And I will utter my judgments against them touching all their wickedness, who have forsaken me, and have burned incense unto other gods, and worshipped the works of their own hands. Thou therefore gird up thy loins, and arise, and speak unto them all that I command thee: be not dismayed at their faces, lest

I confound thee before them. For, behold, I have made thee this day a defenced city, and an iron pillar, and brasen walls against the whole land, against the kings of Judah, against the princes thereof, against the priests thereof, and against the people of the land. And they shall fight against thee; but they shall not prevail against thee; for I am with thee, saith the LORD, to deliver thee. (Jeremiah 1:7-19)

The Call of Jeremiah (7-10): Jeremiah's ministry is a speaking ministry (7). What he is to speak is judgment is coming, thus you have the visions of the almond tree and the seething pot that follow. You will notice the similarity in the call of God here and that of Amos (7:10-17), Isaiah (6:1-6) and Ezekiel (1:1-26). Also see II Peter 1:20, 21.

The Rod of an Almond Tree (11-12): The almond tree blooms in winter (January) and is the first tree to blossom and the last tree to bear fruit. It could be that Jeremiah is shown a "rod" of an almond tree because God is going to correct his children (Proverbs 22:15; 23:13; Rev. 12:5).

The Seething Pot (13-16): The LORD communicates to Jeremiah a second time showing him a seething pot facing the north. The pot is seething, boiling or bubbling. The interpretation of the vision is given, out of the north an evil will break forth (bubbling, heating up) upon the land of Jerusalem for their idolatry and wickedness (14-16). The armies from the north are the Babylonians, who are coming against the land and the people. They come from the north, even though geographically they are west of Jerusalem. This is due to the fact that there is a desert directly west of Jerusalem, therefore when invaders come into the land they come from the north.

Jeremiah's Call to Be Strong (17-19): Jeremiahs ministry is not an easy one as is seen by the words the LORD uses, "gird up thy loins" and "be not dismayed at their faces". However, God is going to strengthen him for the task at hand, thus you have Jeremiah likened to a "defenced city", iron pillar" and a "brazen walls" (18). All these strong against an attacker, this is what God is going to do for Jeremiah, make him that strong tower.

Jeremiah's ministry is against all the corruptness of Judah. The widespread apostasy is seen on those Jeremiah is to speak, "the whole land", "kings of Judah" the "princes" the "priests" and the "people of the land". (Cf. Isaiah 1:4-6)

CHAPTER TWO
The God Israel Had Forsaken

Moreover the word of the LORD came to me, saying, Go and cry in the ears of Jerusalem, saying, Thus saith the LORD; I remember thee, the kindness of thy youth, the love of thine espousals, when thou wentest after me in the wilderness, in a land that was not sown. Israel was holiness unto the LORD, and the firstfruits of his increase: all that devour him shall offend; evil shall come upon them, saith the LORD. Hear ye the word of the LORD, O house of Jacob, and all the families of the house of Israel: (Jeremiah 2:1-4)

What the Nation Was to God (1-4): The relationship between God and the Nation of Israel is that of a marriage relationship (Ezek. 16:6-14; Jer. 31:32). Thus, as Israel begins to turn to other gods, God looks at Israel being that unfaithful wife (20, Ezek. 16:32-34). [1]

---

[1] The book of Hosea covers this issue in great detail; Hosea himself is called to be a living example of Israel and their relationship to the LORD.

Thus saith the LORD, What iniquity have your fathers found in me, that they are gone far from me, and have walked after vanity, and are become vain? Neither said they, Where is the LORD that brought us up out of the land of Egypt, that led us through the wilderness, through a land of deserts and of pits, through a land of drought, and of the shadow of death, through a land that no man passed through, and where no man dwelt? And I brought you into a plentiful country, to eat the fruit thereof and the goodness thereof; but when ye entered, ye defiled my land, and made mine heritage an abomination. The priests said not, Where is the LORD? and they that handle the law knew me not: the pastors also transgressed against me, and the prophets prophesied by Baal, and walked after things that do not profit. (Jeremiah 2:5-8)

The Marriage Relationship Breakdown (5-8): God defends His righteousness in their marriage relationship, He is not to blame. Notice God explains how it was Israel herself that moved from Him and turned to other gods, "What iniquity have your fathers found in me" says the LORD (vs. 5). The LORD was the one that brought them out of the land of Egypt and through the wilderness into a plentiful country. God was faithful in providing and caring for His bride. However what did Israel do? "But when they entered, ye defiled my land and made mine heritage an abomination" (7). The priest did not call upon the LORD and the pastors and prophets prophesied by Baal (8).

Wherefore I will yet plead with you, saith the LORD, and with your children's children will I plead. For pass over the isles of Chittim, and see; and send unto Kedar, and consider diligently, and see if there be such a thing. Hath a nation changed their gods, which are yet no gods? but my people have changed their glory for that which doth not profit. Be astonished, O ye heavens, at this, and be horribly afraid, be ye very desolate, saith the LORD. For my people have committed two evils; they have forsaken me the fountain of living waters, and hewed them out cisterns, broken cisterns, that can hold no water. (Jeremiah 2:9-13)

Two Evils (9-13): God is asking all the land *(from shore to shore concept is used in verse 10)* if anyone has ever seen such a thing as a people trading their glorious relationship to the God of the heavens for gods that are no gods profitable for nothing *(cisterns, broken cisterns that can hold no water)*. It would be evil enough for God's people to have forsaken their God but they turned to other gods. They added insult to injury.

Is Israel a servant? is he a homeborn slave? why is he spoiled? The young lions roared upon him, and

yelled, and they made his land waste: his cities are burned without inhabitant. (Jeremiah 2:14-15)

What became of the Northern Kingdom (14-15): The Northern tribes were conquered by Assyria and took them slaves (vs. 14). Not all Israel however went into slavery some stayed in the land and intermarried with the Assyrians that were transplanted into the land; they became the Samaritans, the mixed race of both Assyria and Israel. [2]

Also the children of Noph and Tahapanes have broken the crown of thy head. Hast thou not procured this unto thyself, in that thou hast forsaken the LORD thy God, when he led thee by the way? And now what hast thou to do in the way of Egypt, to drink the waters of Sihor? or what hast thou to do in the way of Assyria, to drink the waters of the river? Thine own wickedness shall correct thee, and thy backslidings shall reprove thee: know therefore and see that it is an evil thing and bitter, that thou hast forsaken the LORD thy God, and that my fear is not in thee, saith the Lord GOD of hosts. (Jeremiah 2:16-19)

---

[2] It is interesting that in this chapter God is called the "fountain of living waters" (13) a chapter that is dealing with the Samaritan people and it is a Samaritan woman by a well that our Lord presents to her the "living water" (John 4:7-10).

Relationships with Egypt (16-19): Judah is being reminded of their past and how the Northern tribes became captives to the nations around them; starting back when God first brought them out of Egypt "and led thee by the way". The land of Noph and Tahapanes are places of Egypt God is asking what are you doing making alliances with Egypt the very ones I took you out from (18-19), thus you have Israel drinking from the river Sihor which is the Nile (18-19).

For of old time I have broken thy yoke, and burst thy bands; and thou saidst, I will not transgress; when upon every high hill and under every green tree thou wanderest, playing the harlot. Yet I had planted thee a noble vine, wholly a right seed: how then art thou turned into the degenerate plant of a strange vine unto me? For though thou wash thee with nitre, and take thee much soap, yet thine iniquity is marked before me, saith the Lord GOD. How canst thou say, I am not polluted, I have not gone after Baalim? see thy way in the valley, know what thou hast done: thou art a swift dromedary traversing her ways; A wild ass used to the wilderness, that snuffeth up the wind at her pleasure; in her occasion who can turn her away? all they that seek her will not weary themselves; in her month they shall find her. Withhold thy foot from being unshod, and thy throat from thirst: but thou saidst, There is no hope: no; for I have loved strangers, and after them will I go. As the thief is ashamed when he is found, so is the house of Israel ashamed; they, their kings, their princes, and their priests, and their prophets, Saying to a stock, Thou art my father; and to a stone, Thou hast brought me forth: for they have turned their back unto me, and not their face: but in the time of their trouble they will say, Arise, and save us. But where are thy gods that thou hast made thee? let them arise, if they can save thee in the time of thy trouble: for according to the number of thy cities are thy gods, O Judah. Wherefore will ye plead with me? ye all have transgressed against me, saith the LORD. In vain have I smitten your children; they received no correction: your own sword hath devoured your prophets, like a destroying lion. (Jeremiah 2:20-30)

Israel the Unfaithful Wife (20-30): Every time the Nation had transgressed the LORD they cried out to God saying, "I will not transgress" however they "played the harlot" (20). Throughout the prophets the wording is that of the Nation being an unfaithful wife in her relationship to the LORD. Thus throughout the prophets many illustrations are employed to bring this reality to light. Israel is likened to a wild camel (dromedary is an Arabian camel) seeking a mate during the time of heat (23-24).

Israel is repentant only when she is found out by the LORD, i.e. she is told of judgment coming because of her actions (26). Then when she is "found out" she cries unto the LORD for deliverance, however the

LORD says in stern rebuke, "but where are thy gods that thou hast made thee? Let them arise, if they can save thee in the time of thy trouble" (28). God afflicted the children of Israel trying to get them to turn back to Himself; however they are as their children who "received no correction" (29-30).

O generation, see ye the word of the LORD. Have I been a wilderness unto Israel? a land of darkness? wherefore say my people, We are lords; we will come no more unto thee? Can a maid forget her ornaments, or a bride her attire? yet my people have forgotten me days without number. Why trimmest thou thy way to seek love? therefore hast thou also taught the wicked ones thy ways. Also in thy skirts is found the blood of the souls of the poor innocents: I have not found it by secret search, but upon all these. Yet thou sayest, Because I am innocent, surely his anger shall turn from me. Behold, I will plead with thee, because thou sayest, I have not sinned. Why gaddest thou about so much to change thy way? thou also shalt be ashamed of Egypt, as thou wast ashamed of Assyria. Yea, thou shalt go forth from him, and thine hands upon thine head: for the LORD hath rejected thy confidences, and thou shalt not prosper in them. (Jeremiah 2:31-37)

Trusting in Alliances (31-37): The LORD likens Himself to the ornaments of adornments that a bride would wear about her neck (31-32). This is what God was to be to Israel, however "my people have forgotten Me days without number". Israel had forgotten the LORD so long ago that time no longer mattered.

Again Israel is likened to that unfaithful bride who "trimmest"[3] herself for all the other nations about her. Judah would change her God and change her ways for alliances. However all Judah's political compromising to please the nations around her only puts her to shame, "Thou also shalt be ashamed of Egypt as thou wast ashamed of Assyria" (33-37).

---

[3] Trimmest as in the trim of a dress or other clothing is the more ornate part of the garment usually of lace or ribbons. So Israel trimmed or decked herself to please the surrounding heathen nations to her folly Ezekiel 23:40.

CHAPTER THREE
Return Thou Backsliding Israel

They say, If a man put away his wife, and she go from him, and become another man's, shall he return unto her again? shall not that land be greatly polluted? but thou hast played the harlot with many lovers; yet return again to me, saith the LORD. Lift up thine eyes unto the high places, and see where thou hast not been lien with. In the ways hast thou sat for them, as the Arabian in the wilderness; and thou hast polluted the land with thy whoredoms and with thy wickedness. Therefore the showers have been withholden, and there hath been no latter rain; and thou hadst a whore's forehead, thou refusedst to be ashamed. Wilt thou not from this time cry unto me, My father, thou art the guide of my youth? Will he reserve his anger for ever? will he keep it to the end? Behold, thou hast spoken and done evil things as thou couldest. (Jeremiah 3:1-5)

Israel the Unfaithful Wife (1-5): The Law forbade a man to remarry someone whom he has divorced (Deut. 24:1-4). However in these passages God is over-riding this Law, desiring her (Israel) to come back. There were always exceptions to the Laws;[4] like the case with Ruth who was a Moabite which the Law deemed unlawful for a Jew to marry (Deut. 23:3). However she ends up in the lineage of Christ through Boaz (Matt. 1:5). Throughout our studies we will see that God not only desires to still be faithful to Israel but He will perform the doing of it (Jer. 31:31).

The LORD said also unto me in the days of Josiah the king, Hast thou seen that which backsliding Israel hath done? she is gone up upon every high mountain and under every green tree, and there hath played the harlot. And I said after she had done all these things, Turn thou unto me. But she returned not. And her treacherous sister Judah saw it. And I saw, when for all the causes whereby backsliding Israel committed adultery I had put her away, and given her a bill of divorce; yet her treacherous sister Judah feared not, but went and played the harlot also. And it came to pass through the lightness of her whoredom, that she defiled the land, and committed adultery with stones and with stocks. And yet for all this her treacherous sister Judah hath not turned unto me with her whole heart, but feignedly, saith the LORD. And the LORD said unto me, The backsliding Israel hath

---

[4] See Matthew 9:13

justified herself more than treacherous Judah. (Jeremiah 3:6-11)

Two Backsliding Sisters (6-11): In this section Israel and Judah are likened to two adulterous sisters. The Northern Tribes, known as Israel are mentioned first (vss. 6-7). They were the first to be taken away by the Assyrian armies (II Kings 17 – 18:25). Israel was also the first to rebel against the LORD under Jeroboam (I Kings 12:26-33). Israel's ultimate destruction and carrying away into the Assyrian empire was a direct result of their unfaithfulness to God in idolatrous practices (vs. 6 cf. II Kings 18:12). Yet in all this God was and is willing to take her back into the covenant relationship (vs. 7).

Judah with its capital at Jerusalem is still standing during this chapter, Josiah being the first of the last five kings of Judah (vs. 6). However Judah herself is following in her sisters footsteps of idolatry (vss. 7-9). Judah did not fear the judgment of the LORD that fell upon Israel, but rather committed even more atrocities than her sister nation (vss. 10-11).

Go and proclaim these words toward the north, and say, Return, thou backsliding Israel, saith the LORD; and I will not cause mine anger to fall upon you: for I am merciful, saith the LORD, and I will not keep anger for ever. Only acknowledge thine iniquity, that thou hast transgressed against the

LORD thy God, and hast scattered thy ways to the strangers under every green tree, and ye have not obeyed my voice, saith the LORD. Turn, O backsliding children, saith the LORD; for I am married unto you: and I will take you one of a city, and two of a family, and I will bring you to Zion: And I will give you pastors according to mine heart, which shall feed you with knowledge and understanding. And it shall come to pass, when ye be multiplied and increased in the land, in those days, saith the LORD, they shall say no more, The ark of the covenant of the LORD: neither shall it come to mind: neither shall they remember it; neither shall they visit it; neither shall that be done any more. At that time they shall call Jerusalem the throne of the LORD; and all the nations shall be gathered unto it, to the name of the LORD, to Jerusalem: neither shall they walk any more after the imagination of their evil heart. In those days the house of Judah shall walk with the house of Israel, and they shall come together out of the land of the north to the land that I have given for an inheritance unto your fathers. But I said, How shall I put thee among the children, and give thee a pleasant land, a goodly heritage of the hosts of nations? and I said, Thou shalt call me, My father; and shalt not turn away from me. (Jeremiah 3:12-19)

The Restoration of the Two Sisters (12-19): God now calls the Northern Tribes to "return" unto God from their 'backsliding" and "acknowledge" their iniquity and He will "bring you to Zion". When the LORD does this He will establish His nation with pastors that will feed their people with knowledge and understanding[5].

In verse sixteen it is interesting that the Ark of the Covenant is mentioned. The Ark of the Covenant was a coffin shaped box that held inside the Ten Commandments, Arron's Rod that Budded and a pot of Manna. The lid is never mentioned but is rather the Mercy Seat where the blood was to be placed during the Day of Atonement. It is also the place that the Lord's glory resided until it's departing from Solomon's Temple. This verse seems to be stating that the ark will not have a place in the future kingdom to come. The reason for this could be that in the Millennial Temple described in Ezekiel chapters 44 through 48 no ark is mentioned in connection with this future Temple.

So then in the future reestablishment of the kingdom, Jerusalem will be called the "throne of the LORD" (17). Notice it is the "**throne** of the LORD". Ezekiel describes the glory of the LORD returning into the future Temple of the LORD (Ezekiel 43:1-9). What is interesting about that description is that the Glory of

---

[5] When our LORD was here on earth offering this very kingdom to Israel, the state of Israel's religious leaders was that of "blind leaders of the blind" teaching as the doctrines of God the commandments of men (Matthew 15). Therefore our LORD begins to give the disciples right knowledge and understanding, thus they would be those pastors with knowledge and understanding once the kingdom was established. Thus, our LORD tells Peter to "feed my sheep" (John 21:16, 17).

the LORD returns according to the vision Ezekiel had by the river Chebar (Ezekiel 1). And it is in this vision we see the **throne** of God which is the same **throne** that comes down to the Temple when the Glory of the LORD departs (Ezekiel chapters 8-11). In this description the Glory of the LORD is mentioned as coming off the Mercy Seat, which was between the Cherubim (Ezekiel 10:3, 4) and when the Glory of the LORD returns the throne of God comes down and resides in the Temple (Ezekiel 43:1-9), but no Ark of the Covenant is mentioned. So then it could be that in the Millennial temple there will be the throne of God but no Ark of the Covenant.

In those days (the future kingdom) Israel will be one nation again (18). Ezekiel 37 covers this as well.

Once God establishes Israel in their land under the Headship of the LORD, He will be called "My Father" i.e. the two sisters (6-11) will be back under the Headship of the Father (see Luke 15).

Surely as a wife treacherously departeth from her husband, so have ye dealt treacherously with me, O house of Israel, saith the LORD. A voice was heard upon the high places, weeping and supplications of the children of Israel: for they have perverted their way, and they have forgotten the LORD their God. Return, ye backsliding children, and I will heal your backslidings. Behold, we come unto thee; for thou art the LORD our God. Truly in vain is

salvation hoped for from the hills, and from the multitude of mountains: truly in the LORD our God is the salvation of Israel. For shame hath devoured the labour of our fathers from our youth; their flocks and their herds, their sons and their daughters. We lie down in our shame, and our confusion covereth us: for we have sinned against the LORD our God, we and our fathers, from our youth even unto this day, and have not obeyed the voice of the LORD our God. (Jeremiah 3:20-25)

The Hope of Israel (20-25): The LORD graciously offers Israel an open door to return onto Him, remind His nation that the idols they worship upon every high hill and on every mountain cannot save them; for the LORD is the salvation of Israel! (23). Note as well in this section the nation is likened to a wife moved from her husband (20, 21).

CHAPTER FOUR
Judgment from the North

If thou wilt return, O Israel, saith the LORD, return unto me: and if thou wilt put away thine abominations out of my sight, then shalt thou not remove. And thou shalt swear, The LORD liveth, in truth, in judgment, and in righteousness; and the nations shall bless themselves in him, and in him shall they glory. (Jeremiah 4:1-2)

A Continual Call to Return (1-2): Once again in these verses we see the continual call to return back to the LORD. The whole of the ministry of the prophets is to get the nations to turn back to the LORD. Thus the call here and throughout the book of Jeremiah is the call to repent of their ways, return unto the LORD that lives; then shall the nations bless themselves in Him and in Him shall they glory.

For thus saith the LORD to the men of Judah and Jerusalem, Break up your fallow ground, and sow

not among thorns. Circumcise yourselves to the LORD, and take away the foreskins of your heart, ye men of Judah and inhabitants of Jerusalem: lest my fury come forth like fire, and burn that none can quench it, because of the evil of your doings. (Jeremiah 4:3-4)

A Heart Issue (3-4): The LORD is calling Judah and Jerusalem to soften their heart and turn it back to the LORD by using to analogies, one of agriculture and the other of physiology. First God calls them to break up the fallow ground of their heart. No farmer will sow seed on ground that is not plowed. The ground must be first softened to be able to receive the seed. So the LORD calls Judah to soften their heart so growth and blessing can take place in the nation. Next the LORD tells Judah and the people of Jerusalem to circumcise their heart. The call to the nation is to separate themselves to the LORD and cast off that which is hindering them from following their GOD. The idea is along the lines of David after he sinned who said, "Create in me a clean heart": this is the idea here (Deut. 10:16, 30:6; Ezek. 11:19, 36:26).

Declare ye in Judah, and publish in Jerusalem; and say, Blow ye the trumpet in the land: cry, gather together, and say, Assemble yourselves, and let us go into the defenced cities. Set up the standard toward Zion: retire, stay not: for I will bring evil from the north, and a great destruction. The lion is come up from his thicket, and the destroyer of the Gentiles is on his way; he is gone forth from his place to make thy land desolate; and thy cities shall be laid waste, without an inhabitant. For this gird you with sackcloth, lament and howl: for the fierce anger of the LORD is not turned back from us. And it shall come to pass at that day, saith the LORD, that the heart of the king shall perish, and the heart of the princes; and the priests shall be astonished, and the prophets shall wonder. (Jeremiah 4:5-9)

The Lion Has Arisen (5-9): Judah and Jerusalem do not heed the warnings to turn their heart back to the LORD and as such judgment is coming. Thus they are told to sound the alarm and retreat back into their defensed cities (5). This judgment is Babylon who comes from the north (Jer. 25:9). Babylon is likened to a lion (see Daniel 7) for its ferociousness by which it will treat God's people. He is called the "destroyer of the Gentiles" for it is Babylon's destruction of Jerusalem that will mark the beginning of the times of the Gentiles (Luke 21:24). Notice in verse nine that the "heart" of the leadership will be astonished, wonder and perish because they chose not to "break up" and "circumcise" their hearts (4,5).

Then said I, Ah, Lord GOD! surely thou hast greatly deceived this people and Jerusalem, saying, Ye shall have peace; whereas the sword reacheth unto the soul. (Jeremiah 4:10)

A False Prediction of Peace (10): It would seem from this verse that Jeremiah is accusing God of predicting peace to the people, however Jeremiah never prophesied peace, and our LORD did only if the people repented, which they did not. This verse should be interpreted in the light of Jeremiah 14:13.

At that time shall it be said to this people and to Jerusalem, A dry wind of the high places in the wilderness toward the daughter of my people, not to fan, nor to cleanse, Even a full wind from those places shall come unto me: now also will I give sentence against them. Behold, he shall come up as clouds, and his chariots shall be as a whirlwind: his horses are swifter than eagles. Woe unto us! for we are spoiled. (Jeremiah 4:11-13)

The Winds of Change (11-13): The judgment of Babylon from the north is likened in these verses to a wind. This wind is not a refreshing cool wind to fan one's self with or to cleanse the earth with its cool breeze but rather a dry wind, a full wind of judgment. Thus Babylon will come up from the north as "clouds" and with chariots as a "whirlwind" and whose horses are swifter than "eagles"[6] (13 cf. Lam.

---

[6] Babylon is the lion with eagle's wings as in Daniel chapter 7 and as is displayed throughout the Babylonian artifacts. The prophetic significance can be seen in Revelation 12:14.

4:19). The end result of the Babylonian invasion is the people of God are the spoils of war (13).

O Jerusalem, wash thine heart from wickedness, that thou mayest be saved. How long shall thy vain thoughts lodge within thee? For a voice declareth from Dan, and publisheth affliction from mount Ephraim. Make ye mention to the nations; behold, publish against Jerusalem, that watchers come from a far country, and give out their voice against the cities of Judah. As keepers of a field, are they against her round about; because she hath been rebellious against me, saith the LORD. Thy way and thy doings have procured these things unto thee; this is thy wickedness, because it is bitter, because it reacheth unto thine heart. (Jeremiah 4:14-18)

Listen to the Warnings (14-18): Judah and Jerusalem are being warned to listen to the affliction that came from the Northern Tribes[7] when they chose not to "cleanse their heart from wickedness". And now Judah and Jerusalem have "procured" the same judgment unto themselves. Once again it is the issue of the heart (14, 18).

---

[7] Dan to Ephraim, Dan being the most extreme points of Israel, thus from Dan to Ephraim is the whole of the Northern Tribes.

My bowels, my bowels! I am pained at my very heart; my heart maketh a noise in me; I cannot hold my peace, because thou hast heard, O my soul, the sound of the trumpet, the alarm of war. Destruction upon destruction is cried; for the whole land is spoiled: suddenly are my tents spoiled, and my curtains in a moment. How long shall I see the standard, and hear the sound of the trumpet? (Jeremiah 4:19-21)

The Trumpet of Alarm (19-21): Jeremiah is crying out because war has come to the walls of Jerusalem. Jeremiah has heard the trumpet, the alarm of war and cannot contain peace within him but rather his soul cries out "destruction" (19 -20). This is the trumpet of warning of the enemy approaching like in Joel chapter 2.

For my people is foolish, they have not known me; they are sottish children, and they have none understanding: they are wise to do evil, but to do good they have no knowledge. I beheld the earth, and, lo, it was without form, and void; and the heavens, and they had no light. I beheld the mountains, and, lo, they trembled, and all the hills moved lightly. I beheld, and, lo, there was no man, and all the birds of the heavens were fled. I beheld, and, lo, the fruitful place was a wilderness, and all the cities thereof were broken down at the presence of the LORD, and by his fierce anger. For thus hath the LORD said, The whole land shall be desolate; yet will I not make a full end. For this shall the earth mourn, and the heavens above be black: because I have spoken it, I have purposed it, and will not repent, neither will I turn back from it. The whole city shall flee for the noise of the horsemen and bowmen; they shall go into thickets, and climb up upon the rocks: every city shall be forsaken, and not a man dwell therein. (Jeremiah 4:22-29)

The Utter Destruction of Jerusalem (22-29): The children of Israel are wise to do evil (Romans 16:19) and therefore wrath and judgment from God is the only outcome (22). The remaining verses describe the destruction of Jerusalem and the land. Jeremiah paints for us a most horrific depiction of the utter destruction of the land of Jerusalem (23-29). These verses are used to support a pre-adamic earth; however I believe these verses are clearly talking about the total destruction of the land of Jerusalem. Notice Jeremiah talks about beholding how the "fruitful place" became a wilderness no doubt a reference to Jerusalem that fruitful hill (26 cf. Isaiah 5:1). Also "cities" are broken down at the presence of the LORD and His fierce anger (26). And then again in verse 27 "thus hath the LORD said, the whole land shall be desolate" obviously dealing with the whole land of Judah and Jerusalem. It is because of this destruction and the LORD purposing to complete the destruction of the people and the land that the earth mourns and the heavens above are black (The heavens filled with the black smoke of the fires of war). Again in verse 29 Jeremiah tells us that the whole city shall flee for the noise of the horsemen and the bowmen until all men have fled the city that none dwell therein (25 cf. 29).

And when thou art spoiled, what wilt thou do? Though thou clothest thyself with crimson, though thou deckest thee with ornaments of gold, though thou rentest thy face with painting, in vain shalt thou make thyself fair; thy lovers will despise thee, they will seek thy life. For I have heard a voice as of a woman in travail, and the anguish as of her that bringeth forth her first child, the voice of the daughter of Zion, that bewaileth herself, that spreadeth her hands, saying, Woe is me now! for my soul is wearied because of murderers. (Jeremiah 4:30-31)

The Fallacy of Appeasement (30-31): The LORD asks Israel a question, "and when thou art spoiled, what wilt thou do?" This is a rhetorical question, God stating Israel will try to make herself pleasing to her surrounding neighbors but it will be to no avail for these alliances with other nations will only seal her fate (30). Then will she cry out as a woman delivering a child (31).
Though all these passages are dealing with the final destruction of Judah by the invading armies of

Babylon they also have a prophetic significance in the coming destruction of the tribulation period and the Day of the LORD (Ps. 83).

CHAPTER FIVE
No Truth, No Pardon

Run ye to and fro through the streets of Jerusalem, and see now, and know, and seek in the broad places thereof, if ye can find a man, if there be any that executeth judgment, that seeketh the truth; and I will pardon it. And though they say, The LORD liveth; surely they swear falsely. O LORD, are not thine eyes upon the truth? thou hast stricken them, but they have not grieved; thou hast consumed them, but they have refused to receive correction: they have made their faces harder than a rock; they have refused to return. Therefore I said, Surely these are poor; they are foolish: for they know not the way of the LORD, nor the judgment of their God. I will get me unto the great men, and will speak unto them; for they have known the way of the LORD, and the judgment of their God: but these have altogether broken the yoke, and burst the bonds. Wherefore a lion out of the forest shall slay them, and a wolf of the evenings shall spoil them, a leopard shall watch over their cities: every one that goeth out thence shall be torn in pieces: because their transgressions are many, and their backslidings are increased. (Jeremiah 5:1-6)

Seek the Righteous (1-6): Judgment upon Jerusalem is a result of idolatry and the issue mentioned here, unrighteous judgment; a leadership that was ruled by lies. God is sending Jeremiah to see if he can find but one man that executes judgment and seeks after truth and if any are found God will pardon coming judgments (1); he will find none. This is reminiscent of Abraham's plea over Sodom and Gomorrah (Gen. 18:23-33). The people of Jerusalem say the LORD lives but they act as if He does not (2-3). God corrects them with judgments yet they persist in their stubborn rebellion (3 cf. 7:28 cf. Isaiah 48:4). Jeremiah seeks the "great men" of old, the fathers of his people who have known the way of the LORD and the judgment of their God, but these children have broken the godly heritage (5). Therefore God is removing the hedge of protection so that they will be the prey of all the earth[8] (6).

How shall I pardon thee for this? thy children have forsaken me, and sworn by them that are no gods: when I had fed them to the full, they then

---

[8] God had previously warned the Nation way back in Israel's history when God was first bringing them into the promised land that if they did not obey their end of the Law Covenant that various forms of judgments would come upon them as a nation. One of these varying forms of judgments is likened to the things mentioned here (see Lev. 26:21-23).

committed adultery, and assembled themselves by troops in the harlots' houses. They were as fed horses in the morning: every one neighed after his neighbor's wife. Shall I not visit for these things? saith the LORD: and shall not my soul be avenged on such a nation as this? (Jeremiah 5:7-9)

A Life of Ease Leads to Apostasy (7-9): Israel was repeatedly warned that when they came into the Promised Land, a land flowing with milk and honey, which they are not to take those things for granted but keep their heart toward the LORD. However, they did just as the LORD had predicted (Deut. 11:13-16). And in their life of ease they turned unto idols of all kinds (7-8). The end result of all of Israel's apostasy is a nation worthy of the wrath of God[9] (9).

Go ye up upon her walls, and destroy; but make not a full end: take away her battlements; for they are not the LORD'S. For the house of Israel and the house of Judah have dealt very treacherously against me, saith the LORD. They have belied the LORD, and said, It is not he; neither shall evil come upon us; neither shall we see sword nor famine: And the prophets shall become wind, and the word is not in them: thus shall it be done unto them. Wherefore thus saith the LORD God of hosts,

---

[9] What a truth this is, for all of us and nations as well. How many world kingdoms fell because of their overabundance of prosperity? (Prov. 30:8, 9)

Because ye speak this word, behold, I will make my words in thy mouth fire, and this people wood, and it shall devour them. (Jeremiah 5:10-14)

Invaders in the Land (10-14): Israel has reached its end, but not its full end, for the LORD will see to it that Israel will not be utterly annihilated (10). The false prophets in Jerusalem were prophesying that the people will not experience evil, that no famine or sword will come upon them (11-13 cf. 14:13-16). The LORD will make them eat their own words, for Jeremiah's words will be fire and the people the wood and therefore by the words of Jerimiah will the nation be devoured (14).

Lo, I will bring a nation upon you from far, O house of Israel, saith the LORD: it is a mighty nation, it is an ancient nation, a nation whose language thou knowest not, neither understandest what they say. Their quiver is as an open sepulchre, they are all mighty men. And they shall eat up thine harvest, and thy bread, which thy sons and thy daughters should eat: they shall eat up thy flocks and thine herds: they shall eat up thy vines and thy fig trees: they shall impoverish thy fenced cities, wherein thou trustediest, with the sword. Nevertheless in those days, saith the LORD, I will not make a full end with you. (Jeremiah 5:15-18)

The Invaders of Other Tongues: (15-18): The invading army is Babylon from the north. What is interesting is that these invaders are an "ancient nation" and it is Babylon that can trace its origins all the way back to Babel (Gen. 10:10). Babylon is that mother of all things wicked (Rev. 17:5). What is interesting as well is that the "times of the Gentiles" begins with Babylon and ends with Babylon playing a key role in the end times.

Israel will be taken into captivity by those of another tongue, an unknown tongue or foreign language (15). This marks the beginning of the punishment for God's people (Deut. 28:49), the "times of the Gentiles". Isaiah 28:9-13 God tells Israel that He will speak to them through Babylon and other Gentile nations. This is the "stammering lips and another tongue" issue in Isaiah 28:9-13. This is fulfilled once Daniel is in captivity; God gives Daniel the full revelation of Gentile dominion (Daniel 2). The people and the land of Israel will become the spoils of war (17). The LORD ends with the merciful reminder that in all this He will not make a full end, He will not utterly obliterate His people (18).

And it shall come to pass, when ye shall say, Wherefore doeth the LORD our God all these things unto us? then shalt thou answer them, Like as ye have forsaken me, and served strange gods in your land, so shall ye serve strangers in a land that is not yours. Declare this in the house of Jacob, and

publish it in Judah, saying, Hear now this, O foolish people, and without understanding; which have eyes, and see not; which have ears, and hear not: Fear ye not me? saith the LORD: will ye not tremble at my presence, which have placed the sand for the bound of the sea by a perpetual decree, that it cannot pass it: and though the waves thereof toss themselves, yet can they not prevail; though they roar, yet can they not pass over it? But this people hath a revolting and a rebellious heart; they are revolted and gone. Neither say they in their heart, Let us now fear the LORD our God, that giveth rain, both the former and the latter, in his season: he reserveth unto us the appointed weeks of the harvest. Your iniquities have turned away these things, and your sins have withholden good things from you. For among my people are found wicked men: they lay wait, as he that setteth snares; they set a trap, they catch men. (Jeremiah 5:19-26)

Refusing to Listen (19-24): It is an amazing reality that the people of Jerusalem would even say such a thing as "Wherefore doeth the LORD our God all these things unto us?" when they have been repeatedly told. They have had all the prophets; they have seen what has happened to the Northern Tribes and now through prophets like Jeremiah, Daniel and Ezekiel they have been repeatedly warned to turn their heart back to the LORD. However, Judah is a people "without understanding" a people which, "have eyes and see not; which have ears and hear not" (21). They are a deaf and blind people[10] (Isaiah 6:9 cf. Matt. 13:11-23).

The LORD asks, "Fear ye not me? Will ye not tremble at my presence?" Israel had gotten to the place that they did not fear the LORD; the very one that set the bounds of the waters and though the waves roar against the sands the waves will not prevail against the perpetual decree that it cannot pass (22).

Your iniquities have turned away these things, and your sins have withholden good things from you. For among my people are found wicked men: they lay wait, as he that setteth snares; they set a trap, they catch men. As a cage is full of birds, so are their houses full of deceit: therefore they are become great, and waxen rich. They are waxen fat, they shine: yea, they overpass the deeds of the wicked: they judge not the cause, the cause of the fatherless, yet they prosper; and the right of the needy do they not judge. Shall I not visit for these things? saith the LORD: shall not my soul be avenged on such a nation as this? (Jeremiah 5:25-29)

Unjust Leadership (25-29): The LORD of heaven is withholding good things from Israel because their

---

[10] It is interesting to note that Zedekiah is the last of the kings of Judah and is taken away captive blinded (2 Kings 25:70). Then at the stoning of Stephen Israel as a nation is blinded (Rom. 11:7 cf. 2 Cor. 3:14). And in the future the nation will have the vail taken away and be exhorted to "... hear what the Spirit saith unto the churches..." (Revelation 2-3).

leadership is withholding good things and right judgment from the people. The people are rich by means of corruption, lies and deceit (26-27). In judgment they overlook the deeds of the wicked and judge not the cause of the fatherless and the needy all the while they wallow in prosperity (27-28 cf. James 1:27).

A wonderful and horrible thing is committed in the land; the prophets prophesy falsely, and the priests bear rule by their means; and my people love to have it so: and what will ye do in the end thereof? (Jeremiah 5:30-31)

The Love of Lies (30-31): The people love to be told that they will not have judgments laid against them, they love the sound of the false prophets, prophesying peace (Jer. 14:11-16).

CHAPTER SIX
Sound the Alarm

O ye children of Benjamin, gather yourselves to flee out of the midst of Jerusalem, and blow the trumpet in Tekoa, and set up a sign of fire in Bethhaccerem: for evil appeareth out of the north, and great destruction. (Jeremiah 6:1)

Sound the Alarm (1): The children of Benjamin those of the southern tribes, the inhabitants of Jerusalem. The sounding of the trumpet is the sound of an alarm that enemies are spotted coming from the north. The "sign of fire" is the lighting of a bon fire that can be seen from the walls of Jerusalem as a warning to those in Jerusalem that the enemy is on its way. So then, to "blow the trumpet in Tekoa" and "set up a sign of fire in Bethhaccerem" is to warn the inhabitants of coming enemies. Bethhaccerem being the furthest point north of Jerusalem in which the fire would be lit, then in Tekoa the watchmen would see the fire of alarm and would blow the trumpet warning the inhabitants of Jerusalem.

I have likened the daughter of Zion to a comely and delicate woman. The shepherds with their flocks shall come unto her; they shall pitch their tents against her round about; they shall feed everyone in his place. Prepare ye war against her; arise, and let us go up at noon. Woe unto us! for the day goeth away, for the shadows of the evening are stretched out. Arise, and let us go by night, and let us destroy her palaces. (Jeremiah 6:2-5)

A Comely and Delicate Woman (3-5): Jerusalem and the people in it are likened to a comely daughter and the shepherds with their flocks who come to her walls and pitch their tents around her is the Babylonian army. Jeremiah is describing what literally transpired when the armies of Nebuchadnezzar came and lay siege to the city.

For thus hath the LORD of hosts said, Hew ye down trees, and cast a mount against Jerusalem: this is the city to be visited; she is wholly oppression in the midst of her. As a fountain casteth out her waters, so she casteth out her wickedness: violence and spoil is heard in her; before me continually is grief and wounds. Be thou instructed, O Jerusalem, lest my soul depart from thee; lest I make thee desolate, a land not inhabited. (Jeremiah 6:6-8)

Spewing Out Wickedness (6-8): God is calling the armies of Nebuchadnezzar to build bulwarks with the trees, to mount upon the walls of His city (6). The description in verse seven is Israel's wickedness is depicted as a fountain spewing forth wickedness as a fountain that spews forth waters. It could be said as Israel spews out wickedness so God will spew them out of the land!

Thus saith the LORD of hosts, They shall throughly glean the remnant of Israel as a vine: turn back thine hand as a grapegatherer into the baskets. To whom shall I speak, and give warning, that they may hear? behold, their ear is uncircumcised, and they cannot hearken: behold, the word of the LORD is unto them a reproach; they have no delight in it. (Jeremiah 6:9-10)

No Delight in the Word of God (9-10): The LORD is going to allow the remnant in the cities of Jerusalem to be taken so our LORD tells the remnant of Israel to turn back to the LORD "as a grape gatherer into the basket" (9). They will not listen however, for the word of the LORD is unto them as a reproach: they have no delight in it. They would rather hear the words of the false prophets who say Israel will not be judged for their wickedness.

Therefore I am full of the fury of the LORD; I am weary with holding in: I will pour it out upon the children abroad, and upon the assembly of young men together: for even the husband with the wife shall be taken, the aged with him that is full of days. And their houses shall be turned unto others, with their fields and wives together: for I will stretch out my hand upon the inhabitants of the land, saith the LORD. For from the least of them even unto the greatest of them every one is given to covetousness; and from the prophet even unto the priest every one dealeth falsely. They have healed also the hurt of the daughter of my people slightly, saying, Peace, peace; when there is no peace. Were they ashamed when they had committed abomination? nay, they were not at all ashamed, neither could they blush: therefore they shall fall among them that fall: at the time that I visit them they shall be cast down, saith the LORD. Thus saith the LORD, Stand ye in the ways, and see, and ask for the old paths, where is the good way, and walk therein, and ye shall find rest for your souls. But they said, We will not walk therein. Also I set watchmen over you, saying, Hearken to the sound of the trumpet. But they said, We will not hearken. (Jeremiah 6:11-17)

The Fury of the LORD (11-17): Because the people prefer the lies of the false prophets who prophesy peace and because the people say they shall not be held responsible for their wickedness, the LORD will not pour out His fury on the inhabitants of Jerusalem.

Judgment is upon everyone without respect of age or status, from the children to the aged and everyone in between (11-14). And they fell down before their idols so shall they be cast down (15).

The remedy is simply to return unto the "old paths" the "good way" and then they would find rest for their souls (16). They in their stubborn rebellion refuse to heed the warnings, they will not harken (17).

Therefore hear, ye nations, and know, O congregation, what is among them. Hear, O earth: behold, I will bring evil upon this people, even the fruit of their thoughts, because they have not hearkened unto my words, nor to my law, but rejected it. To what purpose cometh there to me incense from Sheba, and the sweet cane from a far country? your burnt offerings are not acceptable, nor your sacrifices sweet unto me. Therefore thus saith the LORD, Behold, I will lay stumblingblocks before this people, and the fathers and the sons together shall fall upon them; the neighbour and his friend shall perish. Thus saith the LORD, Behold, a people cometh from the north country, and a great nation shall be raised from the sides of the earth. They shall lay hold on bow and spear; they are cruel, and have no mercy; their voice roareth like the sea; and they ride upon horses, set in array as men for war against thee, O daughter of Zion. We have heard the fame thereof: our hands wax feeble: anguish hath taken hold of us, and pain, as of a

woman in travail. Go not forth into the field, nor walk by the way; for the sword of the enemy and fear is on every side. (Jeremiah 6:18-25)

The Enemy From the North (18-25): In vain the religious leaders worshiped the LORD in the temple of God (19-20 cf. Isaiah 29:13-15 cf. Matt. 15:8) and therefore the enemy from the north (Babylon) is coming (21-22). Babylon's cruelty and brutality are infamous among the known world (23-24 cf. Ezek. 28:7) which causes the people to tremble with fear (24-25).

O daughter of my people, gird thee with sackcloth, and wallow thyself in ashes: make thee mourning, as for an only son, most bitter lamentation: for the spoiler shall suddenly come upon us. I have set thee for a tower and a fortress among my people, that thou mayest know and try their way. They are all grievous revolters, walking with slanders: they are brass and iron; they are all corrupters. The bellows are burned, the lead is consumed of the fire; the founder melteth in vain: for the wicked are not plucked away. Reprobate silver shall men call them, because the LORD hath rejected them. (Jeremiah 6:26-30)

Lament and Mourn (26-30): In light of what is coming for his people, Jeremiah tells them to "mourn as for an only son, most bitter lamentation". Jeremiah sees the futility of his people repenting and turning back to God for he goes on to say, "They are all grievous revolters, walking with slanders... and the wicked are not plucked away.. Reprobate silver shall men call them, because the LORD hath rejected them." The picture that is given by the word usage is that the inhabitants of Jerusalem are like metals that will be melted down and consumed. This is what the LORD is allowing to happen to Israel, they will be consumed (see Ezek. 22:18-22).

CHAPTER SEVEN
The Den of Robbers

The word that came to Jeremiah from the LORD, saying, Stand in the gate of the LORD'S house, and proclaim there this word, and say, Hear the word of the LORD, all ye of Judah, that enter in at these gates to worship the LORD. Thus saith the LORD of hosts, the God of Israel, Amend your ways and your doings, and I will cause you to dwell in this place. Trust ye not in lying words, saying, The temple of the LORD, The temple of the LORD, The temple of the LORD, are these. For if ye throughly amend your ways and your doings; if ye throughly execute judgment between a man and his neighbour; If ye oppress not the stranger, the fatherless, and the widow, and shed not innocent blood in this place, neither walk after other gods to your hurt: Then will I cause you to dwell in this place, in the land that I gave to your fathers, for ever and ever. (Jeremiah 7:1-7)

The House of Worship (1-7): The Temple at the time of Jeramiah had become nothing more than dead brick and mortar in which corrupt leaders performed religious ceremonies. This is the rebuke throughout this passage. God desires the heart and to worship Him in honesty of heart. Israel believed that because they still had their temple that God was somehow obligated to bless His people regardless of their behavior. However this stern rebuke from Jeremiah says otherwise, "amend your ways and your doings, and I will cause you to dwell in this place" (3). In verse four the people say falsely "The temple of the LORD, The temple of the LORD, The temple of the LORD..." as if the temple in itself holds some kind of supernatural power with God, which is not true for verse five goes on to say, "if ye amend your ways and your doings ... then will I cause you to dwell in this place in the land that I gave to your fathers, for ever and ever" (5 cf. 7).

The amending of their ways would consist of the following list given in verses five through six: If ye thoroughly execute judgment between a man and his neighbor; If you oppress not the stranger, the fatherless and the widow and shed not innocent blood; neither walk after other gods to your hurt. All of which the leadership and people were guilty of.

Behold, ye trust in lying words, that cannot profit. Will ye steal, murder, and commit adultery, and swear falsely, and burn incense unto Baal, and walk after other gods whom ye know not; And come and stand before me in this house, which is called by my

name, and say, We are delivered to do all these abominations? Is this house, which is called by my name, become a den of robbers in your eyes? Behold, even I have seen it, saith the LORD. But go ye now unto my place which was in Shiloh, where I set my name at the first, and see what I did to it for the wickedness of my people Israel. And now, because ye have done all these works, saith the LORD, and I spake unto you, rising up early and speaking, but ye heard not; and I called you, but ye answered not; Therefore will I do unto this house, which is called by my name, wherein ye trust, and unto the place which I gave to you and to your fathers, as I have done to Shiloh. And I will cast you out of my sight, as I have cast out all your brethren, even the whole seed of Ephraim. Therefore pray not thou for this people, neither lift up cry nor prayer for them, neither make intercession to me: for I will not hear thee. (Jeremiah 7:8-16)

As in Shiloh so in Jerusalem (8-16): Shiloh was the first permanent home for the Tabernacle upon the conquest of Canaan (Josh. 18:1). It remained so through the time of the Judges (Judges 18:31). During Samuels early years the Tabernacle was still in Shiloh (I Sam. 1:9, 4:3-4). However, once the Ark is captured by the Philistines (I Sam. 4:11, Ps. 78:60) the Tabernacle at Shiloh ceases to exist and the Ark is kept in Kirjathjearim at the house of Abinadab for 20 years (I Sam. 6:21 – 7:1-2). Upon David ascending to the throne the Ark is brought to Jerusalem at which time Jerusalem becomes the center of worship.

So God in these passages is saying He is going to do to Jerusalem as He did to Shiloh, He is going to allow the place of worship to be destroyed.

Seest thou not what they do in the cities of Judah and in the streets of Jerusalem? The children gather wood, and the fathers kindle the fire, and the women knead their dough, to make cakes to the queen of heaven, and to pour out drink offerings unto other gods, that they may provoke me to anger. Do they provoke me to anger? saith the LORD: do they not provoke themselves to the confusion of their own faces? Therefore thus saith the Lord GOD; Behold, mine anger and my fury shall be poured out upon this place, upon man, and upon beast, and upon the trees of the field, and upon the fruit of the ground; and it shall burn, and shall not be quenched. (Jeremiah 7:17-20)

The Queen of Heaven and Other Gods (17-20): The worship of the Queen of Heaven was a heathen practice that Israel had adopted. Israel being a monotheistic people worshiping only the one true God had taken up the practice of worshiping many gods. The worshiping of the queen of heaven was placed into the very house of God by Manasseh and taking idolatrous worship to the height of apostasy as Jehoiakim introduced it to Judah (2 Kings 21:1-9 cf. 2

Kings 24:3).[11] [12] God's ultimate judgment upon this practice by His people will be judged in the coming Day of the Lord when He comes back in fury (20 cf. Isa. 63:3-6).

Thus saith the LORD of hosts, the God of Israel; Put your burnt offerings unto your sacrifices, and eat flesh. For I spake not unto your fathers, nor commanded them in the day that I brought them out of the land of Egypt, concerning burnt offerings or sacrifices: But this thing commanded I them, saying, Obey my voice, and I will be your God, and ye shall be my people: and walk ye in all the ways that I have commanded you, that it may be well unto you. But they hearkened not, nor inclined their ear, but walked in the counsels and in the imagination of their evil heart, and went backward, and not forward. Since the day that your fathers came forth out of the land of Egypt unto this day I have even sent unto you all my servants the prophets, daily rising up early and sending them: Yet they hearkened not unto me, nor inclined their ear, but hardened their neck: they did worse than their fathers. Therefore thou shalt speak all these words unto them; but they will not hearken to thee: thou

---

[11] What is interesting to note is that Catholicism sees the woman of Revelation 12:1 as Mary and even call her the Queen of Heaven. Yet in this passage the worship of this queen of heaven is sternly rebuked of the LORD.
[12] The worship of gods is strictly forbidden for behind every idol is a devil that receives worship and homage from that act (I Cor. 10:19-22).

shalt also call unto them; but they will not answer thee. But thou shalt say unto them, This is a nation that obeyeth not the voice of the LORD their God, nor receiveth correction: truth is perished, and is cut off from their mouth. (Jeremiah 7:21-28)

To Obey is Better Than Sacrifice (21-28): The LORD surely did communicate unto His people concerning "burnt offerings and sacrifices", but the LORD is saying in verse 22 that He did not communicate to them that those sacrifices and offerings where to supersede listing to and obey the voice of GOD (23). To obey is better than sacrifices Samuel says to Saul, this has always been true and will always be true with God. They were to obey God's voice in doing what He said regarding sacrifices and offerings. However they were not to let those sacrifices and offerings that they performed be a substitute for listening and obeying God.

In verses 24 and 26 we see that they did not obey the voice of the LORD. Though the LORD in His mercy sent the prophets early (right when they started to go astray) they chose not to harken, even unto the very day Jeremiah is speaking to them (27-28).

Cut off thine hair, O Jerusalem, and cast it away, and take up a lamentation on high places; for the LORD hath rejected and forsaken the generation of his wrath. For the children of Judah have done evil

in my sight, saith the LORD: they have set their abominations in the house which is called by my name, to pollute it. And they have built the high places of Tophet, which is in the valley of the son of Hinnom, to burn their sons and their daughters in the fire; which I commanded them not, neither came it into my heart. Therefore, behold, the days come, saith the LORD, that it shall no more be called Tophet, nor the valley of the son of Hinnom, but the valley of slaughter: for they shall bury in Tophet, till there be no place. And the carcases of this people shall be meat for the fowls of the heaven, and for the beasts of the earth; and none shall fray them away. Then will I cause to cease from the cities of Judah, and from the streets of Jerusalem, the voice of mirth, and the voice of gladness, the voice of the bridegroom, and the voice of the bride: for the land shall be desolate. (Jeremiah 7:29-34)

The Valley of Slaughter (29-34): Cut off the hair goes back to the Nazarite vow in which a Nazarite was to grow their hair continually all the time they were consecrated unto the LORD (Num. 6:1-5) if the Nazarite came into contact with a dead body they were to shave their heads (Num. 6:8-9). God is telling Jerusalem that they are going to be a city of dead people, so many that they will not be able to bury them all and Jerusalem will be unclean by the dead bodies; thus "Cut off thine hair, O Jerusalem" (29 cf. 33).

No greater abomination could have been done then to sacrifice one's own children to the fires of heathen gods. Yet this practice is recorded not only here but in multiple other passages in scripture (Lev. 18:21; Deut. 18:10; 2 Kings 16:3, 17:17; Ezek. 20:26, 31 etc.). The Bible states that King Ahaz of Judah, the 12th king from King Solomon, sacrificed his own sons to Molech in his attempt to seek military aid from the pagan god (2 Kings 16:1-3). Tophet means the place of fire and was the location that the heathen god Moloch stood. The valley of the son of Hinnom[13] is a valley (the other is Kidron Valley) surrounding a portion of Old Jerusalem.[14]

---

[13] "Hinnom" in the Hebrew is Gehinnom and in the Greek is "Geheena" which is the Hell of the King James
[14] www.generationword.com/jerusalem101/11-hinnom-valley.html

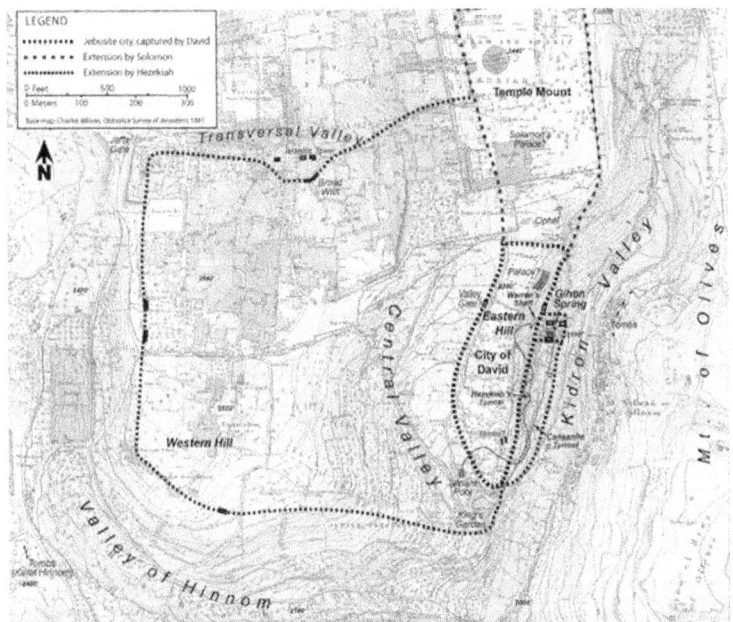

God says that there is going to come a day that the valley of Hinnom will be called the valley of slaughter (32) at which time the birds of the air will consume the bodies of the dead (33). Historically this is referring to the Babylonian invasion but also could have prophetic implications at the Battle of Armageddon.

CHAPTER EIGHT
The Harvest is Past, Summer is Ended And We Are Not Saved

At that time, saith the LORD, they shall bring out the bones of the kings of Judah, and the bones of his princes, and the bones of the priests, and the bones of the prophets, and the bones of the inhabitants of Jerusalem, out of their graves: And they shall spread them before the sun, and the moon, and all the host of heaven, whom they have loved, and whom they have served, and after whom they have walked, and whom they have sought, and whom they have worshipped: they shall not be gathered, nor be buried; they shall be for dung upon the face of the earth. And death shall be chosen rather than life by all the residue of them that remain of this evil family, which remain in all the places whither I have driven them, saith the LORD of hosts. (Jeremiah 8:1-3)

Bring Out the Bones (1-3): Judgment is brought upon all of Jerusalem. In these verses five people groups are mentioned aligning with five adjectives describing their affinity for their false worship: Kings of Judah, Princes, Priests, Prophets and the inhabitants of Jerusalem (2); whom they have loved, served, walked, sought, worshipped (3). The judgment is that the bones of the people will be brought out of the graves and spread before the host of heaven whom they have worshipped; a reference most likely to the sepulchers of the dead being plundered by the Babylonians upon their invasion of the land.

Moreover thou shalt say unto them, Thus saith the LORD; Shall they fall, and not arise? shall he turn away, and not return? Why then is this people of Jerusalem slidden back by a perpetual backsliding? they hold fast deceit, they refuse to return. I hearkened and heard, but they spake not aright: no man repented him of his wickedness, saying, What have I done? every one turned to his course, as the horse rusheth into the battle. Yea, the stork in the heaven knoweth her appointed times; and the turtle and the crane and the swallow observe the time of their coming; but my people know not the judgment of the LORD. How do ye say, We are wise, and the law of the LORD is with us? Lo, certainly in vain made he it; the pen of the scribes is in vain. The wise men are ashamed, they are dismayed and taken: lo, they have rejected the word of the LORD; and what wisdom is in them?

Therefore will I give their wives unto others, and their fields to them that shall inherit them: for everyone from the least even unto the greatest is given to covetousness, from the prophet even unto the priest every one dealeth falsely. For they have healed the hurt of the daughter of my people slightly, saying, Peace, peace; when there is no peace. Were they ashamed when they had committed abomination? nay, they were not at all ashamed, neither could they blush: therefore shall they fall among them that fall: in the time of their visitation they shall be cast down, saith the LORD. (Jeremiah 8:4-12)

The Wisdom of the Wise (4-12): Judah is following the fate of the northern tribes, they have been warned by the LORD by the prophets and yet they refused to receive correction, but rather in the mist of their wickedness they say, "What have I done?" (6). Just as the horse rushes into battle and knows not it's for his life, so Jerusalem is rushing toward destruction (6). How can this be? Jeremiah points out that the birds of heaven know their appointed times but God's people know not the judgment of the LORD (7). The LORD speaking about this to the religious leaders of His day says, "... When it is evening, ye say, It will be fair weather: for the sky is red. And in the morning, It will be foul weather today: for the sky is red and lowring. O ye hypocrites, ye can discern the face of the sky; but can ye not discern the signs of the times?" (Matthew 16:2-3).

Their inability to discern the signs around them are stated plainly, "... they have rejected the word of the LORD ..." (9). Thus, the "pen of the scribes is in vain" (8); they write out the Law of God and know not what it says, they take no heed to it.[15]
Therefore judgment is the only recourse (10). The people preferred to hear the false prophets prophecy peace, however this is only "slightly healing" comfort to the people for destruction is eminent (11).

I will surely consume them, saith the LORD: there shall be no grapes on the vine, nor figs on the fig tree, and the leaf shall fade; and the things that I have given them shall pass away from them. Why do we sit still? assemble yourselves, and let us enter into the defenced cities, and let us be silent there: for the LORD our God hath put us to silence, and given us water of gall to drink, because we have sinned against the LORD. We looked for peace, but no good came; and for a time of health, and behold trouble! The snorting of his horses was heard from Dan: the whole land trembled at the sound of the neighing of his strong ones; for they are come, and have devoured the land, and all that is in it; the city, and those that dwell therein. For, behold, I will send serpents, cockatrices, among you, which will not be charmed, and they shall bite you, saith the LORD. (Jeremiah 8:13-17)

---

[15] The vain religious system of Matthew 15:7-9

The Devouring Army of Babylon (13-17): This is very pictorial if you let the words paint you a picture. The inhabitants are called into the defensed walls (14) for though the false prophets proclaimed peace, and the people sought health, but "trouble" (15). The snorting of the horses was heard and the whole land trembled at the sound of the neighing of the "strong ones" (16); for they are the serpents and the cockatrices that will not be charmed, but bite them. (17).

When I would comfort myself against sorrow, my heart is faint in me. Behold the voice of the cry of the daughter of my people because of them that dwell in a far country: Is not the LORD in Zion? is not her king in her? Why have they provoked me to anger with their graven images, and with strange vanities? The harvest is past, the summer is ended, and we are not saved. For the hurt of the daughter of my people am I hurt; I am black; astonishment hath taken hold on me. Is there no balm in Gilead; is there no physician there? why then is not the health of the daughter of my people recovered? (Jeremiah 8:18-22)

The Harvest is Past, the Summer Ended, and We are Not Saved (18-22): The sorrow in Jeremiah's heart is that the time for his people to be saved from the hands of their enemies is passed. Jeremiah understand that Jerusalem was to be the place that the LORD was to dwell and the king to rule from (19). Those who understand the harvesting of crops is that there was a time to harvest and if you don't harvest by that time it is too late (18-20). The "balm in Gilead" is reference to the pharmaceuticals that Gilead was known for (Gen. 37:25; Jer. 46:11; Ezek. 27:17).

CHAPTER NINE
Glory in the LORD

Oh that my head were waters, and mine eyes a fountain of tears, that I might weep day and night for the slain of the daughter of my people! Oh that I had in the wilderness a lodging place of wayfaring men; that I might leave my people, and go from them! for they be all adulterers, an assembly of treacherous men. And they bend their tongues like their bow for lies: but they are not valiant for the truth upon the earth; for they proceed from evil to evil, and they know not me, saith the LORD. (Jeremiah 9:1-3)

The Weeping Prophet (1-3): Passages like this give Jeremiah the title: "The Weeping Prophet". Jeremiah, at various times, struggles with his calling (Jer. 20:7-9). The language is very pictorial, "they bend their tongues like their bow for lies."

Take ye heed every one of his neighbour, and trust ye not in any brother: for every brother will utterly supplant, and every neighbour will walk with slanders. And they will deceive every one his neighbour, and will not speak the truth: they have taught their tongue to speak lies, and weary themselves to commit iniquity. Thine habitation is in the midst of deceit; through deceit they refuse to know me, saith the LORD. Therefore thus saith the LORD of hosts, Behold, I will melt them, and try them; for how shall I do for the daughter of my people? Their tongue is as an arrow shot out; it speaketh deceit: one speaketh peaceably to his neighbour with his mouth, but in heart he layeth his wait. (Jeremiah 9:4-8)

The Deceitful Neighbor (4-8): All the Law hung on two commandments: Thou shalt love the Lord thy God with all thy heart, and with all thy soul, and with all thy mind and Thou shalt love thy neighbor as thy self (Matt. 22:40, James 2:8). Israel was guilty of both, emphasis here is on the latter.

Shall I not visit them for these things? saith the LORD: shall not my soul be avenged on such a nation as this? For the mountains will I take up a weeping and wailing, and for the habitations of the wilderness a lamentation, because they are burned up, so that none can pass through them; neither can men hear the voice of the cattle; both the fowl of the heavens and the beast are fled; they are gone. And I will make Jerusalem heaps, and a den of dragons;

and I will make the cities of Judah desolate, without an inhabitant. (Jeremiah 9:9-11)

Destruction of Jerusalem (9-11): Theses verses and a host of others foretell of the great suffering the land will endure for Israel's disobedience. Animal life itself will be destroyed from the land of Israel even from within the walls of Jerusalem, the people will suffer from sever starvation.[16]

Who is the wise man, that may understand this? and who is he to whom the mouth of the LORD hath spoken, that he may declare it, for what the land perisheth and is burned up like a wilderness, that none passeth through? And the LORD saith, Because they have forsaken my law which I set before them, and have not obeyed my voice, neither walked therein; But have walked after the imagination of their own heart, and after Baalim, which their fathers taught them: Therefore thus saith the LORD of hosts, the God of Israel; Behold, I will feed them, even this people, with wormwood, and give them water of gall to drink. I will scatter them also among the heathen, whom neither they nor their fathers have known: and I will send a

---

[16] This is why Ezekiel is told to cook his meals with human dung to fuel their fires; for there will be no more animal dung to use for this purpose (Ezek. 4:9-17).

sword after them, till I have consumed them. (Jeremaih 9:12-16)

Scattered in Judgment (12-16): This scattering is the judgment foretold about in Leviticus 26:33. At the tower of Babel the Gentile nations were scattered in judgment (Gen. 11:8, 9). At the destruction of Jerusalem the nation of Israel is scattered among the Gentiles marking the beginning of the Times of the Gentiles (Luke 21:24). There is a return to the land following the 70 year captivity only to be scattered again by Titus in 70 AD. Another re-gathering began in May 14, 1948. I believe that another scattering will take place by the antichrist armies (Dan. 12:7), at which time the LORD will come back and vanquish Israel's enemies and then re-gather the whole nation back into the land (Isaiah 11:10-16). Jeremiah is looking only at the scatter under Babylon at this time but this text does have prophetic utterances. Wormwood and gall are synonymous with bitterness, pain and affliction (Pr. 5:4; Lam. 3:15, Lam. 3:19).

Thus saith the LORD of hosts, Consider ye, and call for the mourning women, that they may come; and send for cunning women, that they may come: And let them make haste, and take up a wailing for us, that our eyes may run down with tears, and our eyelids gush out with waters. For a voice of wailing

is heard out of Zion, How are we spoiled! we are greatly confounded, because we have forsaken the land, because our dwellings have cast us out. Yet hear the word of the LORD, O ye women, and let your ear receive the word of his mouth, and teach your daughters wailing, and every one her neighbour lamentation. For death is come up into our windows, and is entered into our palaces, to cut off the children from without, and the young men from the streets. Speak, Thus saith the LORD, Even the carcases of men shall fall as dung upon the open field, and as the handful after the harvestman, and none shall gather them. (Jer. 9:17-22)

The Spoiling of Jerusalem (17-22): The picture that is described here is that of the mourning women in their homes as the city is invaded. They wail and weep (18) because they are spoiled, their homes in which they sought comfort are casting them out (19-21). The women of the home look out as their young men die in the streets (21-22). This is very visionary of the Babylonian invasion into the city of Jerusalem.

Thus saith the LORD, Let not the wise man glory in his wisdom, neither let the mighty man glory in his might, let not the rich man glory in his riches: But let him that glorieth glory in this, that he understandeth and knoweth me, that I am the LORD which exercise lovingkindness, judgment,

and righteousness, in the earth: for in these things I delight, saith the LORD. (Jeremiah 9:23-24)

Reason to Glory (23-24): The passage lists three positions that (humanly speaking) are glorified positions or the status of individuals: the wise man, mighty man, rich man. All these are warned not to glory in their own state but rather glory in understanding and knowing the LORD. To know the LORD is to understand and know how the LORD exercises lovingkindness, judgment and righteousness in the earth (24). This passage is quoted by Paul in I Corinthians 1:31. The instruction is that God chooses the foolish things to confound the mighty. The foolishness God chooses are things like, Samson defeating the Philistines with a jawbone of an ass, Joshua at the battle of Jericho. Or as Chuck Missler points out, how God would choose the Son of a carpenter crucified on a Roman cross on a hill outside of Jerusalem, that He would be the center of all time, the basis of which all things are judged, the basis by which God will pour His mercy on sinners. [17]

Behold, the days come, saith the LORD, that I will punish all them which are circumcised with the uncircumcised; Egypt, and Judah, and Edom, and the children of Ammon, and Moab, and all that are in the utmost corners, that dwell in the wilderness:

---

[17] The Book of Ezekiel Chuck Missler notes page 58

for all these nations are uncircumcised, and all the house of Israel are uncircumcised in the heart. (Jeremiah 9:25-26)

Judgment by the Uncircumcised (25-26): What is interesting about these verses is that God lays judgment against all the nations; even Judah, and looks at Judah as uncircumcised in heart and therefore is treating them like the heathen nations around them (26).

CHAPTER TEN
But the LORD is the True God

Hear ye the word which the LORD speaketh unto you, O house of Israel: Thus saith the LORD, Learn not the way of the heathen, and be not dismayed at the signs of heaven; for the heathen are dismayed at them. For the customs of the people are vain: for one cutteth a tree out of the forest, the work of the hands of the workman, with the axe. They deck it with silver and with gold; they fasten it with nails and with hammers, that it move not. They are upright as the palm tree, but speak not: they must needs be borne, because they cannot go. Be not afraid of them; for they cannot do evil, neither also is it in them to do good. (Jeremiah 10:1-5)

Learn not the way of the Heathen (1-5): The heathen are dismayed at the signs of the heavens so they go into the woods and cut down a tree, decorate it and pay homage to it asking the idol for good weather, that the idol might provide rain and a fruitful crop.[18] However, it is not in them (idols) to do evil or to do good (5). They are not the God that made the heavens therefore they control them not (11).

Forasmuch as there is none like unto thee, O LORD; thou art great, and thy name is great in might. Who would not fear thee, O King of nations? for to thee doth it appertain: forasmuch as among all the wise men of the nations, and in all their kingdoms, there is none like unto thee. But they are altogether brutish and foolish: the stock is a doctrine of vanities. Silver spread into plates is brought from Tarshish, and gold from Uphaz, the work of the workman, and of the hands of the founder: blue and purple is their clothing: they are all the work of cunning men. But the LORD is the true God, he is the living God, and an everlasting king: at his wrath the earth shall tremble, and the nations shall not be able to abide his indignation. Thus shall ye say unto them, The gods that have not made the heavens and the earth, even they shall perish from the earth, and from under these heavens. He hath made the earth by his power, he hath established the world by his wisdom, and hath stretched out the heavens by his discretion. When he uttereth his voice, there is a

---

[18] Christmas trees are often seen in this passage and while Christmas trees do have their roots in Babylon (page 97 Two Babylons by Alexander Hislop) this passage is clearly referring to idols (14).

multitude of waters in the heavens, and he causeth the vapours to ascend from the ends of the earth; he maketh lightnings with rain, and bringeth forth the wind out of his treasures. Every man is brutish in his knowledge: every founder is confounded by the graven image: for his molten image is falsehood, and there is no breath in them. They are vanity, and the work of errors: in the time of their visitation they shall perish. The portion of Jacob is not like them: for he is the former of all things; and Israel is the rod of his inheritance: The LORD of hosts is his name. (Jeremiah 10:6-16)

The LORD is the True and Living God (6-16): Who would not fear thee, O King of nations? For to thee doth it appertain..." WOW an amazing portion of scriptures, when considered this is what the LORD will establish in the earth (Rev. 19:16). The comparison is made between the previous section (vss. 1-5) and this section. While the idols are unable to do anything regarding the heavens bringing rain and providing sun to yield crops; there is a God who is the maker of the heavens and the earth and as maker He is able to bring rain (12-13). But by the making of their idols they are confounded (14). This section begins with the King over the nations and ends with the LORD of hosts whose inheritance is Israel (16).

Gather up thy wares out of the land, O inhabitant of the fortress. For thus saith the LORD, Behold, I will sling out the inhabitants of the land at this once, and will distress them, that they may find it so. Woe is me for my hurt! my wound is grievous: but I said, Truly this is a grief, and I must bear it. My tabernacle is spoiled, and all my cords are broken: my children are gone forth of me, and they are not: there is none to stretch forth my tent any more, and to set up my curtains. For the pastors are become brutish, and have not sought the LORD: therefore they shall not prosper, and all their flocks shall be scattered. Behold, the noise of the bruit is come, and a great commotion out of the north country, to make the cities of Judah desolate, and a den of dragons. (Jeremiah 10:17-22)

Jerusalem's Grief It Must Bear (17-22): Jeremiah talks as if he is Jerusalem[19], Jerusalem is personified. Likened to man that is hurt and is grievously wounded (19). Whose dwelling is spoiled and his heritage is gone forth from him and broken off so that there is none to carry on his lineage (20). In verses 21 and 22 God is doing what He often does, especially throughout the prophets, He is recompensing onto Israel the very thing they were guilty of: Their pastors were brutish and so God will bring against them a brutish people, Babylon from the north (21-22).

---

[19] Jeremiah was not allowed to marry or have children (Jer. 16:1-2).

O LORD, I know that the way of man is not in himself: it is not in man that walketh to direct his steps. O LORD, correct me, but with judgment; not in thine anger, lest thou bring me to nothing. Pour out thy fury upon the heathen that know thee not, and upon the families that call not on thy name: for they have eaten up Jacob, and devoured him, and consumed him, and have made his habitation desolate. (Jeremiah 10:23-25)

The Plea of Jeremiah for His People (23-25): Jeremiah's plea is for Jerusalem, that God might show judgment but not fury but rather let His fury be poured out on the heathen nations. His plea in some respects is not answered (Jer. 21:5).

CHAPTER ELEVEN
Remember our Covenant

The word that came to Jeremiah from the LORD, saying, Hear ye the words of this covenant, and speak unto the men of Judah, and to the inhabitants of Jerusalem; And say thou unto them, Thus saith the LORD God of Israel; Cursed be the man that obeyeth not the words of this covenant, Which I commanded your fathers in the day that I brought them forth out of the land of Egypt, from the iron furnace, saying, Obey my voice, and do them, according to all which I command you: so shall ye be my people, and I will be your God: That I may perform the oath which I have sworn unto your fathers, to give them a land flowing with milk and honey, as it is this day. Then answered I, and said, So be it, O LORD. Then the LORD said unto me, Proclaim all these words in the cities of Judah, and in the streets of Jerusalem, saying, Hear ye the words of this covenant, and do them. For I earnestly protested unto your fathers in the day that I brought them up out of the land of Egypt, even unto this day, rising early and protesting, saying, Obey my voice.

Yet they obeyed not, nor inclined their ear, but walked everyone in the imagination of their evil heart: therefore I will bring upon them all the words of this covenant, which I commanded them to do; but they did them not. And the LORD said unto me, A conspiracy is found among the men of Judah, and among the inhabitants of Jerusalem. They are turned back to the iniquities of their forefathers, which refused to hear my words; and they went after other gods to serve them: the house of Israel and the house of Judah have broken my covenant which I made with their fathers. Therefore thus saith the LORD, Behold, I will bring evil upon them, which they shall not be able to escape; and though they shall cry unto me, I will not hearken unto them. (Jeremiah 11:1-11)

The Covenant With God (1-11): God's people have reached a pivotal point in their judgment from the LORD. The tribes of Judah are about to be carried away into Babylonian captivity. This captivity was a prophetic chastisement from the LORD for their disobedience to the Law contract given to them at Mount Sinai (Leviticus 26:33, 34). This is why the LORD, in this portion of scripture, is going all the way back to the time he brought them out of Egypt (4). When the LORD brought His people out of Egypt, at Mount Sinai He made a Covenant with them. That Covenant was based upon "obedience" to the words contained in the Covenant (Notice vss. 3, 4, 7, 8). If they "obeyed the voice of the LORD" they would receive the Promised Land and blessings associated with that; however if they did not "obey the voice of the LORD" they would receive the curses associated with disobedience. The "blessings" and the "curses" are summarized in Deuteronomy 28. Thus, the LORD through Jeremiah is basically saying, "you have merited the curses of the Law."

Then shall the cities of Judah and inhabitants of Jerusalem go, and cry unto the gods unto whom they offer incense: but they shall not save them at all in the time of their trouble. For according to the number of thy cities were thy gods, O Judah; and according to the number of the streets of Jerusalem have ye set up altars to that shameful thing, even altars to burn incense unto Baal. Therefore pray not thou for this people, neither lift up a cry or prayer for them: for I will not hear them in the time that they cry unto me for their trouble. What hath my beloved to do in mine house, seeing she hath wrought lewdness with many, and the holy flesh is passed from thee? when thou doest evil, then thou rejoicest. The LORD called thy name, A green olive tree, fair, and of goodly fruit: with the noise of a great tumult he hath kindled fire upon it, and the branches of it are broken. For the LORD of hosts, that planted thee, hath pronounced evil against thee, for the evil of the house of Israel and of the house of Judah, which they have done against themselves to provoke me to anger in offering incense unto Baal. (Jeremiah 11:12-17)

Pronouncement of Evil Upon Both Houses of Israel (12-17): Once again we see the reason for the judgment of the Babylonian captivity was due in part to the idolatry that Israel and Judah partook of; for every city and every street Israel had a god to worship (12-13). Jeremiah was told "pray not thou for this people neither lift up a cry or prayer for them; for I will not hear them ..." (14), the LORD is not going to turn back from this judgment. The evil of both the house of Israel and of Judah have provoked the LORD to anger against Jerusalem the "green olive tree" (16).

And the LORD hath given me knowledge of it, and I know it: then thou shewedst me their doings. But I was like a lamb or an ox that is brought to the slaughter; and I knew not that they had devised devices against me, saying, Let us destroy the tree with the fruit thereof, and let us cut him off from the land of the living, that his name may be no more remembered. But, O LORD of hosts, that judgest righteously, that triest the reins and the heart, let me see thy vengeance on them: for unto thee have I revealed my cause. Therefore thus saith the LORD of the men of Anathoth, that seek thy life, saying, Prophesy not in the name of the LORD, that thou die not by our hand: Therefore thus saith the LORD

of hosts, Behold, I will punish them: the young men shall die by the sword; their sons and their daughters shall die by famine: And there shall be no remnant of them: for I will bring evil upon the men of Anathoth, even the year of their visitation. (Jeremiah 11:18-23)

Silence the Messenger (18-23): Anathoth is the home town of Jeremiah (Jer. 1:1, 29:27; 32:7-9) a city of Benjamin. Jeremiah's own family and home town seek a plot to take Jeremiah's life for his message God gave him to proclaim (vs. 19 cf. Jer. 12:6, 18:18). Thus, a curse is placed upon them (22). What is interesting in this portion of scripture is that Jeremiah is likened to the future Nation of Israel and the plot to exterminate them from the Arab Confederacy (Psalm 83).

CHAPTER TWELVE
The Prosperity of the Wicked

Righteous art thou, O LORD, when I plead with thee: yet let me talk with thee of thy judgments: Wherefore doth the way of the wicked prosper? wherefore are all they happy that deal very treacherously? Thou hast planted them, yea, they have taken root: they grow, yea, they bring forth fruit: thou art near in their mouth, and far from their reins. But thou, O LORD, knowest me: thou hast seen me, and tried mine heart toward thee: pull them out like sheep for the slaughter, and prepare them for the day of slaughter. How long shall the land mourn, and the herbs of every field wither, for the wickedness of them that dwell therein? the beasts are consumed, and the birds; because they said, He shall not see our last end. (Jeremiah 12:1-4)

Jeremiah's Question (1-4): Jeremiah asks a question of God, "Yet let me talk with thee of thy judgments: Wherefore doth the way of the wicked prosper?" (1). This question has been asked many times in the Bible (Job 12; 21; Psalms 37; 49; 73; Hab. 1; Mal. 2:17; 3:15) as it is by many people today. The answer of course is not an easy one to answer, however Asaph comes the closest (Psalm 73).

Jeremiah compares his trials that God has chosen him for to the seeming prosperity of the wicked (3) and so Jeremiah desires that God deal with them like "sheep for the slaughter" (3). For the wicked rulers abuse the land and say, "He (God) shall not see our last end" (4). The wicked prosper because they think God does not see what they do to His inheritance. However what follows in verses 7-13 shows something very contrary.

If thou hast run with the footmen, and they have wearied thee, then how canst thou contend with horses? and if in the land of peace, wherein thou trustedst, they wearied thee, then how wilt thou do in the swelling of Jordan? For even thy brethren, and the house of thy father, even they have dealt treacherously with thee; yea, they have called a multitude after thee: believe them not, though they speak fair words unto thee. (Jeremiah 12:5-6)

The Question to Jeremiah (5-6): The LORD's answer to Jeremiah is not what you might think. Instead of answering the question right away, the LORD focuses on Jeremiah, and basically says, "You are finite" and then gives example of this. You might have been able to run with footmen but how can you contend with horses or the swelling of the Jordan (5). For even those of your own house seek thy life (6). This line of rebuke is similar to God's rebuke of Job (Job 38-41).

I have forsaken mine house, I have left mine heritage; I have given the dearly beloved of my soul into the hand of her enemies. Mine heritage is unto me as a lion in the forest; it crieth out against me: therefore have I hated it. Mine heritage is unto me as a speckled bird, the birds round about are against her; come ye, assemble all the beasts of the field, come to devour. Many pastors have destroyed my vineyard, they have trodden my portion under foot, they have made my pleasant portion a desolate wilderness. They have made it desolate, and being desolate it mourneth unto me; the whole land is made desolate, because no man layeth it to heart. The spoilers are come upon all high places through the wilderness: for the sword of the LORD shall devour from the one end of the land even to the other end of the land: no flesh shall have peace. They have sown wheat, but shall reap thorns: they have put themselves to pain, but shall not profit: and they shall be ashamed of your revenues because of the fierce anger of the LORD. (Jeremiah 12:7-13)

The Answer From the LORD (7-13): The LORD does answer Jeremiah by explaining that He has "forsaken" His own house (7), He has left His "heritage" and has given his "dearly beloved of My soul into the hand of her enemies" (7). God tells Jeremiah what His "heritage" is become unto Him: they are as a lion roaring against Him (8). Israel has become a "speckled bird" and the "birds" (Israel's own people) with the "beasts of the field" (other surrounding nations) devour her (9). The land Israel occupied is the LORDS' and was only loaned out to His people (Lev. 25:18-24). They, however, abused the LORD'S land by not letting it rest (10-13) and therefore the LORD is removing them from His land (vs. 14 cf. Lev. 26:33-35 cf. 2 Chron. 36:21).

Thus saith the LORD against all mine evil neighbours, that touch the inheritance which I have caused my people Israel to inherit; Behold, I will pluck them out of their land, and pluck out the house of Judah from among them. And it shall come to pass, after that I have plucked them out I will return, and have compassion on them, and will bring them again, every man to his heritage, and every man to his land. And it shall come to pass, if they will diligently learn the ways of my people, to swear by my name, The LORD liveth; as they taught my people to swear by Baal; then shall they be built in the midst of my people. But if they will not obey, I will utterly pluck up and destroy that nation, saith the LORD. (Jeremiah 12:14-17)

A Glimmer of Hope with a Stark Warning (14-17): Judah is "plucked" out of their land (vs. 14 cf. 2

Chron. 36:21; 2 Kings 25:8-11). However, the LORD goes on to tell His people that "after that" He will "bring them again, every man to his heritage, and every man to his land (15). This gathering happened during the times of Ezra and Nehemiah (Ezra 1:1; Neh. 7:5-6). The LORD also gives His people a stark warning to "obey" the voice of the LORD in following the words of the Commandments of the LORD (17). The nation does not "obey the voice of the LORD" and in 70 AD the city is once again destroyed and the people are scattered.

CHAPTER THIRTEEN
A Linen Girdle

Thus saith the LORD unto me, Go and get thee a linen girdle, and put it upon thy loins, and put it not in water. So I got a girdle according to the word of the LORD, and put it on my loins. And the word of the LORD came unto me the second time, saying, Take the girdle that thou hast got, which is upon thy loins, and arise, go to Euphrates, and hide it there in a hole of the rock. So I went, and hid it by Euphrates, as the LORD commanded me. And it came to pass after many days, that the LORD said unto me, Arise, go to Euphrates, and take the girdle from thence, which I commanded thee to hide there. Then I went to Euphrates, and digged, and took the girdle from the place where I had hid it: and, behold, the girdle was marred, it was profitable for nothing. Then the word of the LORD came unto me, saying, Thus saith the LORD, After this manner will I mar the pride of Judah, and the great pride of Jerusalem. This evil people, which refuse to hear my words, which walk in the imagination of their heart, and walk after other gods, to serve them, and to worship them, shall even be as this girdle, which is good for nothing. For as the girdle cleaveth to the loins of a man, so have I caused to cleave unto me the whole house of Israel and the whole house of Judah, saith the LORD; that they might be unto me for a people, and for a name, and for a praise, and for a glory: but they would not hear. (Jeremiah 13:1-11)

The Linen Girdle (1-11): Jeremiah is going to do a living object lesson much as Ezekiel has done for the bulk of his ministry. Jeremiah is prophesying following the first siege on Jerusalem and the final siege of which the time was about 19 years; there would therefore have been plenty of time to travel to the Euphrates to fulfill this request of the LORD.

The interpretation to this section is found in verses 8-11. The linen girdle that Jeremiah placed upon his loins (1) represents the close relationship that was and did exist between the LORD and the whole house of Israel and Judah (11). The burying of the girdle in the Euphrates and it being marred (6-7) represents what the nation had become in the sight of the LORD (10) and because of this the LORD is carrying them beyond the Euphrates river to Babylon.

Therefore thou shalt speak unto them this word; Thus saith the LORD God of Israel, Every bottle shall be filled with wine: and they shall say unto thee, Do we not certainly know that every bottle

shall be filled with wine? Then shalt thou say unto them, Thus saith the LORD, Behold, I will fill all the inhabitants of this land, even the kings that sit upon David's throne, and the priests, and the prophets, and all the inhabitants of Jerusalem, with drunkenness. And I will dash them one against another, even the fathers and the sons together, saith the LORD: I will not pity, nor spare, nor have mercy, but destroy them. (Jeremiah 13:12-14)

Drink of the Wrath of God (12-14): Because God's people would not cleave unto the LORD and harken unto the words (11), God is giving them to drink the wine of the wrath of the LORD (13-14). This portion is similar to Jeremiah 25:15-28 and Revelation 16:19.

Hear ye, and give ear; be not proud: for the LORD hath spoken. Give glory to the LORD your God, before he cause darkness, and before your feet stumble upon the dark mountains, and, while ye look for light, he turn it into the shadow of death, and make it gross darkness. But if ye will not hear it, my soul shall weep in secret places for your pride; and mine eye shall weep sore, and run down with tears, because the LORD'S flock is carried away captive. Say unto the king and to the queen, Humble yourselves, sit down: for your principalities shall come down, even the crown of your glory. The cities of the south shall be shut up, and none shall open them: Judah shall be carried away captive all of it, it shall be wholly carried away captive. Lift up your eyes, and behold them that come from the north: where is the flock that was given thee, thy beautiful flock? What wilt thou say when he shall punish thee? for thou hast taught them to be captains, and as chief over thee: shall not sorrows take thee, as a woman in travail? (Jeremiah 13:15-21)

The Prideful People Taken Captive (15-21): In pride the leadership of God's people chose not to listen to the words of the LORD and will suffer the judgment of the Babylonian captivity. The issue in these verses is Judah's pride and specifically their leadership, "Say unto the king and to the queen, humble your selves..." (18). It is God that will "humble" them causing them to be taken into captivity; beholding the eyes of them that "come from the north".

And if thou say in thine heart, Wherefore come these things upon me? For the greatness of thine iniquity are thy skirts discovered, and thy heels made bare. Can the Ethiopian change his skin, or the leopard his spots? then may ye also do good, that are accustomed to do evil. Therefore will I scatter them as the stubble that passeth away by the wind of the wilderness. This is thy lot, the portion of thy measures from me, saith the LORD; because thou hast forgotten me, and trusted in falsehood. Therefore will I discover thy skirts upon thy face,

that thy shame may appear. I have seen thine adulteries, and thy neighings, the lewdness of thy whoredom, and thine abominations on the hills in the fields. Woe unto thee, O Jerusalem! wilt thou not be made clean? when shall it once be? (Jeremiah 13:22-27)

Can an Ethiopian Change His Skin or the Leopard His Spots (22-27): The inhabitants of Jerusalem have corrupted themselves by committing all kinds of immoral acts in the worshipping of their idols and the LORD saw it all (22, 27). The idiom used in verse 23 is basically saying, just as an Ethiopian can't change his color or the leopard his spots so His people cannot cease from doing evil (23). Therefore the LORD is going to "scatter" them as stubble (25). Just as Belshazzar was weighed in the balances and found wanting (Dan. 5:27) so Judah is measured out their portion of the judgment of God (25).

CHAPTER FOURTEEN
Drought and False Prophets

The word of the LORD that came to Jeremiah concerning the dearth. Judah mourneth, and the gates thereof languish; they are black unto the ground; and the cry of Jerusalem is gone up. And their nobles have sent their little ones to the waters: they came to the pits, and found no water; they returned with their vessels empty; they were ashamed and confounded, and covered their heads. Because the ground is chapt, for there was no rain in the earth, the plowmen were ashamed, they covered their heads. Yea, the hind also calved in the field, and forsook it, because there was no grass. And the wild asses did stand in the high places, they snuffed up the wind like dragons; their eyes did fail, because there was no grass. (Jeremiah 14:1-6)

The Judgment of Drought (1-6): God had set before His people, blessings and curses. If they obeyed the voice of the LORD they would receive the blessings if they did not they would receive the curses. One such judgment is the issue of causing the rain to cease bringing drought and famine. Notice these blessings and curses as they pertained to rainfall:

> *The LORD shall open unto thee his good treasure, the heaven to give the rain unto thy land in his season, and to bless all the work of thine hand: and thou shalt lend unto many nations, and thou shalt not borrow.* (Deuteronomy 28:12)

> *And thy heaven that is over thy head shall be brass, and the earth that is under thee shall be iron. The LORD shall make the rain of thy land powder and dust: from heaven shall it come down upon thee, until thou be destroyed.* (Deuteronomy 28:23-24)

Jerusalem, more than other places, was dependent on rain fall. Thus, they were to be dependent on God to sustain them (see. Deut. 11:10-12). Prophetically, drought will be used in the future as a judgment from God brought on by the two witnesses (Revelation 11:2, 3, 6) of which Elijah was a type (I Kings 17 cf. James 5:17).

O LORD, though our iniquities testify against us, do thou it for thy name's sake: for our backslidings are many; we have sinned against thee. O the hope of Israel, the saviour thereof in time of trouble, why shouldest thou be as a stranger in the land, and as a wayfaring man that turneth aside to tarry for a night? Why shouldest thou be as a man astonied, as a mighty man that cannot save? yet thou, O LORD,

art in the midst of us, and we are called by thy name; leave us not. (Jeremiah 14:7-9)

The Prayer of the People (7-9): The people understood that the great famine was a result of their sins, their backsliding. The people look at God as a stranger in the land and as a wayfaring man that turns aside to tarry for the night (7-8). God is unto them as a man astonished even as a mighty man that cannot save (9). All these are similes that tell how the people look at God: He is as a stranger, someone they don't even know. He is as a wayfaring man turned away for the night; God has turned from them. He is as an astonished man, someone who does not respond for reason of shock and last He is as a mighty man that cannot save; though strong and mighty, He is commanded to refrain from helping (8-9).

Thus saith the LORD unto this people, Thus have they loved to wander, they have not refrained their feet, therefore the LORD doth not accept them; he will now remember their iniquity, and visit their sins. Then said the LORD unto me, Pray not for this people for their good. When they fast, I will not hear their cry; and when they offer burnt offering and an oblation, I will not accept them: but I will consume them by the sword, and by the famine, and by the pestilence. (Jeremiah 14:10-12)

Pray Not for this People (10-12): Jeremiah is told to "pray not for this people for their good" (11) for the "LORD doth not accept them" (10), when the people fast, the LORD will not "hear their cry" (12).

When God's people first came into the Promised Land they sent 12 spies into the land of Canaan. Ten brought an evil report and the people listened and refused to take the land God had promised them. However, when judgment was pronounced against the people and the 10 men that brought an evil report died; the people decided to obey the LORD and go up to take the Promised Land, but it was too late. The chance to obey was over, and they were smitten before their enemies (Num. 14).

The lesson to learn from these passages is that there is a season to obey the voice of the LORD. Once that is passed, it is passed and judgment is all that will follow. The LORD says:

God is not a man, that he should lie; neither the son of man, that he should repent: hath he said, and shall he not do it? or hath he spoken, and shall he not make it good? **(Numbers 23:19)**

The idea is that God has an end to His longsuffering and mercy and grace for those who refuse to take heed to the voice of God. And when judgment is set the time for repentance is over. [20]

---

[20] This is the truth of Hebrews 6:1-6. See "The Tribulation Saint" by author.

Then said I, Ah, Lord GOD! behold, the prophets say unto them, Ye shall not see the sword, neither shall ye have famine; but I will give you assured peace in this place. Then the LORD said unto me, The prophets prophesy lies in my name: I sent them not, neither have I commanded them, neither spake unto them: they prophesy unto you a false vision and divination, and a thing of nought, and the deceit of their heart. Therefore thus saith the LORD concerning the prophets that prophesy in my name, and I sent them not, yet they say, Sword and famine shall not be in this land; By sword and famine shall those prophets be consumed. And the people to whom they prophesy shall be cast out in the streets of Jerusalem because of the famine and the sword; and they shall have none to bury them, them, their wives, nor their sons, nor their daughters: for I will pour their wickedness upon them. (Jeremiah 14:13-16)

The False Prophets of Peace (13-16): The false prophets directly opposed God's words, saying, "Ye shall not see the sword neither shall ye have famine: but I will give you assured peace in this place" (13 cf. 12). The LORD however did not call these prophets[21] (14). In verse 15 we see the LORD bringing upon the people the very opposite of what the false prophets said would come, sword, famine (15-16).

---

[21] How to discern a true prophet of the LORD see Jer. 28:9; Isa. 8:20; Num. 12:6.

Therefore thou shalt say this word unto them; Let mine eyes run down with tears night and day, and let them not cease: for the virgin daughter of my people is broken with a great breach, with a very grievous blow. If I go forth into the field, then behold the slain with the sword! and if I enter into the city, then behold them that are sick with famine! yea, both the prophet and the priest go about into a land that they know not. Hast thou utterly rejected Judah? hath thy soul lothed Zion? why hast thou smitten us, and there is no healing for us? we looked for peace, and there is no good; and for the time of healing, and behold trouble! We acknowledge, O LORD, our wickedness, and the iniquity of our fathers: for we have sinned against thee. Do not abhor us, for thy name's sake, do not disgrace the throne of thy glory: remember, break not thy covenant with us. Are there any among the vanities of the Gentiles that can cause rain? or can the heavens give showers? art not thou he, O LORD our God? therefore we will wait upon thee: for thou hast made all these things. (Jeremiah 14:17-22)

The Cry of Jeremiah for the People (17-22): Jeremiah is told to say these words unto the people. As you read over the verses it is as Jeremiah is crying out for the people themselves (the "we" of verse 20 and "us" of verse 21 etc.), as if God is saying, "this is what you should be crying out to Me". Notice that the people cry out to God to remember His covenant with them (21) which is very fitting because it is in response to this covenant that God is pouring out this judgment they are experiencing. They have not obeyed the Law of God and therefore the curses are upon them. What they should be crying out is for God to have mercy upon them; for God to make a "New Covenant" with them, one not based upon their performance, but based on something better (Hebrews 7).

CHAPTER FIFTEEN
A Response to Jeremiah

Then said the LORD unto me, Though Moses and Samuel stood before me, yet my mind could not be toward this people: cast them out of my sight, and let them go forth. (Jeremiah 15:1)

Moses and Samuel (1): This chapter is a response to Jeremiah as a spokesman for God's people, trying to get the people to turn back to God. God is angry in this chapter. He brings up several people that were prominent in Israel. The first two are Moses and Samuel (1) who were intercessors between the people and God. God is saying that even Moses and Samuel could not get the people to turn back to God (Ex. 32:11-14, 30-38; Num. 14:13-23; Deut. 9:18-20, 25-29; I Sam. 7:5-9; 12:19-25 and Ps. 99:6-8). Moses and Samuel petitioned the LORD on behalf of the people but the LORD'S judgment was set.

And it shall come to pass, if they say unto thee, Whither shall we go forth? then thou shalt tell them,

Thus saith the LORD; Such as are for death, to death; and such as are for the sword, to the sword; and such as are for the famine, to the famine; and such as are for the captivity, to the captivity. And I will appoint over them four kinds, saith the LORD: the sword to slay, and the dogs to tear, and the fowls of the heaven, and the beasts of the earth, to devour and destroy. (Jeremiah 15:2-3)

Every Man According to His Deeds (2-3): The idea in these verses is that the people ask what is going to be our end, "Whither shall we go forth?", and the LORD tells them those that are ordained to death, death shall they get, those that are ordained to sword, by the sword they shall die, those ordained to famine, by famine they shall die and those ordained to captivity, into captivity shall they go (2 cf. 43:11). The LORD will appoint over these people: the sword to slay, the dogs to tear, the fowls and the beasts to devour and destroy (3). The remaining will be carried away into captivity (4).

And I will cause them to be removed into all kingdoms of the earth, because of Manasseh the son of Hezekiah king of Judah, for that which he did in Jerusalem. (Jeremiah 15:4)

The Judgment of Manasseh (4): Manasseh was responsible for setting up idols in the very house of the LORD (2 Kings 21:1-9) and because of this great wickedness God pronounces judgment on Jerusalem and Judah (2 Kings 21:10-16) of which at the time of Jeremiah is now transpiring. Manasseh will be forever remembered as the one who sealed the fate of Jerusalem and Judah for his evil deeds (2 Kings 23:26; 24:3)[22].

For who shall have pity upon thee, O Jerusalem? or who shall bemoan thee? or who shall go aside to ask how thou doest? Thou hast forsaken me, saith the LORD, thou art gone backward: therefore will I stretch out my hand against thee, and destroy thee; I am weary with repenting. And I will fan them with a fan in the gates of the land; I will bereave them of children, I will destroy my people, since they return not from their ways. Their widows are increased to me above the sand of the seas: I have brought upon them against the mother of the young men a spoiler at noonday: I have caused him to fall upon it suddenly, and terrors upon the city. She that hath borne seven languisheth: she hath given up the ghost; her sun is gone down while it was yet day: she hath been ashamed and confounded: and the residue of them will I deliver to the sword before their enemies, saith the LORD. (Jeremiah 15:5-9)

---

[22] This is not to overlook how in Babylonian captivity he repented and cried out to God and the LORD harkened unto him and brought him back into the land of Jerusalem (2 Chron. 33:15-20) and restored him to his position and allowed him to do a work for the LORD.

Widows and Mothers (5-9): The coming judgment from the LORD would be likened to separating the chaff from the wheat (5-7). The inhabitants of the city of Jerusalem are the chaff that the wind will drive away (Isaiah 41:15, 16 cf. Matt. 3:12). The wives will become widows as the sand of the sea and the mothers will be bereaved of their children. A woman with seven sons would be considered blessed, however if all die in battle she will languish, it would be as if the day was cut short and the light of her life (given up the ghost) would be gone because the future of the family is gone (8-9).

Woe is me, my mother, that thou hast borne me a man of strife and a man of contention to the whole earth! I have neither lent on usury, nor men have lent to me on usury; yet every one of them doth curse me. The LORD said, Verily it shall be well with thy remnant; verily I will cause the enemy to entreat thee well in the time of evil and in the time of affliction. Shall iron break the northern iron and the steel? Thy substance and thy treasures will I give to the spoil without price, and that for all thy sins, even in all thy borders. And I will make thee to pass with thine enemies into a land which thou knowest not: for a fire is kindled in mine anger, which shall burn upon you. (Jeremiah 15:10-14)

Jeremiah's Lament (10-14): Jeremiah is lamenting over the treatment he was receiving by the hands of the people. He is being treated as a traitor to his own people for the message he is called to proclaim (10). However the LORD promises that Jeremiah will be entreated well in the time of evil and the time of affliction (11)[23]. The message that Jeremiah is called to proclaim, that is causing him such persecution is listed in verses 12-13; which is to say: no one is able to stop the Babylonians from coming against Jerusalem (12) and therefore all the substance and treasures of Babylon will be given into his hand (13).

O LORD, thou knowest: remember me, and visit me, and revenge me of my persecutors; take me not away in thy longsuffering: know that for thy sake I have suffered rebuke. Thy words were found, and I did eat them; and thy word was unto me the joy and rejoicing of mine heart: for I am called by thy name, O LORD God of hosts. I sat not in the assembly of the mockers, nor rejoiced; I sat alone because of thy hand: for thou hast filled me with indignation. Why is my pain perpetual, and my wound incurable, which refuseth to be healed? wilt thou be altogether unto me as a liar, and as waters that fail? (Jeremiah 15:15-18)

The Turmoil in Jeremiah's Heart (15-18): Jeremiah is asking for a reprieve from those who are persecuting him (15). He is arguing on his own behalf why God

---

[23] See Jeremiah 38:28; 39:11-14; 40:1-6

should not only deal with those who are persecuting him, but when judgment does come from God, why it is that he should be spared (16 -17). Jeremiah has digested the words of the LORD and proclaimed them faithfully, just as Ezekiel is told to do (Ezek. 3:1-3)[24]. Jeremiah is upset in these passages even asking God if He is going to be unto him as a "liar" or as "waters that fail" (18).

Therefore thus saith the LORD, If thou return, then will I bring thee again, and thou shalt stand before me: and if thou take forth the precious from the vile, thou shalt be as my mouth: let them return unto thee; but return not thou unto them. And I will make thee unto this people a fenced brasen wall: and they shall fight against thee, but they shall not prevail against thee: for I am with thee to save thee and to deliver thee, saith the LORD. And I will deliver thee out of the hand of the wicked, and I will redeem thee out of the hand of the terrible. (Jeremiah 15:19-21)

God's Response to Jeremiah (19-21): Some commentators look at this as the recommissioning of Jeremiah. It seems Jeremiah was moving away from the LORD in his heart, however, after these verses Jeremiah will complain no more. The LORD assures him that if he returns to the LORD, He will set

---

[24] See also Matt. 4:4

Jeremiah before Him and will continue to be the mouthpiece of God (19). God assures Jeremiah that He will strengthen Jeremiah against the people as a brazen wall so they shall not prevail. Jeremiah is assured from the LORD repeatedly that He will save and deliver Jeremiah out of the hand of the enemies (20-21), which the LORD does.

CHAPTER SIXTEEN
That They Might Know, that My Name is the LORD

The word of the LORD came also unto me, saying, Thou shalt not take thee a wife, neither shalt thou have sons or daughters in this place. For thus saith the LORD concerning the sons and concerning the daughters that are born in this place, and concerning their mothers that bare them, and concerning their fathers that begat them in this land; They shall die of grievous deaths; they shall not be lamented; neither shall they be buried; but they shall be as dung upon the face of the earth: and they shall be consumed by the sword, and by famine; and their carcases shall be meat for the fowls of heaven, and for the beasts of the earth. For thus saith the LORD, Enter not into the house of mourning, neither go to lament nor bemoan them: for I have taken away my peace from this people, saith the LORD, even lovingkindness and mercies. Both the great and the small shall die in this land: they shall not be buried, neither shall men lament for them, nor cut themselves, nor make themselves bald for them: Neither shall men tear themselves for them in mourning, to comfort them for the dead; neither shall men give them the cup of consolation to drink for their father or for their mother. Thou shalt not also go into the house of feasting, to sit with them to eat and to drink. For thus saith the LORD of hosts, the God of Israel; Behold, I will cause to cease out of this place in your eyes, and in your days, the voice of mirth, and the voice of gladness, the voice of the bridegroom, and the voice of the bride. (Jeremiah 16:1-9)

No Comfort, No Mourning (1-9): Once again in these chapters we see both the judgment on Jerusalem and its inhabitants. There will be none that will escape the judgment from the LORD, from the sons and daughters even to the mother and father (3-4). The LORD has removed His peace from the people, "even lovingkindness and mercies" (5). It would seem that the issue of the people mourning by cutting themselves and making themselves bald and tearing themselves is a heathen practice they were performing (6-7 cf. I Kings 18:28). If this is the case, God is saying that you will not perform your heathen practices any more.

And it shall come to pass, when thou shalt shew this people all these words, and they shall say unto thee, Wherefore hath the LORD pronounced all this great evil against us? or what is our iniquity? or what is our sin that we have committed against the LORD our God? Then shalt thou say unto them, Because your fathers have forsaken me, saith the LORD, and have walked after other gods, and have served them, and have worshipped them, and have forsaken me, and have not kept my law; And ye have done worse than your fathers; for, behold, ye walk every one after the imagination of his evil heart, that they may not hearken unto me: Therefore will I cast you out of this land into a land that ye know not, neither ye nor your fathers; and there shall ye serve other gods day and night; where I will not shew you favour. (Jeremiah 16:10-13)

Why the Judgment Against the People of Jerusalem (10-13): We have seen this throughout Jeremiah already; the judgment against them is because of the people's gross idolatry in not keeping with the Laws of God (11). It is a truth contained in scripture and in life experience that each generation will sink deeper into sin than the previous generation if repentance doesn't take place in the heart of the people; thus, "ye have done worse than your fathers" (12).[25]

Therefore, behold, the days come, saith the LORD, that it shall no more be said, The LORD liveth, that

---

[25] Thus, the admonition to "teach them thy sons, and thy sons sons" the Law (Deut. 4:5-9).

brought up the children of Israel out of the land of Egypt; But, The LORD liveth, that brought up the children of Israel from the land of the north, and from all the lands whither he had driven them: and I will bring them again into their land that I gave unto their fathers. Behold, I will send for many fishers, saith the LORD, and they shall fish them; and after will I send for many hunters, and they shall hunt them from every mountain, and from every hill, and out of the holes of the rocks. For mine eyes are upon all their ways: they are not hid from my face, neither is their iniquity hid from mine eyes. And first I will recompense their iniquity and their sin double; because they have defiled my land, they have filled mine inheritance with the carcases of their detestable and abominable things. O LORD, my strength, and my fortress, and my refuge in the day of affliction, the Gentiles shall come unto thee from the ends of the earth, and shall say, Surely our fathers have inherited lies, vanity, and things wherein there is no profit. Shall a man make gods unto himself, and they are no gods? Therefore, behold, I will this once cause them to know, I will cause them to know mine hand and my might; and they shall know that my name is The LORD. (Jeremiah 16:14-21)

A Lesson to Learn, Again (14-21): When the LORD brought His people out of the land of Egypt, He had done so that Israel would know that the LORD, Jehovah was their God and that He alone was the

God of all the earth (Ex. 6:1-8, 9:14 cf. Josh. 2:9-11). Israel's history, however, is a dismal testimony to the reality that they did not appreciate the LORD that liveth (14) and as a result of these perpetual judgments they are going to go into captivity once again and be delivered. This judgment of the Babylonian captivity is so they might learn the lesson that "the LORD liveth" (15) and that He is the God of all the earth. In the latter verses God is promising they will return unto the land He promised them (Ezra 1:1) once their recompense is complete. This happens under Ezra and Nehemiah, but also looks out into the future of a coming deliverance in which all the Gentile world may know that, "my name is The LORD" (17-21).

CHAPTER SEVENTEEN
Remember the Sabbath and Keep it

The sin of Judah is written with a pen of iron, and with the point of a diamond: it is graven upon the table of their heart, and upon the horns of your altars; Whilst their children remember their altars and their groves by the green trees upon the high hills. O my mountain in the field, I will give thy substance and all thy treasures to the spoil, and thy high places for sin, throughout all thy borders. And thou, even thyself, shalt discontinue from thine heritage that I gave thee; and I will cause thee to serve thine enemies in the land which thou knowest not: for ye have kindled a fire in mine anger, which shall burn for ever. (Jeremiah 17:1-4)

A Discontinued Inheritance (1-4): The sin of Judah is forever recorded, for we are reading it today (cf. Job 19:24). This is the idea in these verses, God has written their sins with an iron pen with a diamond point emphasizing the aspect that their sins are not erasable. Their sins are also engraved on their hearts;

thus, the LORD will give them a new heart (Ezek. 36). However, prior to this the LORD will discontinue their inheritance in the land: they're going out of the land (3-4 cf. 2 Chron. 36:21).

Thus saith the LORD; Cursed be the man that trusteth in man, and maketh flesh his arm, and whose heart departeth from the LORD. For he shall be like the heath in the desert, and shall not see when good cometh; but shall inhabit the parched places in the wilderness, in a salt land and not inhabited. Blessed is the man that trusteth in the LORD, and whose hope the LORD is. For he shall be as a tree planted by the waters, and that spreadeth out her roots by the river, and shall not see when heat cometh, but her leaf shall be green; and shall not be careful in the year of drought, neither shall cease from yielding fruit. (Jeremiah 17:5-8)

The Cursed and Blessed Man (5-8): These verses are similar to Psalm 1:3 and may refer to Jehoiakim or Zedekiah who both trusted in making alliances with Egypt rather than trusting in the LORD's provision by yielding to the Chaldean army.

The heart is deceitful above all things, and desperately wicked: who can know it? I the LORD search the heart, I try the reins, even to give every

man according to his ways, and according to the fruit of his doings. As the partridge sitteth on eggs, and hatcheth them not; so he that getteth riches, and not by right, shall leave them in the midst of his days, and at his end shall be a fool. (Jeremiah 17:9-11)

The Deceitful Heart (9-11): The heart of man is deceitful and desperately wicked who can know it? (9) The LORD knows it (10) and it is by the heart that all men will be judged (I Cor. 4:1-5).

A glorious high throne from the beginning is the place of our sanctuary. O LORD, the hope of Israel, all that forsake thee shall be ashamed, and they that depart from me shall be written in the earth, because they have forsaken the LORD, the fountain of living waters. Heal me, O LORD, and I shall be healed; save me, and I shall be saved: for thou art my praise. Behold, they say unto me, Where is the word of the LORD? let it come now. As for me, I have not hastened from being a pastor to follow thee: neither have I desired the woeful day; thou knowest: that which came out of my lips was right before thee. Be not a terror unto me: thou art my hope in the day of evil. Let them be confounded that persecute me, but let not me be confounded: let them be dismayed, but let not me be dismayed: bring upon them the day of evil, and destroy them with double destruction. (Jeremiah 17:12-18)

Written in the Earth (12-18): Those that forsake the LORD shall be written in the earth, verses written in the book of life (Ex. 32:32; Rev. 20:12). They are forsaken because they have rejected the fountain of living waters (13).

Jeremiah is not so, however (15-18), for he has not stopped from following the LORD and the words that proceeded out of his mouth were right (16). Therefore, Jeremiah's plea is for the LORD to judge those wrong doers, but spare him when they are judged (17-18).

Thus said the LORD unto me; Go and stand in the gate of the children of the people, whereby the kings of Judah come in, and by the which they go out, and in all the gates of Jerusalem; And say unto them, Hear ye the word of the LORD, ye kings of Judah, and all Judah, and all the inhabitants of Jerusalem, that enter in by these gates: Thus saith the LORD; Take heed to yourselves, and bear no burden on the sabbath day, nor bring it in by the gates of Jerusalem; Neither carry forth a burden out of your houses on the sabbath day, neither do ye any work, but hallow ye the sabbath day, as I commanded your fathers. But they obeyed not, neither inclined their ear, but made their neck stiff, that they might not hear, nor receive instruction. And it shall come to pass, if ye diligently hearken unto me, saith the LORD, to bring in no burden through the gates of this city on the sabbath day, but hallow the sabbath day, to do no work therein; Then shall there enter into the gates of this city kings and princes sitting upon the throne of David, riding in chariots and on horses, they, and their princes, the men of Judah, and the inhabitants of Jerusalem: and this city shall remain for ever. And they shall come from the cities of Judah, and from the places about Jerusalem, and from the land of Benjamin, and from the plain, and from the mountains, and from the south, bringing burnt offerings, and sacrifices, and meat offerings, and incense, and bringing sacrifices of praise, unto the house of the LORD. But if ye will not hearken unto me to hallow the sabbath day, and not to bear a burden, even entering in at the gates of Jerusalem on the sabbath day; then will I kindle a fire in the gates thereof, and it shall devour the palaces of Jerusalem, and it shall not be quenched. (Jeremiah 17:19-27)

Keep the Sabbath Day (19-27): Jeremiah is to preach before all the gates of the city regarding the Sabbath Day. The Sabbath day was God's day, a day to commemorate God, for it was on the seventh day that God rested (Ex. 20:8-10). The emphasis in these verses is on not bearing burdens through the **GATES** of Jerusalem *(Gates mentioned 7 times in these verses)*, i.e. not working or doing the business of the day with God's people. Thus, from sundown the day before the Sabbath to the day following the Sabbath the gates of the city were to be closed (Neh. 13:19). Nehemiah upon coming out of the Babylonian captivity and reinstituting right worship deals with some that would do this very thing again. They are met with a stern rebuke by Nehemiah (Neh. 13:17-21). The reward for obedience to the Sabbath is that kings and princes and the people of the land would bring burnt offerings and incense and sacrifices of praise, unto the house of the LORD (25-26). This will be literally fulfilled in the Millennium when the LORD fulfills all His promises to the city of Jerusalem and its inhabitants.

CHAPTER EIGHTEEN
The Potter's House

The word which came to Jeremiah from the LORD, saying, Arise, and go down to the potter's house, and there I will cause thee to hear my words. Then I went down to the potter's house, and, behold, he wrought a work on the wheels. And the vessel that he made of clay was marred in the hand of the potter: so he made it again another vessel, as seemed good to the potter to make it. Then the word of the LORD came to me, saying, O house of Israel, cannot I do with you as this potter? saith the LORD. Behold, as the clay is in the potter's hand, so are ye in mine hand, O house of Israel. At what instant I shall speak concerning a nation, and concerning a kingdom, to pluck up, and to pull down, and to destroy it; If that nation, against whom I have pronounced, turn from their evil, I will repent of the evil that I thought to do unto them. And at what instant I shall speak concerning a nation, and concerning a kingdom, to build and to plant it; If it do evil in my sight, that it obey not my voice, then I will repent of the good, wherewith I said I would benefit them. (Jeremiah 18:1-10)

The Potter's House (1-10): Jeremiah is instructed to go down to the potter's house to hear the words of the LORD (1-2). Jeremiah sees a potter make a work on the wheel that is marred in his hands, so he made it again as it seemed good to the potter (4). Then the word of the LORD came to Jeremiah about what he just witnessed (5), saying "O house of Israel, cannot I do with you as this potter? Behold, as the clay is in the potter's hand so are ye in mine hand, O house of Israel" (6).

The interpretation of what Jeremiah saw was that like the clay, Israel had become marred. He, the great Potter, would not mend the nation; but would make a new nation, a new Israel in whom He could put a new spirit, and write His law on their hearts (Jer. 31:31-37). This new nation is what our LORD referred to while He was on earth, addressing the nation of His day (Matthew 21:43). That nation will be the same clay, but re-made "another vessel as seemed good to the potter to make it."

The eternal truth of this passage is that God does not just patch up things that are marred but He makes all things new, from the New Covenant, to the New Heaven and New Earth[26].

---

[26] See Bullinger's work "How to enjoy the Bible" pgs. 307-402

Now therefore go to, speak to the men of Judah, and to the inhabitants of Jerusalem, saying, Thus saith the LORD; Behold, I frame evil against you, and devise a device against you: return ye now every one from his evil way, and make your ways and your doings good. And they said, There is no hope: but we will walk after our own devices, and we will every one do the imagination of his evil heart. Therefore thus saith the LORD; Ask ye now among the heathen, who hath heard such things: the virgin of Israel hath done a very horrible thing. Will a man leave the snow of Lebanon which cometh from the rock of the field? or shall the cold flowing waters that come from another place be forsaken? Because my people hath forgotten me, they have burned incense to vanity, and they have caused them to stumble in their ways from the ancient paths, to walk in paths, in a way not cast up; To make their land desolate, and a perpetual hissing; every one that passeth thereby shall be astonished, and wag his head. I will scatter them as with an east wind before the enemy; I will shew them the back, and not the face, in the day of their calamity. (Jeremiah 18:11-17)

Turn a Back to the People (11-17): We have seen similar passages through Jeremiah. The LORD is commenting; asking how can it be that His people, the virgin of Israel, (13) has chosen to follow after their own evil devises, (12) in turning away from the place of blessing (14) unto idols (15). Therefore, as

Israel has devised evil in their heart (12) so the LORD has devised evil against them (11).

Then said they, Come, and let us devise devices against Jeremiah; for the law shall not perish from the priest, nor counsel from the wise, nor the word from the prophet. Come, and let us smite him with the tongue, and let us not give heed to any of his words. Give heed to me, O LORD, and hearken to the voice of them that contend with me. Shall evil be recompensed for good? for they have digged a pit for my soul. Remember that I stood before thee to speak good for them, and to turn away thy wrath from them. Therefore deliver up their children to the famine, and pour out their blood by the force of the sword; and let their wives be bereaved of their children, and be widows; and let their men be put to death; let their young men be slain by the sword in battle. Let a cry be heard from their houses, when thou shalt bring a troop suddenly upon them: for they have digged a pit to take me, and hid snares for my feet. Yet, LORD, thou knowest all their counsel against me to slay me: forgive not their iniquity, neither blot out their sin from thy sight, but let them be overthrown before thee; deal thus with them in the time of thine anger. (Jeremiah 18:18-23)

The People's Revolt against Jeremiah (18-23): The people cannot fight God so they go after God's mouth-piece, Jeremiah. The people think that by silencing the messenger the message of judgment against Jerusalem will be stopped: however, all this shows is their stiff-necked rebellion to the warnings of the LORD (18). Jeremiah's reference to the pit (20, 21) is telling, because he will be let down into a dungeon by cords (Jer. 38). Jeremiah seeks the judgment of the LORD upon those who seek his life (21-23).

CHAPTER NINETEEN
A Pronouncement of Coming Evil

Thus saith the LORD, Go and get a potter's earthen bottle, and take of the ancients of the people, and of the ancients of the priests; And go forth unto the valley of the son of Hinnom, which is by the entry of the east gate, and proclaim there the words that I shall tell thee, And say, Hear ye the word of the LORD, O kings of Judah, and inhabitants of Jerusalem; Thus saith the LORD of hosts, the God of Israel; Behold, I will bring evil upon this place, the which whosoever heareth, his ears shall tingle. (Jeremiah 19:1-3)

Jeremiah's Pronouncement in the Valley of Hinnom (1-3): This dramatic illustration carried out by Jeremiah before the "ancient of the people and the ancient of the priests" will result in Jeremiah being beaten and spending a night in the stocks. Jeremiah goes down to the potters house and takes an earthen vessel and gathers the ancient of the people and of the priests and goes out unto the Valley of the son of

Hinnom which is by the entering of the east gate and he proclaims judgment on the kings of Judah and the inhabitants of Jerusalem (1-3). The leadership being brought outside the city unto the Valley of Hinnom is purposely done in light of the pronouncement of judgment for their idolatrous practices performed in that valley (see notes on Jeremiah 7:29-34).

Because they have forsaken me, and have estranged this place, and have burned incense in it unto other gods, whom neither they nor their fathers have known, nor the kings of Judah, and have filled this place with the blood of innocents; They have built also the high places of Baal, to burn their sons with fire for burnt offerings unto Baal, which I commanded not, nor spake it, neither came it into my mind: Therefore, behold, the days come, saith the LORD, that this place shall no more be called Tophet, nor The valley of the son of Hinnom, but The valley of slaughter. And I will make void the counsel of Judah and Jerusalem in this place; and I will cause them to fall by the sword before their enemies, and by the hands of them that seek their lives: and their carcases will I give to be meat for the fowls of the heaven, and for the beasts of the earth. And I will make this city desolate, and an hissing; every one that passeth thereby shall be astonished and hiss because of all the plagues thereof. And I will cause them to eat the flesh of their sons and the flesh of their daughters, and they shall eat every one

the flesh of his friend in the siege and straitness, wherewith their enemies, and they that seek their lives, shall straiten them. (Jeremiah 19:4-9)

The Valley of Slaughter (4-9): The LORD through Jeremiah is telling the kings of Judah and the inhabitants of Jerusalem, that the God of Israel is bringing judgment upon these in direct proportion to the evil that they performed for their false gods. As they sacrificed their sons to the fires of Baal in the Valley of Hinnom, at the place of Tophet so God will sacrifice the kings of Judah and the inhabitants of Jerusalem in this very valley; so that the valley will be known as "The Valley of Slaughter" i.e. the slaughter of the inhabitants of Jerusalem (5-6).

The judgment against the people of Jerusalem will be so horrific that those that pass by the city will be "astonished and hiss because of all the plagues" they will encounter (7-8). The LORD will also cause them to "eat the flesh of their sons and the flesh of their daughters, and they shall eat everyone the flesh of his friend" (9). This judgment took place when the siege was laid against the city by Babylon (Lam. 4:10), and is a fulfillment of the prophecy in Leviticus 26:29.

Then shalt thou break the bottle in the sight of the men that go with thee, And shalt say unto them, Thus saith the LORD of hosts; Even so will I break this people and this city, as one breaketh a potter's

vessel, that cannot be made whole again: and they shall bury them in Tophet, till there be no place to bury. Thus will I do unto this place, saith the LORD, and to the inhabitants thereof, and even make this city as Tophet: And the houses of Jerusalem, and the houses of the kings of Judah, shall be defiled as the place of Tophet, because of all the houses upon whose roofs they have burned incense unto all the host of heaven, and have poured out drink offerings unto other gods. (Jeremiah 19:10-13)

Jeremiah's Dramatic Illustration (10-13): Jeremiah is told to break the clay bottle in the sight of the ancients (10). It is this event and what it represents that causes Pashur in the next chapter to have Jeremiah beaten and placed in stocks (20). The breaking of the bottle is representative of God "breaking" the city of Jerusalem and its people (11-12). In verse 11 through 14 the emphasis of bringing the ancients to the valley of Hinnom is seen by the repetition of the word "Tophet" (11, 12, 13, and 14). God will make this city like Tophet (12). As God's people defiled their houses by heathen practices upon their rooftops so God will defile their houses and the inhabitants of the city by the Chaldeans (13).

Then came Jeremiah from Tophet, whither the LORD had sent him to prophesy; and he stood in the court of the LORD'S house; and said to all the people, Thus saith the LORD of hosts, the God of

Israel; Behold, I will bring upon this city and upon all her towns all the evil that I have pronounced against it, because they have hardened their necks, that they might not hear my words. (Jeremiah 19:14-15)

Jeremiah's Pronouncement in the Court of the LORD'S House (14-15): Jeremiah now goes into the court of the LORD'S house to declare the judgment to all the people; the judgment that he had previously told the ancients of the city.

CHAPTER TWENTY
Pashur and Jeremiah's Persecution

Now Pashur the son of Immer the priest, who was also chief governor in the house of the LORD, heard that Jeremiah prophesied these things. Then Pashur smote Jeremiah the prophet, and put him in the stocks that were in the high gate of Benjamin, which was by the house of the LORD. (Jeremiah 20:1-2)

Pashur's Persecution of Jeremiah (1-2): When Jeremiah was in the house of the LORD prophesying of the coming judgment (19:14-15), Pashur heard him (20:1), and smote him and placed him in the stocks that were in the high gate of Benjamin (2).

And it came to pass on the morrow, that Pashur brought forth Jeremiah out of the stocks. Then said Jeremiah unto him, The LORD hath not called thy name Pashur, but Magormissabib. For thus saith the LORD, Behold, I will make thee a terror to thyself, and to all thy friends: and they shall fall by the sword of their enemies, and thine eyes shall behold it: and I will give all Judah into the hand of the king of Babylon, and he shall carry them captive into Babylon, and shall slay them with the sword. Moreover I will deliver all the strength of this city, and all the labours thereof, and all the precious things thereof, and all the treasures of the kings of Judah will I give into the hand of their enemies, which shall spoil them, and take them, and carry them to Babylon. And thou, Pashur, and all that dwell in thine house shall go into captivity: and thou shalt come to Babylon, and there thou shalt die, and shalt be buried there, thou, and all thy friends, to whom thou hast prophesied lies. (Jeremiah 20:3-6)

From Pashur to Magormissabib (3-6): Pashur brings forth Jeremiah from the stocks and the LORD, through Jeremiah tells Pashur, that his name has changed to Magormissabib (3). Magormissabib means terror or terror on every side (4). Then Jeremiah does what he had not done up to this point; Jeremiah names the country that will come from the north, Babylon (4-6). Babylon being mentioned by name in this chapter is telling, for up to this point Jeremiah had only mentioned the enemy from the north (chapters 1-19), however once Jeremiah does the symbolic act of breaking the vessel of clay (chapter 19), he then specifically announces that the terror from the north is Babylon; for from this point on their fate is sealed (4-6). Pashur himself will die in Babylonian captivity (6). Notice that this judgment against Pashur and his friends is because they "prophesied lies" (6), they are those false prophets who predict, peace and safety.

O LORD, thou hast deceived me, and I was deceived: thou art stronger than I, and hast prevailed: I am in derision daily, every one mocketh me. For since I spake, I cried out, I cried violence and spoil; because the word of the LORD was made a reproach unto me, and a derision, daily. Then I said, I will not make mention of him, nor speak any more in his name. But his word was in mine heart as a burning fire shut up in my bones, and I was weary with forbearing, and I could not stay. (Jeremiah 20:7-9)

Jeremiah's Inner Struggle (7-9): In these verses we see Jeremiah's inner struggles with his calling to preach about coming judgment. The reproach from the people and his own countrymen that he has and will encounter has caused him to quit preaching; But notice that once he ate the word of the LORD (15:16), it was burning inside him and he was weary with forbearing, so he had to proclaim it (9). It was more wearisome to not do the calling that God gave him.

For I heard the defaming of many, fear on every side. Report, say they, and we will report it. All my familiars watched for my halting, saying, Peradventure he will be enticed, and we shall prevail against him, and we shall take our revenge on him. But the LORD is with me as a mighty terrible one: therefore my persecutors shall stumble, and they shall not prevail: they shall be greatly ashamed; for they shall not prosper: their everlasting confusion shall never be forgotten. But, O LORD of hosts, that triest the righteous, and seest the reins and the heart, let me see thy vengeance on them: for unto thee have I opened my cause. Sing unto the LORD, praise ye the LORD: for he hath delivered the soul of the poor from the hand of evildoers. (Jeremiah 20:10-13)

Jeremiah Encouraging Himself in the LORD (10-13): These passages show the turmoil that Jeremiah is experiencing. First we see him struggling not to preach the word (7-9), now we see him encouraging himself in the LORD (I Sam. 30:6). He is reminding himself that the LORD is with him (11) and will avenge his enemies (12-13).

Cursed be the day wherein I was born: let not the day wherein my mother bare me be blessed. Cursed be the man who brought tidings to my father, saying, A man child is born unto thee; making him very glad. And let that man be as the cities which the LORD overthrew, and repented not: and let him hear the cry in the morning, and the shouting at noontide; Because he slew me not from the womb; or that my mother might have been my grave, and her womb to be always great with me. Wherefore came I forth out of the womb to see labour and sorrow, that my days should be consumed with shame? (Jeremiah 20:14-18)

Jeremiah Curses His Day (14-18): What a rollercoaster ride of emotions Jeremiah's personal calling and persecution have caused. What we are seeing in this chapter is a real man, not some super human person without fears and doubts, but a man full of human emotion and insecurities. Jeremiah curses his day, much like Job and Elijah (Job 3:1; I Kings 19:1-14). Jeremiah is faithful to his calling however it is not without its doubts and fears all of which the LORD sees and understands.

CHAPTER TWENTY-ONE
Zedekiah's Inquiry

The word which came unto Jeremiah from the LORD, when king Zedekiah sent unto him Pashur the son of Melchiah, and Zephaniah the son of Maaseiah the priest, saying, Inquire, I pray thee, of the LORD for us; for Nebuchadrezzar king of Babylon maketh war against us; if so be that the LORD will deal with us according to all his wondrous works, that he may go up from us. (Jeremiah 21:1-2)

Zedekiah's Inquiry (1-2): As mentioned at the outset of this study, the book of Jeremiah is not chronological. Zedekiah is the last king of Judah, setting the time frame for this chapter. Zedekiah sends Pashur and Zephaniah to Jeremiah to seek what he hopes is favorable prophecy from the LORD concerning the advancing Babylonians. The message from the LORD is not favorable and rather than respond by humbling himself he will rebel sealing his own demise (2 Chron. 36:12-13). The Pashur in this chapter is different than the Pashur in chapter 20 but is the same as in chapter 38. Zephaniah the priest is slain by Nebuchadnezzar at Riblah (Jer. 52:24-27).

Then said Jeremiah unto them, Thus shall ye say to Zedekiah: Thus saith the LORD God of Israel; Behold, I will turn back the weapons of war that are in your hands, wherewith ye fight against the king of Babylon, and against the Chaldeans, which besiege you without the walls, and I will assemble them into the midst of this city. And I myself will fight against you with an outstretched hand and with a strong arm, even in anger, and in fury, and in great wrath. And I will smite the inhabitants of this city, both man and beast: they shall die of a great pestilence. And afterward, saith the LORD, I will deliver Zedekiah king of Judah, and his servants, and the people, and such as are left in this city from the pestilence, from the sword, and from the famine, into the hand of Nebuchadrezzar king of Babylon, and into the hand of their enemies, and into the hand of those that seek their life: and he shall smite them with the edge of the sword; he shall not spare them, neither have pity, nor have mercy. (Jeremiah 21:3-7)

The LORD'S Response from Jeremiah (3-7): The response from the LORD to Zedekiah from Jeremiah is not as the king had hoped for. The LORD is going to see to it that Zedekiah will be forced to withdraw his troops into the walls of Jerusalem (4). Within the walls of the city the outstretched hand and the strong arm of the LORD is going to turn against the inhabitants of the city, smiting it with pestilence (5-6). And those within the city walls that do not die of pestilence, sword or famine will be delivered into the hand of Nebuchadnezzar (7).

And unto this people thou shalt say, Thus saith the LORD; Behold, I set before you the way of life, and the way of death. He that abideth in this city shall die by the sword, and by the famine, and by the pestilence: but he that goeth out, and falleth to the Chaldeans that besiege you, he shall live, and his life shall be unto him for a prey. For I have set my face against this city for evil, and not for good, saith the LORD: it shall be given into the hand of the king of Babylon, and he shall burn it with fire. (Jeremiah 21:8-10)

Surrender and Live (8-10): Jeremiah is telling them if they resist against the Babylonian army you will die, however if you surrender to them you will live. Why is this so?, because the LORD has "set his face against this city for evil and not for good" (10). Because of Jeremiah's prophesying to surrender and live he is labeled a traitor (38:17-18) and is charged with treachery (Chap. 37; 38).

And touching the house of the king of Judah, say, Hear ye the word of the LORD; O house of David, thus saith the LORD; Execute judgment in the morning, and deliver him that is spoiled out of the hand of the oppressor, lest my fury go out like fire, and burn that none can quench it, because of the evil of your doings. Behold, I am against thee, O inhabitant of the valley, and rock of the plain, saith the LORD; which say, Who shall come down against us? or who shall enter into our habitations? But I will punish you according to the fruit of your doings, saith the LORD: and I will kindle a fire in the forest thereof, and it shall devour all things round about it. (Jeremiah 21:11-14)

Judgment Against the House of David (11-14): God had promised David that his descendants would sit on the thrown of David forever (II Sam. 7:12-17). This Covenant was an everlasting covenant (II Sam. 23:1-5). However if the kings of David's lineage did evil, they would be chastened (II Sam. 7:14 cf. Jer. 22:1-9). What the nation is experiencing is the direct result of the kings of David's dynasty being chastised. Zedekiah the last king of Judah is soon taken into captivity.

CHAPTER TWENTY-TWO
The Curse on Jeconiah

Thus saith the LORD; Go down to the house of the king of Judah, and speak there this word, And say, Hear the word of the LORD, O king of Judah, that sittest upon the throne of David, thou, and thy servants, and thy people that enter in by these gates: Thus saith the LORD; Execute ye judgment and righteousness, and deliver the spoiled out of the hand of the oppressor: and do no wrong, do no violence to the stranger, the fatherless, nor the widow, neither shed innocent blood in this place. For if ye do this thing indeed, then shall there enter in by the gates of this house kings sitting upon the throne of David, riding in chariots and on horses, he, and his servants, and his people. But if ye will not hear these words, I swear by myself, saith the LORD, that this house shall become a desolation. For thus saith the LORD unto the king's house of Judah; Thou art Gilead unto me, and the head of Lebanon: yet surely I will make thee a wilderness, and cities which are not inhabited. And I will prepare destroyers against thee, every one with his weapons: and they shall cut down thy choice cedars, and cast them into the fire. And many nations shall pass by this city, and they shall say every man to his neighbour, Wherefore hath the LORD done thus unto this great city? Then they shall answer, Because they have forsaken the covenant of the LORD their God, and worshipped other gods, and served them. (Jeremiah 22:1-9)

The LORD'S Promised Judgment (1-9): Jeremiah speaks to the king of Judah that sits upon the throne (2). The kings of Judah were held accountable for executing proper judgment and righteousness toward the stranger, the fatherless and the widow (3). Theses righteous judgments were according to the covenant that God made with them (9). The LORD offers a severe warning for their disobedience by saying, "I swear by myself, saith the LORD that this house shall become a desolation" (5). Though Jerusalem (the king's house of Judah) is unto the LORD as Gilead and the head of Lebanon,[27] yet the LORD will make it a wilderness (7). He will prepare destroyers against it who will cut down the choice cedars in their war campaigns (7). Once this is accomplished those who passed by will wonder at what the LORD had done to this great city (8-9).

---

[27] Gilead and Lebanon where both made desolate by the Assyrian armies when they invaded the 10 Northern tribes (2 Kings 15:29).

Weep ye not for the dead, neither bemoan him: but weep sore for him that goeth away: for he shall return no more, nor see his native country. For thus saith the LORD touching Shallum the son of Josiah king of Judah, which reigned instead of Josiah his father, which went forth out of this place; He shall not return thither any more: But he shall die in the place whither they have led him captive, and shall see this land no more. (Jeremiah 22:10-12)

Jehoahaz, Son of Josiah (10-12): Shallum is Jehoahaz (I Chron. 3:15) son to Josiah (11). Jehoahaz was deposed in three months and exiled to Egypt by Pharaohnechoh (2 Kings 23:31-34). According to these verses what happened to Jehoahaz was the result of the judgment of God.

Woe unto him that buildeth his house by unrighteousness, and his chambers by wrong; that useth his neighbour's service without wages, and giveth him not for his work; That saith, I will build me a wide house and large chambers, and cutteth him out windows; and it is cieled with cedar, and painted with vermilion. Shalt thou reign, because thou closest thyself in cedar? did not thy father eat and drink, and do judgment and justice, and then it was well with him? He judged the cause of the poor and needy; then it was well with him: was not this to know me? saith the LORD. But thine eyes and thine heart are not but for thy covetousness, and for to shed innocent blood, and for oppression, and for violence, to do it. Therefore thus saith the LORD concerning Jehoiakim the son of Josiah king of Judah; They shall not lament for him, saying, Ah my brother! or, Ah sister! they shall not lament for him, saying, Ah lord! or, Ah his glory! He shall be buried with the burial of an ass, drawn and cast forth beyond the gates of Jerusalem. (Jeremiah 22:13-19)

Jehoiakim, Son of Josiah (13-19): These verses are dealing with Jehoiakim (18). The LORD is rebuking Jehoiakim for building his house using forced labor without wages (13-14). This action was prohibited by the Law (Lev. 19:13; Deut. 24:14-15). Jeremiah points out that Jehoiakim's father, Josiah executed right judgment and justice and then it was well with him (15). He heard the cause of the poor and the needy and because of this he was taken care of by the LORD (16). Jehoiakim however sought riches and wealth on the backs of the people and therefore God judges him (18-19). Jehoiakim dies in the first siege against Jerusalem, though he is bound in fetters for transport to Babylon he ends up being drawn and cast forth beyond the gates of Jerusalem (Jer. 36:30-31; 2 Chron. 36:5-7).

Go up to Lebanon, and cry; and lift up thy voice in Bashan, and cry from the passages: for all thy lovers are destroyed. I spake unto thee in thy prosperity; but thou saidst, I will not hear. This hath been thy

manner from thy youth, that thou obeyedst not my voice. The wind shall eat up all thy pastors, and thy lovers shall go into captivity: surely then shalt thou be ashamed and confounded for all thy wickedness. O inhabitant of Lebanon, that makest thy nest in the cedars, how gracious shalt thou be when pangs come upon thee, the pain as of a woman in travail! As I live, saith the LORD, though Coniah the son of Jehoiakim king of Judah were the signet upon my right hand, yet would I pluck thee thence; And I will give thee into the hand of them that seek thy life, and into the hand of them whose face thou fearest, even into the hand of Nebuchadrezzar king of Babylon, and into the hand of the Chaldeans. And I will cast thee out, and thy mother that bare thee, into another country, where ye were not born; and there shall ye die. But to the land whereunto they desire to return, thither shall they not return. Is this man Coniah a despised broken idol? is he a vessel wherein is no pleasure? wherefore are they cast out, he and his seed, and are cast into a land which they know not? O earth, earth, earth, hear the word of the LORD. Thus saith the LORD, Write ye this man childless, a man that shall not prosper in his days: for no man of his seed shall prosper, sitting upon the throne of David, and ruling any more in Judah. (Jeremiah 22:20-30)

Coniah, Son of Jehoiakim (20-30): Jeremiah is told to go up to Labanon and cry from the passages of Bashan against all thy lovers, Jerusalem (20-23). For

Jerusalem whom they have sought alliances with are going into captivity (22).

The LORD uses the name Coniah (24) in place of Jeconiah removing the reference to God in his name[28] [29]. Coniah is told that he and his seed will be given into the hands of Nebuchadnezzar king of Babylon (25-28) and he will die in captivity (25-27 cf. 2 Kings 24:8-17; Jer. 52:31-34).

The LORD writes, or declares Jeconiah "childless" (30). This is childless only in the sense that none of Jeconiah's seed will sit on the throne of David, a man that shall not prosper (29-30); for Jeconiah does have several sons (2 Chron. 3:17-18)[30]. This is exactly what takes place, for none of his seed ascends to the throne of David. Matthew's genealogy testifies to this fact (Matthew 1:11, 12). Zerubbabel grandson to Jeconiah who comes back into the land following the Babylonian Captivity is only a governor and never sits on the throne and Zedekiah who does sit on the throne is uncle to Jeconiah not a son.

---

[28] "Je" for Jehovah, see Chuck Missler Jeremiah notes 100, 101.

[29] Coniah, Jeconiah and Jehoiachin are all the same person just variant spellings.

[30] Notice that passage even says "seed" in reference to his decedents being taken into captivity (28).

CHAPTER TWENTY-THREE
The Righteous Branch

Woe be unto the pastors that destroy and scatter the sheep of my pasture! saith the LORD. Therefore thus saith the LORD God of Israel against the pastors that feed my people; Ye have scattered my flock, and driven them away, and have not visited them: behold, I will visit upon you the evil of your doings, saith the LORD. And I will gather the remnant of my flock out of all countries whither I have driven them, and will bring them again to their folds; and they shall be fruitful and increase. And I will set up shepherds over them which shall feed them: and they shall fear no more, nor be dismayed, neither shall they be lacking, saith the LORD. Behold, the days come, saith the LORD, that I will raise unto David a righteous Branch, and a King shall reign and prosper, and shall execute judgment and justice in the earth. In his days Judah shall be saved, and Israel shall dwell safely: and this is his name whereby he shall be called, THE LORD OUR RIGHTEOUSNESS. Therefore, behold, the days come, saith the LORD, that they shall no more say,

The LORD liveth, which brought up the children of Israel out of the land of Egypt; But, The LORD liveth, which brought up and which led the seed of the house of Israel out of the north country, and from all countries whither I had driven them; and they shall dwell in their own land. (Jeremiah 23:1-8)

Scatter and Re-gather (1-4): This portion of Scripture is looking at both the scattering that is taking place historically at the time of Jeremiah and at a future time in which the armies of the antichrist will scatter God's people. At both of these events a regathering takes place. It is often said that God replays world events.

Historically, at the time of Jeremiah, the nation will experience a scattering in judgment into the land of the Chaldeans (the North Country 8). Following the seventy year captivity however they enter back into the Promised Land by the decree of Cyrus under Zerubabel and Joshua the priest (2 Chron. 36:21-23; Ezra 1; 2). However, these passages of Scripture look beyond this time, for once they come back into the Promised Land they never really gain any foothold as a people; and remain subservient to Gentile powers from the time of the Maccabees to Rome; they never truly "dwell in safety" (6). And the leadership that is responsible for driving them away only becomes more corrupt, as is seen in the Pharisees and Sadducees of our Lord's Day. And though the Righteous Branch did come and He did begin to call forth His righteous judges that will be over His new nation (Matt. 19:28); those judges (the Apostles) would soon pass away not seeing the establishment of any kingdom. The Lord Himself would not reign as King executing judgment and justice in the earth (5), but would be crucified. Nor can it be said that the re-gathering of May 14, 1948 has fulfilled any of these passages to their totality as well.

However, these passages will transpire just as the LORD predicts by the mouth of Jeremiah. The fact that Jeremiah is prophesying of a future event is proven by the fact that Zechariah when prophesying to the people that was re-gathered following the Babylonian captivity, tells of a time when the "BRANCH" will come (Zech. 3:8-10). So, there will be another scattering by the armies of the Antichrist, from the north[31] (Daniel 8:9; Daniel 11; 12:1-4; Matt. 24:15-31) at which time the Lord, the Righteous Branch, will return and re-gather Israel and Judah into the Promised Land (Ezek. 36). The LORD will sit as King with His twelve judges, executing righteous judgment and justice in the earth through the Nation of Israel (5-6; Isaiah 4; Matt. 21:43; Isaiah 33; 15, 11:12).

Mine heart within me is broken because of the prophets; all my bones shake; I am like a drunken man, and like a man whom wine hath overcome,

---

[31] He is the "king of the north" Daniel 11

because of the LORD, and because of the words of his holiness. For the land is full of adulterers; for because of swearing the land mourneth; the pleasant places of the wilderness are dried up, and their course is evil, and their force is not right. For both prophet and priest are profane; yea, in my house have I found their wickedness, saith the LORD. Wherefore their way shall be unto them as slippery ways in the darkness: they shall be driven on, and fall therein: for I will bring evil upon them, even the year of their visitation, saith the LORD. And I have seen folly in the prophets of Samaria; they prophesied in Baal, and caused my people Israel to err. I have seen also in the prophets of Jerusalem an horrible thing: they commit adultery, and walk in lies: they strengthen also the hands of evildoers, that none doth return from his wickedness: they are all of them unto me as Sodom, and the inhabitants thereof as Gomorrah. Therefore thus saith the LORD of hosts concerning the prophets; Behold, I will feed them with wormwood, and make them drink the water of gall: for from the prophets of Jerusalem is profaneness gone forth into all the land. Thus saith the LORD of hosts, Hearken not unto the words of the prophets that prophesy unto you: they make you vain: they speak a vision of their own heart, and not out of the mouth of the LORD. They say still unto them that despise me, The LORD hath said, Ye shall have peace; and they say unto every one that walketh after the imagination of his own heart, No evil shall come upon you. For who hath stood in the counsel of the LORD, and hath perceived and heard his word? who hath marked his word, and heard it? Behold, a whirlwind of the LORD is gone forth in fury, even a grievous whirlwind: it shall fall grievously upon the head of the wicked. The anger of the LORD shall not return, until he have executed, and till he have performed the thoughts of his heart: in the latter days ye shall consider it perfectly. I have not sent these prophets, yet they ran: I have not spoken to them, yet they prophesied. But if they had stood in my counsel, and had caused my people to hear my words, then they should have turned them from their evil way, and from the evil of their doings. Am I a God at hand, saith the LORD, and not a God afar off? Can any hide himself in secret places that I shall not see him? saith the LORD. Do not I fill heaven and earth? saith the LORD. I have heard what the prophets said, that prophesy lies in my name, saying, I have dreamed, I have dreamed. How long shall this be in the heart of the prophets that prophesy lies? yea, they are prophets of the deceit of their own heart; Which think to cause my people to forget my name by their dreams which they tell every man to his neighbour, as their fathers have forgotten my name for Baal. The prophet that hath a dream, let him tell a dream; and he that hath my word, let him speak my word faithfully. What is the chaff to the wheat? saith the LORD. Is not my word like as a fire? saith the LORD; and like a hammer that breaketh the rock in pieces? Therefore, behold,

I am against the prophets, saith the LORD, that steal my words every one from his neighbour. Behold, I am against the prophets, saith the LORD, that use their tongues, and say, He saith. Behold, I am against them that prophesy false dreams, saith the LORD, and do tell them, and cause my people to err by their lies, and by their lightness; yet I sent them not, nor commanded them: therefore they shall not profit this people at all, saith the LORD. (Jeremiah 23:9-32)

Condemnation of the False Prophets (9-32): Jeremiah is lamenting over the profane lies coming from the prophets. The prophets of God were to be the spokesmen or mouth piece for God to keep the people living in accordance to God's way. However the land was filled with prophets that were devising words out of their own hearts (14-17, 26). They prophesy to the people saying, "Ye shall have peace; no evil will come upon you" (17). The LORD states clearly that He has not sent these prophets, He has not sent them unto His people (21). For if these prophets had heard from God they would turn from their evil ways (22). These false prophets cause the people to forget the name of the LORD as their fathers have forgotten the name of the LORD for Baal (25-27). The LORD is against these false prophets saying, "The prophet that hath a dream, let him tell a dream; and he that hath my word let him speak it faithfully. What is the chaff to the wheat?" The answer is nothing. The voice of the false prophets are as chaff the wind will drive away, it will amount to nothing, while the wheat will stand (28-32).[32]

And when this people, or the prophet, or a priest, shall ask thee, saying, What is the burden of the LORD? thou shalt then say unto them, What burden? I will even forsake you, saith the LORD. And as for the prophet, and the priest, and the people, that shall say, The burden of the LORD, I will even punish that man and his house. Thus shall ye say every one to his neighbour, and every one to his brother, What hath the LORD answered? and, What hath the LORD spoken? And the burden of the LORD shall ye mention no more: for every man's word shall be his burden; for ye have perverted the words of the living God, of the LORD of hosts our God. Thus shalt thou say to the prophet, What hath the LORD answered thee? and, What hath the LORD spoken? But since ye say, The burden of the LORD; therefore thus saith the LORD; Because ye say this word, The burden of the LORD, and I have sent unto you, saying, Ye shall not say, The burden of the LORD; Therefore, behold, I, even I, will utterly forget you, and I will forsake you, and the city that I gave you and your fathers, and cast you out of my presence: And I will

---

[32] See Deut. 18:20-22 for things pertaining to the false prophet. Also Isaiah 30:9-14; Jer. 5:31.

bring an everlasting reproach upon you, and a perpetual shame, which shall not be forgotten. (Jeremiah 23:33-40)

The Burden of the LORD (33-40): The "people, prophet and the priest" are all prophesying a "burden of the LORD" (34). The true prophet when speaking for the LORD carries this burden. This burden of the message is seen especially in prophets like Jeremiah[33] and Ezekiel that are called upon to prophesy judgment and destruction. However these people are prophesying lies and claim their burden is from the LORD (35). The LORD warned them to not prophesy falsely but they refused to listen: as a result judgment will come upon them (37-40).

---

[33] Jeremiah 20:8,9

CHAPTER TWENTY-FOUR
The Two Baskets of Figs

The LORD shewed me, and, behold, two baskets of figs were set before the temple of the LORD, after that Nebuchadrezzar king of Babylon had carried away captive Jeconiah the son of Jehoiakim king of Judah, and the princes of Judah, with the carpenters and smiths, from Jerusalem, and had brought them to Babylon. One basket had very good figs, even like the figs that are first ripe: and the other basket had very naughty figs, which could not be eaten, they were so bad. Then said the LORD unto me, What seest thou, Jeremiah? And I said, Figs; the good figs, very good; and the evil, very evil, that cannot be eaten, they are so evil. Again the word of the LORD came unto me, saying, Thus saith the LORD, the God of Israel; Like these good figs, so will I acknowledge them that are carried away captive of Judah, whom I have sent out of this place into the land of the Chaldeans for their good. For I will set mine eyes upon them for good, and I will bring them again to this land: and I will build them, and not pull them down; and I will plant them, and not pluck them up. And I will give them an heart to know me, that I am the LORD: and they shall be my people, and I will be their God: for they shall return unto me with their whole heart. And as the evil figs, which cannot be eaten, they are so evil; surely thus saith the LORD, So will I give Zedekiah the king of Judah, and his princes, and the residue of Jerusalem, that remain in this land, and them that dwell in the land of Egypt: And I will deliver them to be removed into all the kingdoms of the earth for their hurt, to be a reproach and a proverb, a taunt and a curse, in all places whither I shall drive them. And I will send the sword, the famine, and the pestilence, among them, till they be consumed from off the land that I gave unto them and to their fathers. (Jeremiah 24:1-10)

The Two Figs (1-10): The placing of the two baskets of figs before the temple of the LORD is representative of the people of the city that were taken captive under the second siege by Nebuchadrezzar (vs. 1, 5 cf. 2 Kings 24:12-14). In this second siege against Jerusalem king Jeconiah is taken along with all the princes, carpenters and smiths (vs. 1, cf. 2 Kings 24:14), these are the good of the people, those who have a trade and or of nobility represented by the good basket of figs (2, 5). These good baskets are also representative of the "good" the LORD will show them taken in this second siege by not only preserving them favorably in captivity but also allowing them to return out of captivity to their land once again (5-7).

The second basket of figs, the naughty figs that could not be eaten represent those taken under the third siege under the leadership of Zedekiah (8 cf. 2 Kings 25:1-7). These are those who reject the warnings of the prophets Ezekiel and Jeremiah to submit to the king of Babylon, to go into captivity without resistance for your own good. These "naughty figs" do resist and are treated evil, suffering a great famine, pestilence and death (8-10). Again the "evil" figs are represented by the evil the LORD will allow those in this final siege to experience.

CHAPTER TWENTY-FIVE
Prophetic Pronouncements on Two World Empires

The word that came to Jeremiah concerning all the people of Judah in the fourth year of Jehoiakim the son of Josiah king of Judah, that was the first year of Nebuchadrezzar king of Babylon; The which Jeremiah the prophet spake unto all the people of Judah, and to all the inhabitants of Jerusalem, saying, From the thirteenth year of Josiah the son of Amon king of Judah, even unto this day, that is the three and twentieth year, the word of the LORD hath come unto me, and I have spoken unto you, rising early and speaking; but ye have not hearkened. And the LORD hath sent unto you all his servants the prophets, rising early and sending them; but ye have not hearkened, nor inclined your ear to hear. They said, Turn ye again now every one from his evil way, and from the evil of your doings, and dwell in the land that the LORD hath given unto you and to your fathers for ever and ever: And go not after other gods to serve them, and to worship them, and provoke me not to anger with the works of your hands; and I will do you no hurt. Yet ye have not hearkened unto me, saith the LORD; that ye might provoke me to anger with the works of your hands to your own hurt. (Jeremiah 25:1-7)

Jeremiah and the Prophets' Faithfulness (1-7): This chapter is "In the first year of Nebuchadrezzar king of Babylon..." (1), which is recorded in 2 Kings 24:1-2. This is the first siege against Jerusalem in which the king of Judah, Jehoiakim is taken marking the beginning of the 70 years captivity (11). Jeremiah is reviewing twenty-three years of ministry in these verses, from the thirteenth year of Josiah unto this day (the fourth year of Jehoiakim) the "three and twentieth year" (3). He is reviewing not only his ministry to the nation, but also the ministry of all the prophets contemporary with him ("all the servants the prophets" – Ezekiel, Daniel, Zephaniah, Habakkuk). Jeremiah's summary of this twenty-three years of ministry to the nation is that they have turned a deaf ear to the prophets of the LORD (7).

Therefore thus saith the LORD of hosts; Because ye have not heard my words, Behold, I will send and take all the families of the north, saith the LORD, and Nebuchadrezzar the king of Babylon, my servant, and will bring them against this land, and against the inhabitants thereof, and against all these

nations round about, and will utterly destroy them, and make them an astonishment, and an hissing, and perpetual desolations. Moreover I will take from them the voice of mirth, and the voice of gladness, the voice of the bridegroom, and the voice of the bride, the sound of the millstones, and the light of the candle. And this whole land shall be a desolation, and an astonishment; and these nations shall serve the king of Babylon seventy years. (Jeremiah 25:8-11)

Nubuchadrezzar, My Servant (8-11): The judgment of the LORD against Jerusalem and its inhabitants is a 70 year captivity (11). The nation will fulfill all of its 70 years in servitude to Babylon. For 490 years Israel failed to give the land its Sabbatical rest. The LORD forgave them 70 x 7 (Matt. 18:22) and now calls in the debt. Nebuchadnezzar is the servant of the LORD in this act (9) doing the will of the LORD. Babylon will "serve" themselves of Jerusalem and its inhabitants (11). This captivity also marks the beginning of the "Times of the Gentiles" [34] (Luke 21:24 cf. Daniel 2) which will not cease until the LORD Jesus Christ comes and destroys all dominion over His nation (Daniel 2:44).

---

[34] This is not to be confused with the "fullness of the Gentiles" Romans 11:25.

And it shall come to pass, when seventy years are accomplished, that I will punish the king of Babylon, and that nation, saith the LORD, for their iniquity, and the land of the Chaldeans, and will make it perpetual desolations. And I will bring upon that land all my words which I have pronounced against it, even all that is written in this book, which Jeremiah hath prophesied against all the nations. For many nations and great kings shall serve themselves of them also: and I will recompense them according to their deeds, and according to the works of their own hands. (Jeremiah 25:12-14)

Judgment Against Babylon (12-14): An interesting thing the LORD does consistently, He will raise up a nation to judge Israel; then once that judgment is complete He will judge the nation He used in disciplining His nation (12). In this case Babylon will be judged by the LORD once the 70 years of captivity is complete. Though Babylon did fall into a state of desolation later in history, its role in world affairs is far from complete. Babylon as a nation will rise to power once again and God will judge them to where they will not rise again (Isaiah 13:19-22 cf. Rev. 14:8). Also notice that just as other nations were allowed to "serve" themselves of the nation of Israel, so those nations will be "served" by others (14).

For thus saith the LORD God of Israel unto me; Take the wine cup of this fury at my hand, and cause all the nations, to whom I send thee, to drink it. And they shall drink, and be moved, and be mad, because of the sword that I will send among them. Then took I the cup at the LORD'S hand, and made all the nations to drink, unto whom the LORD had sent me: To wit, Jerusalem, and the cities of Judah, and the kings thereof, and the princes thereof, to make them a desolation, an astonishment, an hissing, and a curse; as it is this day; Pharaoh king of Egypt, and his servants, and his princes, and all his people; And all the mingled people, and all the kings of the land of Uz, and all the kings of the land of the Philistines, and Ashkelon, and Azzah, and Ekron, and the remnant of Ashdod, Edom, and Moab, and the children of Ammon, And all the kings of Tyrus, and all the kings of Zidon, and the kings of the isles which are beyond the sea, Dedan, and Tema, and Buz, and all that are in the utmost corners, And all the kings of Arabia, and all the kings of the mingled people that dwell in the desert, And all the kings of Zimri, and all the kings of Elam, and all the kings of the Medes, And all the kings of the north, far and near, one with another, and all the kingdoms of the world, which are upon the face of the earth: and the king of Sheshach shall drink after them. Therefore thou shalt say unto them, Thus saith the LORD of hosts, the God of Israel; Drink ye, and be drunken, and spue, and fall, and rise no more, because of the sword which I will send among you. And it shall be, if they refuse to take the cup at thine hand to drink, then shalt thou say unto them, Thus saith the LORD of hosts; Ye shall certainly drink. For, lo, I begin to bring evil on the city which is called by my name, and should ye be utterly unpunished? Ye shall not be unpunished: for I will call for a sword upon all the inhabitants of the earth, saith the LORD of hosts. Therefore prophesy thou against them all these words, and say unto them, The LORD shall roar from on high, and utter his voice from his holy habitation; he shall mightily roar upon his habitation; he shall give a shout, as they that tread the grapes, against all the inhabitants of the earth. A noise shall come even to the ends of the earth; for the LORD hath a controversy with the nations, he will plead with all flesh; he will give them that are wicked to the sword, saith the LORD. Thus saith the LORD of hosts, Behold, evil shall go forth from nation to nation, and a great whirlwind shall be raised up from the coasts of the earth. And the slain of the LORD shall be at that day from one end of the earth even unto the other end of the earth: they shall not be lamented, neither gathered, nor buried; they shall be dung upon the ground. (Jeremiah 25:15-33)

The Wine Cup of Fury against the Gentile Nations (15-33): As mentioned in the previous section, the LORD not only will judge those nations that He uses to judge Israel but the LORD also replays world events. Especially in relation to Babylon. Because of

Israel's disobedience God allowed His people to be taken into Babylonian captivity. Following the 70 years of servitude they came back out into the land, however never gained any spiritual fortitude and remained subservient to Gentile nations surrounding them. Even at this present time they are far from the picture God has painted for them in the Word of God. Nor has the judgment befallen the Gentile nations as seen in the Word of God congruent to what we see today. So then we must understand that while some of the prophecies concerning the judgment of these Gentile nations has taken place, and some Scripture has been fulfilled, there is a host of Scripture concerning the judgment of the Gentile nations that is awaiting a future fulfillment (We will see this especially in chapters 46-51 of Jeremiah).

Here, then, is a prophetic pronouncement against all those Gentile nations that "served" themselves of Israel. The judgment against these Gentile nations is that they are to drink of the wrath of God (15-17, 26-28; 49:12, 51:7). Again, though judgment has befallen these nations at some time in history, these passages and others will find their ultimate fulfillment in the future when the LORD Himself will come and "trample them in His fury" (Isaiah 63:1-4). It will be the day in which He will "tread the grapes, against all the inhabitants of the earth" (30 cf. Isiah 63:3 cf. Rev. 14:19-20, 19:15).

Howl, ye shepherds, and cry; and wallow yourselves in the ashes, ye principal of the flock: for the days of your slaughter and of your dispersions are accomplished; and ye shall fall like a pleasant vessel. And the shepherds shall have no way to flee, nor the principal of the flock to escape. A voice of the cry of the shepherds, and an howling of the principal of the flock, shall be heard: for the LORD hath spoiled their pasture. And the peaceable habitations are cut down because of the fierce anger of the LORD. He hath forsaken his covert, as the lion: for their land is desolate because of the fierceness of the oppressor, and because of his fierce anger. (Jeremiah 25:34-38)

Judgment of the Shepherds, the Principle of the Flock (34-38): The shepherds of the flock are the leadership of God's people. The Kings were to lead the people physically and the Priests were to lead the people spiritually. They both had failed the people, leading them astray. Therefore this scattering is going to take place, as it will again in the future.

For one to understand fully the doctrine of the shepherds of Israel a thorough study of Ezekiel 34 and John 10:1-18 is needed. It is in Ezekiel chapter 34 that the nature of the shepherds ruling Israel are taught (Ezek. 34:1-6). The judgment against the shepherds will be the scattering of the sheep (Ezek. 34:5). However the true Shepherd will come and seek the sheep (Gospels) and will deliver them

(Tribulation) and then bring them into their pastures (Millennium).

CHAPTER TWENTY-SIX
Jeremiah's Close Call

In the beginning of the reign of Jehoiakim the son of Josiah king of Judah came this word from the LORD, saying, Thus saith the LORD; Stand in the court of the LORD'S house, and speak unto all the cities of Judah, which come to worship in the LORD'S house, all the words that I command thee to speak unto them; diminish not a word: If so be they will hearken, and turn every man from his evil way, that I may repent me of the evil, which I purpose to do unto them because of the evil of their doings. And thou shalt say unto them, Thus saith the LORD; If ye will not hearken to me, to walk in my law, which I have set before you, To hearken to the words of my servants the prophets, whom I sent unto you, both rising up early, and sending them, but ye have not hearkened; Then will I make this house like Shiloh, and will make this city a curse to all the nations of the earth. So the priests and the prophets and all the people heard Jeremiah speaking these words in the house of the LORD. (Jeremiah 26:1-7)

Judgment Pronounced in the Court of the House of the LORD (1-7): This chapter is during the reign of Jehoiakim. It was during the beginning of his reign that the first siege takes place (2 Kings 24:1-4). Jeremiah is told to go in the court of the house of the LORD and pronounce coming judgment if they do not turn from their evil ways. It would seem that this act was done during feast time given the location Jeremiah is placed and that he is told to "speak unto all the cities of Judah, which come to worship in the LORD's house" (2).

His pronouncement of judgment is against the House of the LORD, specifically the place of worship in which Jeremiah is standing. Israel's place of worship will be removed as when worship was removed from Shiloh (6). The reference to Shiloh all of Judah knew too well, as is seen by their response (8 - 9). The Ark rested in Shiloh until it was captured and eventually brought to rest in Jerusalem and Shiloh was left in desolation, so the LORD will allow that to happen in Jerusalem. The people had a misplaced idea that because they had the Ark of the Covenant that God would not destroy the place of worship; however Ezekiel had already seen the glory of the LORD depart the temple (Ezekiel 9-11).

Now it came to pass, when Jeremiah had made an end of speaking all that the LORD had commanded him to speak unto all the people, that the priests and

the prophets and all the people took him, saying, Thou shalt surely die. Why hast thou prophesied in the name of the LORD, saying, This house shall be like Shiloh, and this city shall be desolate without an inhabitant? And all the people were gathered against Jeremiah in the house of the LORD. When the princes of Judah heard these things, then they came up from the king's house unto the house of the LORD, and sat down in the entry of the new gate of the LORD'S house. Then spake the priests and the prophets unto the princes and to all the people, saying, This man is worthy to die; for he hath prophesied against this city, as ye have heard with your ears. (Jeremiah 26:8-11)

The Priests' and the Prophets' Response (8-11): Throughout the remainder of this chapter you will notice that it is the prophets (false) and the priests that call for the death of Jeremiah, while the princes oppose this decision (16). The opposition of the prophets would be natural since they prophesy a false peace. The prophets along with the priests seek to persuade the princes in their decision to have Jeremiah killed (11).

Then spake Jeremiah unto all the princes and to all the people, saying, The LORD sent me to prophesy against this house and against this city all the words that ye have heard. Therefore now amend your ways and your doings, and obey the voice of the

LORD your God; and the LORD will repent him of the evil that he hath pronounced against you. As for me, behold, I am in your hand: do with me as seemeth good and meet unto you. But know ye for certain, that if ye put me to death, ye shall surely bring innocent blood upon yourselves, and upon this city, and upon the inhabitants thereof: for of a truth the LORD hath sent me unto you to speak all these words in your ears. (Jeremiah 26:12-15)

Jeremiah's Determination (12-15): Jeremiah is resolved in the words he has spoken, for they were not his but the LORD'S (15). Jeremiah says in so many words, go ahead and kill me but if you do, you will be killing innocent blood (14, 15).

Then said the princes and all the people unto the priests and to the prophets; This man is not worthy to die: for he hath spoken to us in the name of the LORD our God. Then rose up certain of the elders of the land, and spake to all the assembly of the people, saying, Micah the Morasthite prophesied in the days of Hezekiah king of Judah, and spake to all the people of Judah, saying, Thus saith the LORD of hosts; Zion shall be plowed like a field, and Jerusalem shall become heaps, and the mountain of the house as the high places of a forest. Did Hezekiah king of Judah and all Judah put him at all to death? did he not fear the LORD, and besought the LORD, and the LORD repented him of the evil which he had pronounced against them? Thus might we procure great evil against our souls. And there was also a man that prophesied in the name of the LORD, Urijah the son of Shemaiah of Kirjathjearim, who prophesied against this city and against this land according to all the words of Jeremiah: And when Jehoiakim the king, with all his mighty men, and all the princes, heard his words, the king sought to put him to death: but when Urijah heard it, he was afraid, and fled, and went into Egypt; And Jehoiakim the king sent men into Egypt, namely, Elnathan the son of Achbor, and certain men with him into Egypt. And they fetched forth Urijah out of Egypt, and brought him unto Jehoiakim the king; who slew him with the sword, and cast his dead body into the graves of the common people. Nevertheless the hand of Ahikam the son of Shaphan was with Jeremiah, that they should not give him into the hand of the people to put him to death. (Jeremiah 26:16-24)

The Elders Intercede (16-24): The princes declare Jeremiah not worthy of death (16) and to settle this issue the elders of the land are successful in delivering Jeremiah from the hands of his enemies. They bring up the case from two other prophets of God, Micah and Urijah. It would seem from the two examples given that the elders were merely showing that there is a precedent for both putting Jeremiah to death and delivering him. However, calmer heads prevail and Jeremiah is spared. The reasoning of the elders is as follows:

The prophet Micah prophesied destruction on Jerusalem to King Hezekiah and he did not put Micah to death, but rather repented and God stayed His hand of judgment for a time (Micah 3:12 cf. 2 Kings 18:3-6).

The prophet Urijah's account is only found here in Scripture. A true prophet nonetheless, he prophesied "against the city and the land according to the words of Jeremiah" (20). Jehoiakim however did not spare his life. Urijah flees to Egypt for safety, only to be hunted by Jehoiakim's men and brought back to Jerusalem and killed.

CHAPTER TWENTY-SEVEN
Submit

In the beginning of the reign of Jehoiakim the son of Josiah king of Judah came this word unto Jeremiah from the LORD, saying, Thus saith the LORD to me; Make thee bonds and yokes, and put them upon thy neck, And send them to the king of Edom, and to the king of Moab, and to the king of the Ammonites, and to the king of Tyrus, and to the king of Zidon, by the hand of the messengers which come to Jerusalem unto Zedekiah king of Judah; And command them to say unto their masters, Thus saith the LORD of hosts, the God of Israel; Thus shall ye say unto your masters; I have made the earth, the man and the beast that are upon the ground, by my great power and by my outstretched arm, and have given it unto whom it seemed meet unto me. And now have I given all these lands into the hand of Nebuchadnezzar the king of Babylon, my servant; and the beasts of the field have I given him also to serve him. And all nations shall serve him, and his son, and his son's son, until the very time of his land come: and then many nations and great kings shall serve themselves of him. And it shall come to pass, that the nation and kingdom which will not serve the same Nebuchadnezzar the king of Babylon, and that will not put their neck under the yoke of the king of Babylon, that nation will I punish, saith the LORD, with the sword, and with the famine, and with the pestilence, until I have consumed them by his hand. Therefore hearken not ye to your prophets, nor to your diviners, nor to your dreamers, nor to your enchanters, nor to your sorcerers, which speak unto you, saying, Ye shall not serve the king of Babylon: For they prophesy a lie unto you, to remove you far from your land; and that I should drive you out, and ye should perish. But the nations that bring their neck under the yoke of the king of Babylon, and serve him, those will I let remain still in their own land, saith the LORD; and they shall till it, and dwell therein. (Jeremiah 27:1-11)

Submit and Survive (1-11): Jeremiah does a symbolic act of submission. Jeremiah is told to "make thee bonds and yokes and put them upon thy neck" (2). He is then told to send theses by the hand of a messenger to all the kings that will be subject to Nebuchadnezzar (3). Jeremiah made "bonds and yokes," plural, showing that he had made these to be distributed to these kings over time; especially given that he is first told to do this during the reign of Jehoiakim and yet King Zedekiah is to receive one (3).

The messengers from Jeremiah that are to deliver these "bonds and yokes" are told to say in essence: I, God, that made all living things to inhabit My land am allowing Nebuchadnezzar, king of Babylon to take control of My land and all living things therein are to be subservient to him (4-6). However there will be an end to Nebuchadnezzar's reign. It will be "until the very time of his land come", a reference to the seventy-year rest captivity in which the land was to rest. Then at that time Nebuchadnezzar will be overtaken and "many nations and great kings shall serve themselves of him" (7).

The stark warning by Jeremiah's symbolic act is that if they try to resist they will suffer the punishment of the LORD by the sword, famine and pestilence until they are consumed (8). Therefore they are not to take heed to the false prophets, diviners nor your dreamers or to the enchanters nor sorcerers which speak lies, saying "Ye shall not serve the king of Babylon" (9). King Zedekiah resists, fulfilling this verse.

I spake also to Zedekiah king of Judah according to all these words, saying, Bring your necks under the yoke of the king of Babylon, and serve him and his people, and live. Why will ye die, thou and thy people, by the sword, by the famine, and by the pestilence, as the LORD hath spoken against the nation that will not serve the king of Babylon?

Therefore hearken not unto the words of the prophets that speak unto you, saying, Ye shall not serve the king of Babylon: for they prophesy a lie unto you. For I have not sent them, saith the LORD, yet they prophesy a lie in my name; that I might drive you out, and that ye might perish, ye, and the prophets that prophesy unto you. Also I spake to the priests and to all this people, saying, Thus saith the LORD; Hearken not to the words of your prophets that prophesy unto you, saying, Behold, the vessels of the LORD'S house shall now shortly be brought again from Babylon: for they prophesy a lie unto you. Hearken not unto them; serve the king of Babylon, and live: wherefore should this city be laid waste? But if they be prophets, and if the word of the LORD be with them, let them now make intercession to the LORD of hosts, that the vessels which are left in the house of the LORD, and in the house of the king of Judah, and at Jerusalem, go not to Babylon. For thus saith the LORD of hosts concerning the pillars, and concerning the sea, and concerning the bases, and concerning the residue of the vessels that remain in this city, Which Nebuchadnezzar king of Babylon took not, when he carried away captive Jeconiah the son of Jehoiakim king of Judah from Jerusalem to Babylon, and all the nobles of Judah and Jerusalem; Yea, thus saith the LORD of hosts, the God of Israel, concerning the vessels that remain in the house of the LORD, and in the house of the king of Judah and of Jerusalem; They shall be carried to Babylon, and there shall they be until the day that I visit them, saith the LORD; then will I bring them up, and restore them to this place. (Jeremiah 27:12-22)

Zedekiah and the False Prophets (12-18): Zedekiah was taken in by these false prophets for they used an apparent contradiction in the prophetic announcements of both Jeremiah and Ezekiel concerning the fate of Zedekiah to bolster their prophetic announcements of peace (Jer. 32:4 cf. Ezek. 12:13). The LORD says, He "has not sent them... yet they prophesy lies in my name" (15). Jeremiah is also to speak to the "priests" concerning what the false prophets that prophesy saying, "the vessels of the LORD'S house shall now shortly be brought again from Babylon" (16). The vessels were taken during the second siege under the reign of Jehoiachin. The false prophets are prophesying that the vessels taken into Babylon will return, i.e. God is going to bring them back. However the reality is that they will resist the yoke of Babylon and there will be a final siege. At that time the remaining vessels and items of worth will be "carried to Babylon" (19-22). However the LORD will bring them up and restore them to this place (22 cf. Ezra 5:14).

CHAPTER TWENTY-EIGHT
Confronting a False Prophet

And it came to pass the same year, in the beginning of the reign of Zedekiah king of Judah, in the fourth year, and in the fifth month, that Hananiah the son of Azur the prophet, which was of Gibeon, spake unto me in the house of the LORD, in the presence of the priests and of all the people, saying, Thus speaketh the LORD of hosts, the God of Israel, saying, I have broken the yoke of the king of Babylon. Within two full years will I bring again into this place all the vessels of the LORD'S house, that Nebuchadnezzar king of Babylon took away from this place, and carried them to Babylon: And I will bring again to this place Jeconiah the son of Jehoiakim king of Judah, with all the captives of Judah, that went into Babylon, saith the LORD: for I will break the yoke of the king of Babylon. (Jeremiah 28:1-4)

Hananiah's False Prophesying (1-4): Hananiah is a false prophet proclaiming what was previously mentioned in the last chapter, which was that in two years all the things stolen from the temple will be returned. He also falsely predicts that Jeconiah and all the captives of Judah will return (4).

Then the prophet Jeremiah said unto the prophet Hananiah in the presence of the priests, and in the presence of all the people that stood in the house of the LORD, Even the prophet Jeremiah said, Amen: the LORD do so: the LORD perform thy words which thou hast prophesied, to bring again the vessels of the LORD'S house, and all that is carried away captive, from Babylon into this place. Nevertheless hear thou now this word that I speak in thine ears, and in the ears of all the people; The prophets that have been before me and before thee of old prophesied both against many countries, and against great kingdoms, of war, and of evil, and of pestilence. The prophet which prophesieth of peace, when the word of the prophet shall come to pass, then shall the prophet be known, that the LORD hath truly sent him. (Jeremiah 28:5-9)

Jeremiah's Challenge (5-9): Jeremiah sarcastically is agreeing, saying, Amen, he too wishes all the vessels of the LORD'S house and the captives of Judah would return (5-6). However Jeremiah points out that other prophets besides him prophesied of this judgment against the city and its people (7-8). Jeremiah adds a warning, that according to the Law if a prophet prophesy and it does not come to pass he is branded a false prophet (9) and all false prophets are to be put to death (Deut. 18:21-22).

Then Hananiah the prophet took the yoke from off the prophet Jeremiah's neck, and brake it. And Hananiah spake in the presence of all the people, saying, Thus saith the LORD; Even so will I break the yoke of Nebuchadnezzar king of Babylon from the neck of all nations within the space of two full years. And the prophet Jeremiah went his way. (Jeremiah 28:10-11)

The Persistence of Hananiah (10 – 11): Hananiah does not heed the warning of Jeremiah and persists in his false prophetic announcement by the graphic illustration of breaking the yoke of "wood" from off Jeremiah's neck.

Then the word of the LORD came unto Jeremiah the prophet, after that Hananiah the prophet had broken the yoke from off the neck of the prophet Jeremiah, saying, Go and tell Hananiah, saying, Thus saith the LORD; Thou hast broken the yokes of wood; but thou shalt make for them yokes of iron. For thus saith the LORD of hosts, the God of Israel; I have put a yoke of iron upon the neck of all these nations, that they may serve Nebuchadnezzar king of Babylon; and they shall serve him: and I have given him the beasts of the field also. (Jeremiah 28:12-14)

Yokes of Iron (12-14): The LORD through Jeremiah tells Hananiah that you have broken yokes of "wood", but the LORD will make yokes of "Iron" for the nations. The issue of placing a yoke of iron is a prophetic announcement given in Deuteronomy 28:48; Israel is meriting the curses of the Law. In other words the LORD is not going to deliver God's people from the Babylonian Captivity, Hananiah's prophecy is false.

Then said the prophet Jeremiah unto Hananiah the prophet, Hear now, Hananiah; The LORD hath not sent thee; but thou makest this people to trust in a lie. Therefore thus saith the LORD; Behold, I will cast thee from off the face of the earth: this year thou shalt die, because thou hast taught rebellion against the LORD. So Hananiah the prophet died the same year in the seventh month. (Jeremiah 28:15-17)

Judgment on Hananiah (15-17): Hananiah receives the just recompense of his ways: he will die by the end of the year as prophesied by the true prophet of God (16-17).

CHAPTER TWENTY-NINE
Writing Letters

Now these are the words of the letter that Jeremiah the prophet sent from Jerusalem unto the residue of the elders which were carried away captives, and to the priests, and to the prophets, and to all the people whom Nebuchadnezzar had carried away captive from Jerusalem to Babylon; (After that Jeconiah the king, and the queen, and the eunuchs, the princes of Judah and Jerusalem, and the carpenters, and the smiths, were departed from Jerusalem;) By the hand of Elasah the son of Shaphan, and Gemariah the son of Hilkiah, (whom Zedekiah king of Judah sent unto Babylon to Nebuchadnezzar king of Babylon) saying, Thus saith the LORD of hosts, the God of Israel, unto all that are carried away captives, whom I have caused to be carried away from Jerusalem unto Babylon; Build ye houses, and dwell in them; and plant gardens, and eat the fruit of them; Take ye wives, and beget sons and daughters; and take wives for your sons, and give your daughters to husbands, that they may bear sons and daughters; that ye may be increased there, and not diminished.

And seek the peace of the city whither I have caused you to be carried away captives, and pray unto the LORD for it: for in the peace thereof shall ye have peace. For thus saith the LORD of hosts, the God of Israel; Let not your prophets and your diviners, that be in the midst of you, deceive you, neither hearken to your dreams which ye cause to be dreamed. For they prophesy falsely unto you in my name: I have not sent them, saith the LORD. For thus saith the LORD, That after seventy years be accomplished at Babylon I will visit you, and perform my good word toward you, in causing you to return to this place. For I know the thoughts that I think toward you, saith the LORD, thoughts of peace, and not of evil, to give you an expected end. Then shall ye call upon me, and ye shall go and pray unto me, and I will hearken unto you. And ye shall seek me, and find me, when ye shall search for me with all your heart. And I will be found of you, saith the LORD: and I will turn away your captivity, and I will gather you from all the nations, and from all the places whither I have driven you, saith the LORD; and I will bring you again into the place whence I caused you to be carried away captive. (Jeremiah 29:1-14)

Letter From Jeremiah to the Exiles in Babylon (1-14): This chapter records various letters to and from Babylon during the reign of Zedekiah (3). This first letter is written to the captives in Babylon that were brought there under the first two sieges. Daniel and Ezekiel are the most prominent of those taken captive. In the first deportation to Babylon captives were taken to the main city and palace proper. Daniel was one of them taken at this time along with all those skillful and gifted in knowledge (the educated see Daniel 1:1-4). Under the second deportation in which Ezekiel was taken, the captives were taken to an agricultural area by the river Chebar to do manual labor (Ezekiel 1:1-3).

This letter was carried to Babylon by the hand of Shaphan, and Gemariah (3). The letter was to encourage those in captivity to "build ye houses, and dwell in them; and plant gardens, and eat the fruit of them; take ye wives, and beget daughters; and give your daughters to husbands, that they may bear sons and daughters; that ye may be increased there and not diminished" (5-6). Jeremiah also instructs them to pray for peace (7). Jeremiah also gives them warning not to believe the false prophets who are claiming a revelation from God (8-9). *What happens next is important for both defending the accuracy of Scripture and having great prophetic significance.* Jeremiah gives the captives in Babylon the duration of their captivity (10). Seventy years will be the duration before God will allow His people to return to the land of their nativity (10-14). It is this information that Daniel will read (Daniel 9:1, 2). Daniel will not only understand the seventy years of Babylonian captivity but will also be given understanding of the whole time period that Israel will experience oppression by Gentile powers. The time until their Messiah comes to remove all sin and establish their long awaited kingdom (see Daniel 9).[35]

Because ye have said, The LORD hath raised us up prophets in Babylon; Know that thus saith the LORD of the king that sitteth upon the throne of David, and of all the people that dwelleth in this city, and of your brethren that are not gone forth with you into captivity; Thus saith the LORD of hosts; Behold, I will send upon them the sword, the famine, and the pestilence, and will make them like vile figs, that cannot be eaten, they are so evil. And I will persecute them with the sword, with the famine, and with the pestilence, and will deliver them to be removed to all the kingdoms of the earth, to be a curse, and an astonishment, and an hissing, and a reproach, among all the nations whither I have driven them: Because they have not hearkened to my words, saith the LORD, which I sent unto them by my servants the prophets, rising up early and sending them; but ye would not hear, saith the LORD. (Jeremiah 29:15-19)

---

[35] This time schedule given to Daniel (Chapter 9) is very important, for it is the reason that Daniel understood the time of the coming Messiah's birth when he conveyed to the wise men under his care, the coming of the Messiah and the star that was to mark his birth. This time schedule given to Daniel is also important because now there was a timeline to place all prophetic passages given to the prophets.

Jeremiah Gives the Results of the Words of the False Prophets in Babylon (15-19): Jeremiah communicates in this letter to the false prophets in Babylon that because of their words those left in Jerusalem who were not taken away captive will suffer the fate of the sword, famine and pestilence because they listened to these false prophets. If they had listened to the real prophets of the LORD they would have submitted to the king of Babylon and lived. [36]

Hear ye therefore the word of the LORD, all ye of the captivity, whom I have sent from Jerusalem to Babylon: Thus saith the LORD of hosts, the God of Israel, of Ahab the son of Kolaiah, and of Zedekiah the son of Maaseiah, which prophesy a lie unto you in my name; Behold, I will deliver them into the hand of Nebuchadrezzar king of Babylon; and he shall slay them before your eyes; And of them shall be taken up a curse by all the captivity of Judah which are in Babylon, saying, The LORD make thee like Zedekiah and like Ahab, whom the king of Babylon roasted in the fire; Because they have committed villany in Israel, and have committed adultery with their neighbours' wives, and have

---

[36] Nebuchadnezzar used the common method of attack known as – a siege wall. A siege wall was intended to surround the city, preventing all business and trade from entering the city, and to eventually starve out the population into surrender. He also placed watch towers allowing those who wished to leave to do so.

spoken lying words in my name, which I have not commanded them; even I know, and am a witness, saith the LORD. (Jeremiah 29:20-23)

The Curse of Ahab and Zedekiah, False Prophets in Babylon (20-23): Jeremiah, in his letter, specifically addresses two false prophets prophesying to the captivity in Babylon; Ahab and Zedekiah. Jeremiah's prophesy against them is that the king of Babylon will slay them and roast them in the fires of Babylon. Following this event there will be a saying that people would use if they wanted to curse someone, "The LORD make thee like Zedekiah and like Ahab, whom the king of Babylon roasted in the fire" (22).

Thus shalt thou also speak to Shemaiah the Nehelamite, saying, Thus speaketh the LORD of hosts, the God of Israel, saying, Because thou hast sent letters in thy name unto all the people that are at Jerusalem, and to Zephaniah the son of Maaseiah the priest, and to all the priests, saying, The LORD hath made thee priest in the stead of Jehoiada the priest, that ye should be officers in the house of the LORD, for every man that is mad, and maketh himself a prophet, that thou shouldest put him in prison, and in the stocks. Now therefore why hast thou not reproved Jeremiah of Anathoth, which maketh himself a prophet to you? For therefore he sent unto us in Babylon, saying, This captivity is long: build ye houses, and dwell in them; and plant

gardens, and eat the fruit of them. And Zephaniah the priest read this letter in the ears of Jeremiah the prophet. Then came the word of the LORD unto Jeremiah, saying, Send to all them of the captivity, saying, Thus saith the LORD concerning Shemaiah the Nehelamite; Because that Shemaiah hath prophesied unto you, and I sent him not, and he caused you to trust in a lie: Therefore thus saith the LORD; Behold, I will punish Shemaiah the Nehelamite, and his seed: he shall not have a man to dwell among this people; neither shall he behold the good that I will do for my people, saith the LORD; because he hath taught rebellion against the LORD. (Jeremiah 29:24-32)

Condemnation of Shemaiah the False Prophet (24-32): As Jeremiah closes this letter he addresses a false prophet named Shemaiah the Nehelamite who falsely prophesied in letters sent to Jerusalem (25), saying, that Zephaniah the priest should be priest instead of Jehoiada and that Zephaniah with other priests should reprove Jeremiah who makes himself to be a prophet and cast him in prison (26-28). This is what Zephaniah the priest read before the ears of Jeremiah the prophet (29).

Jeremiah responds from the LORD with these final words written to those in captivity saying, "Thus saith the LORD concerning Shemaiah the Nehelamite; Because that Shemaiah hath prophesied unto you, and I sent him not, and he caused you to trust in a lie: Therefore thus saith the LORD; Behold,

I will punish Shemaiah the Nehelamite, and his seed: he shall not have a man to dwell among this people; neither shall he behold the good that I will do for my people" (32). Shemaiah had propagated a lie saying to the people, you will return shortly to the land of your nativity. The truth however taught by God from Jeremiah is that they will be in captivity seventy years, so seek peace and build lives together (4-10).

CHAPTER THIRTY
In the Latter Days Ye Shall Consider It

These next three chapters (30-33) contain some of the most prophetically profound passages in all of Jeremiah. The return of God's people to the land God has promised them is what is in view. This magnificent day, however, will precede a coming day in which they will suffer their greatest persecution yet under the Antichrist and his armies; a time known as Jacob's Trouble, the Great Tribulation and Daniel's Seventieth Week.[37] However, in these chapters is also the promise that the LORD will ransom them and deliver them from the hands of their enemies and establish a New Covenant with them whereby He will remember their sins no more. It will be at this

---

[37] Daniel is given the totality of the Gentile dominion lasting 70 x 7 of weeks or 490 years. It is the last seven years that are remaining until the LORD comes to deliver Israel, destroys Gentile dominion over them and establishes His Theocratic Kingdom on the earth. See Daniel study by same author for details to this time.

time that the nation of Israel will be that "head of all the nations" promised to them (Deut. 28:13).

The word that came to Jeremiah from the LORD, saying, Thus speaketh the LORD God of Israel, saying, Write thee all the words that I have spoken unto thee in a book. For, lo, the days come, saith the LORD, that I will bring again the captivity of my people Israel and Judah, saith the LORD: and I will cause them to return to the land that I gave to their fathers, and they shall possess it. (Jeremiah 30:1-3)

The Book of Jeremiah (1-3): Jeremiah is told to write down "all the words I have spoken unto thee in a book". The book of Jeremiah is that book. The reason that Jeremiah is to write down all the words of the LORD, is to make it known that the LORD will be instrumentally involved in bringing into the land both Israel and Judah. The LORD will see to it that all things He promised will come to pass. Notice that both Israel and Judah are in view. The LORD will see to it that both tribes, Israel and Judah will occupy the totality of the land God promised them. As we will see in these next chapters, this is not only referring to the faithfulness of God to bring them into the land following the Babylonian captivity under Ezra and Nehemiah; but also has a much further fulfillment in view, in which the LORD will accomplish His covenant with them in its totality.

And these are the words that the LORD spake concerning Israel and concerning Judah. For thus saith the LORD; We have heard a voice of trembling, of fear, and not of peace. Ask ye now, and see whether a man doth travail with child? wherefore do I see every man with his hands on his loins, as a woman in travail, and all faces are turned into paleness? Alas! for that day is great, so that none is like it: it is even the time of Jacob's trouble; but he shall be saved out of it. For it shall come to pass in that day, saith the LORD of hosts, that I will break his yoke from off thy neck, and will burst thy bonds, and strangers shall no more serve themselves of him: But they shall serve the LORD their God, and David their king, whom I will raise up unto them. (Jeremiah 30:4-9)

Jacob's Trouble and the Davidic Throne (4-9): Notice again these highly prophetic portions of Scripture are concerning "Israel and Judah". The LORD has all the house of Israel in view.

The nation is asked if they have ever seen a man in travail as a women with child, the answer would be no. The LORD then asks, why do I see every man with his hands on his loins as a woman in travail and all faces are turned to paleness (5-6). The answer is the LORD is looking at a time called "Jacob's Trouble"; a time so horrific that men's hearts shall fail them (Luke 21:26). This time known as "Jacob's Trouble" is spoken of throughout the Scriptures (Isa. 2:12-21; Joel 2:10-11; Amos 5:18-20; Mich. 1:1-5; Zeph. 1:14-18).

Notice it is Jacob's Trouble, i.e. the trouble to befall all the tribes that come from Jacob (7). Notice also the day is "great so none is like it" (7), it is the book of Revelation, Matthew 24 & 25 with a host of other prophetic passages scattered throughout the prophets that tell of this time (Matt. 24:21; Dan. 12:1). The phrase, "woman in travail" is used throughout Scripture of the coming Tribulation Period because of the great upheaval that the world and the nations will experience (Ps. 48:6; Jer. 4:31; I Thess. 5:12)[38]. Now the emphasis is placed on a woman in travail because it is when this climactic time is transpiring that Jacob will be delivered, just as a woman that travails and then delivers her child. So it is recorded that "he shall be saved out of it" (7). The reality of all this can be seen in such passages as Revelation 12:1-6; Daniel 12:1; Malachi 3:16 [39] in which the LORD will deliver His people (Zech. 14:3) and will once and for all break the yoke of Gentile dominance over them (vs 8; Daniel 2:44-45). Then the God of Heaven will setup His Theocratic Kingdom establishing the throne of David in which king David himself will be

---

[38] However the phrase "as a woman in travail" is not exclusive for just the Tribulation Period.

[39] The issue of the Remnant of Israel being delivered from Jacob's Trouble is taught in the following Scriptures: *Zeph. 2:2-3; Luke 21:36; Joel 2:31, 32;* they are hid in Babylon for the latter 3 ½ years *(Rev. 12:13-17; Mich. 4:10)* and are removed before its destruction *(Rev. 18:4).*

resurrected as Prince over the people (vs. 9 cf. Ezek. 34:24, Ezek. 37:25). [40]

Therefore fear thou not, O my servant Jacob, saith the LORD; neither be dismayed, O Israel: for, lo, I will save thee from afar, and thy seed from the land of their captivity; and Jacob shall return, and shall be in rest, and be quiet, and none shall make him afraid. For I am with thee, saith the LORD, to save thee: though I make a full end of all nations whither I have scattered thee, yet will I not make a full end of thee: but I will correct thee in measure, and will not leave thee altogether unpunished. For thus saith the LORD, Thy bruise is incurable, and thy wound is grievous. There is none to plead thy cause, that thou mayest be bound up: thou hast no healing medicines. All thy lovers have forgotten thee; they seek thee not; for I have wounded thee with the wound of an enemy, with the chastisement of a cruel one, for the multitude of thine iniquity; because thy sins were increased. Why criest thou for thine affliction? thy sorrow is incurable for the multitude of thine iniquity: because thy sins were increased, I have done these things unto thee. Therefore all they that devour thee shall be

---

[40] David will rule in the coming Theocratic Kingdom as Prince of the people while the LORD will sit on the throne of David as the King of kings. Notice the difference of these words used in Ezekiel 28 where "Prince" is used in connection with the human ruler of Tyrus and later in the chapter the title "king" is used referring to Satan, the one ruling behind the scenes.

devoured; and all thine adversaries, every one of them, shall go into captivity; and they that spoil thee shall be a spoil, and all that prey upon thee will I give for a prey. For I will restore health unto thee, and I will heal thee of thy wounds, saith the LORD; because they called thee an Outcast, saying, This is Zion, whom no man seeketh after. (Jeremiah 30:10-17)

I Will Not Make a Full End of Thee (10-17): Once again all of Israel is in view (both southern and northern). These words are encouraging words, for "lo, I will save thee from afar, and thy seed from the land of their captivity" (10). Historically this happened under Ezra and Nehemiah however, these passages look far beyond that event, for notice the following statements: "and Jacob shall return and be at rest, and be quiet, and none shall make him afraid" (10). At the time of this event, the LORD will make a full end of the Gentile nations that have ruled over Israel, but will not make a full end of His chosen people Israel (11). The destruction of Gentile dominion will take place once the Rock cut without hands comes and smites Daniel's image (Dan. 2:44-45); thus when the LORD comes and sets up His Theocratic Kingdom on the earth.

At that time the LORD will avenge Israel's enemies. Israel will continue to reap the fruits of their sins. However one day the LORD will recompense all the nations that have punished Israel (16), and Israel will be healed (Mal. 4:2).

Thus saith the LORD; Behold, I will bring again the captivity of Jacob's tents, and have mercy on his dwellingplaces; and the city shall be builded upon her own heap, and the palace shall remain after the manner thereof. And out of them shall proceed thanksgiving and the voice of them that make merry: and I will multiply them, and they shall not be few; I will also glorify them, and they shall not be small. Their children also shall be as aforetime, and their congregation shall be established before me, and I will punish all that oppress them. And their nobles shall be of themselves, and their governor shall proceed from the midst of them; and I will cause him to draw near, and he shall approach unto me: for who is this that engaged his heart to approach unto me? saith the LORD. And ye shall be my people, and I will be your God. Behold, the whirlwind of the LORD goeth forth with fury, a continuing whirlwind: it shall fall with pain upon the head of the wicked. The fierce anger of the LORD shall not return, until he have done it, and until he have performed the intents of his heart: in the latter days ye shall consider it. (Jeremiah 30:18-24)

God's People and Their God (18-24): The context is again the same throughout this chapter; a future time in which the LORD will deliver His people from captivity and establish them in the land forever. We also see a double fulfillment; historically the LORD did bring again the captivity of "Jacob's tents" and established them before the LORD; however as the last verse of this section states, "The fierce anger of the LORD shall not return, until He have done it, and until He have performed the intents of His heart: <u>in the latter days ye shall consider it</u>" (24). The latter days referring to the time when the LORD will execute His fury upon the head of the wicked (Jacob's Trouble) and then out of Israel will proceed thanksgiving at which time the LORD will multiply them and glorify them, the Millennium Reign of verse 22 will be a reality: **"And ye shall be my people, and I will be your God"**. (Jeremiah 30:22)

CHAPTER THIRTY-ONE
A New Covenant

At the same time, saith the LORD, will I be the God of all the families of Israel, and they shall be my people. Thus saith the LORD, The people which were left of the sword found grace in the wilderness; even Israel, when I went to cause him to rest. The LORD hath appeared of old unto me, saying, Yea, I have loved thee with an everlasting love: therefore with lovingkindness have I drawn thee. Again I will build thee, and thou shalt be built, O virgin of Israel: thou shalt again be adorned with thy tabrets, and shalt go forth in the dances of them that make merry. Thou shalt yet plant vines upon the mountains of Samaria: the planters shall plant, and shall eat them as common things. For there shall be a day, that the watchmen upon the mount Ephraim shall cry, Arise ye, and let us go up to Zion unto the LORD our God. For thus saith the LORD; Sing with gladness for Jacob, and shout among the chief of the nations: publish ye, praise ye, and say, O LORD, save thy people, the remnant of Israel. Behold, I will bring them from the north country, and gather them from the coasts of the earth, and with them the blind and the lame, the woman with child and her that travaileth with child together: a great company shall return thither. They shall come with weeping, and with supplications will I lead them: I will cause them to walk by the rivers of waters in a straight way, wherein they shall not stumble: for I am a father to Israel, and Ephraim is my firstborn. (Jeremiah 31:1-9)

Father to Israel and Ephraim My Firstborn (1-9): Once again the main thrust of this section is the future re-gathering of the whole house of Israel. Even a casual read of these passages will show that the subject goes well beyond the re-gathering under Ezra and Nehemiah. It would seem the historical account of the re-gathering following Babylonian captivity and the future re-gathering are intertwined throughout these passages. Notice that they are to be re-gathered from not only the "north country" but also from "the coasts of the earth" (8); showing that more than only the Babylonian captivity is in view. Also notice that they are told to plant vines upon the mountains of Samaria (5). Those of Samaria were not allowed to partake of the temple rebuilding under the first re-gathering (Ezra 4:1-6), placing this in the yet future time when the LORD will gather Israel from among the nations and lead them back into the land God has promised them (See Isaiah 11:12-16 for the path of the redeemed).

Ephraim is Joseph's second born son, Manasseh being the first born (Gen. 41:51). However, Ephraim is the first born as to preeminence; the blessing of the first born goes to Ephraim; he gets the blessing associated with that position (vs. 9 cf. Gen. 48:13-22). Just as Jesus Christ is said to be the "first born of every creature" He is not born in the sense that He had a beginning, as though He is not eternal, but first born as to preeminence: "…that in all things he might have the preeminence" (Col. 1:16, 18).

Hear the word of the LORD, O ye nations, and declare it in the isles afar off, and say, He that scattered Israel will gather him, and keep him, as a shepherd doth his flock. For the LORD hath redeemed Jacob, and ransomed him from the hand of him that was stronger than he. Therefore they shall come and sing in the height of Zion, and shall flow together to the goodness of the LORD, for wheat, and for wine, and for oil, and for the young of the flock and of the herd: and their soul shall be as a watered garden; and they shall not sorrow any more at all. Then shall the virgin rejoice in the dance, both young men and old together: for I will turn their mourning into joy, and will comfort them, and make them rejoice from their sorrow. And I will satiate the soul of the priests with fatness, and my people shall be satisfied with my goodness, saith the LORD. (Jeremiah 31:10-14)

The Song of the Redeemed of the LORD (10-14): As has been stated in the previous section the LORD will gather His redeemed from the isles afar off, ransoming them from he that is stronger than he (10-11). The LORD will bring back the remnant of Israel from the lands where they have been scattered and when He does they will sing of the goodness of the LORD (12-14 cf. Isaiah 12).

Thus saith the LORD; A voice was heard in Ramah, lamentation, and bitter weeping; Rahel weeping for her children refused to be comforted for her children, because they were not. Thus saith the LORD; Refrain thy voice from weeping, and thine eyes from tears: for thy work shall be rewarded, saith the LORD; and they shall come again from the land of the enemy. And there is hope in thine end, saith the LORD that thy children shall come again to their own border. (Jeremiah 31:15-17)

The Comfort of Rahel (15-17): The Gospel of Matthew applies this verse to those who died by the hand of Herod (Matt. 2:17-18). The context is of those taken away in Babylonian Captivity, Ramah was the assembling place for those being taken away captive (Jer. 40:1); thus, Jeremiah hears weeping in Ramah (15). The weeping is from Rahel (Rachel) who gave birth to Joseph (Manasseh and Ephraim) and Benjamin. Thus, Rachel is weeping for Ephraim (northern tribes) who were taken into captivity by the Assyrians and now Benjamin (southern tribes) are being taken away as well, she is robbed of her children! (15). The LORD'S comforting word however is, "refrain thy voice from weeping and thine eyes from tears: for thy work shall be rewarded saith the LORD and they shall come again from the land of the enemy" (16) and that "thy children shall come again from the land of the enemy" (17).

I have surely heard Ephraim bemoaning himself thus; Thou h ast chastised me, and I was chastised, as a bullock unaccustomed to the yoke: turn thou me, and I shall be turned; for thou art the LORD my God. Surely after that I was turned, I repented; and after that I was instructed, I smote upon my thigh: I was ashamed, yea, even confounded, because I did bear the reproach of my youth. Is Ephraim my dear son? is he a pleasant child? for since I spake against him, I do earnestly remember him still: therefore my bowels are troubled for him; I will surely have mercy upon him, saith the LORD. Set thee up waymarks, make thee high heaps: set thine heart toward the highway, even the way which thou wentest: turn again, O virgin of Israel, turn again to these thy cities. (Jeremiah 31:18-21)

Bemoaning of Ephraim (18-21): The northern tribes were the first to suffer greatly under the chastisement (18) from the LORD. Having been conquered over

100 years earlier, the northern tribes bore the reproach of their youth (19). However, the LORD will set up waymarks toward the highway and bring them back into their city (21).

How long wilt thou go about, O thou backsliding daughter? for the LORD hath created a new thing in the earth, A woman shall compass a man. Thus saith the LORD of hosts, the God of Israel; As yet they shall use this speech in the land of Judah and in the cities thereof, when I shall bring again their captivity; The LORD bless thee, O habitation of justice, and mountain of holiness. And there shall dwell in Judah itself, and in all the cities thereof together, husbandmen, and they that go forth with flocks. For I have satiated the weary soul, and I have replenished every sorrowful soul. Upon this I awaked, and beheld; and my sleep was sweet unto me. (Jeremiah 31:22-26)

I Shall Bring Again the Captivity (22-26): Once again we see these verses reaching beyond the return from the Babylonian captivity at the time of Ezra and Nehemiah for these verses deal with a time in which the LORD will restore onto them a pure language, the Hebrew language (see Zeph. 3:9).

Behold, the days come, saith the LORD, that I will sow the house of Israel and the house of Judah with

the seed of man, and with the seed of beast. And it shall come to pass, that like as I have watched over them, to pluck up, and to break down, and to throw down, and to destroy, and to afflict; so will I watch over them, to build, and to plant, saith the LORD. In those days they shall say no more, The fathers have eaten a sour grape, and the children's teeth are set on edge. But every one shall die for his own iniquity: every man that eateth the sour grape, his teeth shall be set on edge. (Jeremiah 31:27-30)

The Cease of a Proverb (27-30): The whole house of Israel, both Israel and Judah are in view. They both will be brought back into their land, just as a farmer casts his seed through his fields to plant his crop; the LORD will sow the "house of Israel and the house of Judah" to plant them in the land of Israel (27, 28). Verse 29 & 30 deal with a proverb that was commonly used in the land. The issue of this proverb is discussed in Ezekiel 18. [41] The idea conveyed in this proverb is that the sons of the fathers are only experiencing the judgment of God because of the sins of the fathers and not as a result of any iniquity on their part. Thus, the fathers have eaten sour grapes and the children's teeth are set on edge (the children are reaping the consequences). The argument against this is briefly stated in verse 30, that everyone is accountable for his own actions. The more detailed argument against this idea is in Ezekiel 18.

---

[41] See Commentary of Ezekiel by author.

Behold, the days come, saith the LORD, that I will make a new covenant with the house of Israel, and with the house of Judah: Not according to the covenant that I made with their fathers in the day that I took them by the hand to bring them out of the land of Egypt; which my covenant they brake, although I was an husband unto them, saith the LORD: But this shall be the covenant that I will make with the house of Israel; After those days, saith the LORD, I will put my law in their inward parts, and write it in their hearts; and will be their God, and they shall be my people. And they shall teach no more every man his neighbour, and every man his brother, saying, Know the LORD: for they shall all know me, from the least of them unto the greatest of them, saith the LORD: for I will forgive their iniquity, and I will remember their sin no more. (Jeremiah 31:31-34)

The New Covenant (31-34): To fully understand these passages and the idea of a New Covenant one needs to understand all the covenants and their relationship to each other. The following is a brief overview of these covenants:

• The **Abrahamic Covenant** is an unconditional covenant made with Abraham and his seed. Given in Genesis 12, the statement by God is that God would bless Abraham and his seed above all other nations:
Now the LORD had said unto Abram,
Get thee out of thy country, and from thy

> kindred, and from thy father's house, unto a land that I will shew thee: And <u>I will make of thee a great nation</u>, and I will bless thee, <u>and make thy name great</u>; and thou shalt be a blessing: And I will bless them that bless thee, and curse him that curseth thee: and in thee shall all families of the earth be blessed. (Genesis 12:1-3)

Their greatness is the issue in this covenant. Great not only because of their multiplied seed but also great as to their exaltation above all people and nations. This greatness issue is a result of the greatness of the One sitting and ruling in their midst, the LORD Himself. It will be the LORD that will accomplish His will through them, hence the "I will" in the above passages.

It is important to note that all other covenants are given to accomplish the Abrahamic covenant. They are the means by which the LORD will accomplish making Abraham and his seed that great nation.

• The **Mosaic Covenant** given at Mount Sinai was originally given to Abraham's seed because of their desire to be all that the Abrahamic covenant called for in their own strength. This covenant was based on their performance in keeping all of its laws. As the nation gathered at the bottom of Mount Sinai, Moses rehearsed the Law to the people and they replied (too their own folly) "all that the LORD hath spoken we will do" (Ex. 19:8, 24:3, 7). Even before Moses came down from the mount the people had already broken the covenant they had made with God (Ex. 32). This covenant was meant to be done away with, for if Abraham's seed was going to be all that the Abrahamic covenant called for they would need to be dealt with in another way; they will need to be dealt with by grace. We will deal with how the LORD solved this issue in the last covenant.

• The **Land Covenant** is given in Deut. 29 & 30. This covenant is given to Abraham and his seed, and its view is the land, the land in which they are to be that "great nation." Though Abraham's seed is to be blessed in the land only upon their obedience to the Law Covenant, their obtaining the land is *unconditional*. The LORD will see that they inherit the land forever (Ezek. 37:20-23).

• The **Davidic Covenant** is given to accomplish the "greatness" issue as to who will be ruling through them. To be the head over all the nations requires a throne of all authority. They are going to be the blessing to all the nations because the Blessed One will be ruling in their midst. For the nation to be ruling over all the earth would also require an eternal throne. This eternal throne issue is also dealt with through this covenant. The issue of death has to be resolved and it is that issue that is resolved through this covenant. This covenant given in 2 Samuel 7 promises an eternal seed and an eternal throne. Originally given to David and his seed it extends to an unbroken bloodline that flows to our LORD Jesus Christ who will sit on the throne of David as King of kings and LORD of lords. Having conquered death He has the power to resurrect those to whom the covenants of promise are made.

• The last covenant is the **New Covenant** and it is this covenant that Jeremiah 31:31-34 is dealing with. The New Covenant is the covenant that is to replace the Law Covenant. It is the means by which the LORD will make Abraham's seed spiritually fit to be that "great nation" that the Abrahamic covenant calls for[42]. The Law Covenant was based on the performance of the flesh, the New Covenant will be based on the inner man, the heart. It is an unconditional covenant (Jer. 31:35-37) whereby Abraham's seed will be dealt with by grace and not according to their performance. The New Covenant is in Jeremiah 31:31-34, Jeremiah 32:36-41; Ezekiel 36:24-28, Hebrews 8 & 10. It is provided for by the atoning work of our Lord Jesus Christ on the cross and His resurrection. It is a time in which our LORD will remove from Abraham's seed their sins and write His laws in their heart, and give them His Spirit and making them spiritually fit to function as that

---

[42] This covenant is for both the house of Israel and house of Judah Ezekiel 37:15-19.

"great nation" (Jer. 31:33 cf. Heb. 10:16-18). This will begin with a remnant prior to the establishment of the Kingdom, but will come to full bloom during the Millennial Kingdom (Zech. 12:10-13:1).

Thus saith the LORD, which giveth the sun for a light by day, and the ordinances of the moon and of the stars for a light by night, which divideth the sea when the waves thereof roar; The LORD of hosts is his name: If those ordinances depart from before me, saith the LORD, then the seed of Israel also shall cease from being a nation before me for ever. Thus saith the LORD; If heaven above can be measured, and the foundations of the earth searched out beneath, I will also cast off all the seed of Israel for all that they have done, saith the LORD. (Jeremiah 31:35-37)

An Unconditional Covenant (35-37): These verses reinforce the idea that this covenant is an everlasting covenant, it is immutable (see Hebrews 6:13 cf. Hebrews 6:18). The LORD's dependability is directly associated with the fulfillment of all these promises given to the nation of Israel (Jer. 33:19-22; Rom. 11:1).

Behold, the days come, saith the LORD, that the city shall be built to the LORD from the tower of Hananeel unto the gate of the corner. And the measuring line shall yet go forth over against it

upon the hill Gareb, and shall compass about to Goath. And the whole valley of the dead bodies, and of the ashes, and all the fields unto the brook of Kidron, unto the corner of the horse gate toward the east, shall be holy unto the LORD; it shall not be plucked up, nor thrown down any more for ever. (Jeremiah 31:38-40)

A Future City Built For the LORD (38-40): This could not be a reference to the rebuilding following the Babylonian captivity for this city shall "not be plucked up, nor thrown down any more for ever" (40). What is given in these verses is the future city: dimensions of the city of New Jerusalem.

CHAPTER THIRTY-TWO
A Promise to Return

The word that came to Jeremiah from the LORD in the tenth year of Zedekiah king of Judah, which was the eighteenth year of Nebuchadrezzar. For then the king of Babylon's army besieged Jerusalem: and Jeremiah the prophet was shut up in the court of the prison, which was in the king of Judah's house. For Zedekiah king of Judah had shut him up, saying, Wherefore dost thou prophesy, and say, Thus saith the LORD, Behold, I will give this city into the hand of the king of Babylon, and he shall take it; And Zedekiah king of Judah shall not escape out of the hand of the Chaldeans, but shall surely be delivered into the hand of the king of Babylon, and shall speak with him mouth to mouth, and his eyes shall behold his eyes; And he shall lead Zedekiah to Babylon, and there shall he be until I visit him, saith the LORD: though ye fight with the Chaldeans, ye shall not prosper? (Jeremiah 32:1-5)

The Prophesy of Zedekiah's Demise (1-6): Not in chronological order this chapter takes place one year before Nebuchadnezzar's armies breach the walls of Jerusalem (cf. Jer. 39:1-2). Jeremiah is "shut up in the court of the prison, which was in the king of Judah's house"; this is a type of house arrest (2). Jeremiah remains in prison all during the siege even until the Chaldean armies take the city (38:28). The reason for Jeremiah's imprisonment is treason. He was declaring the fall of King Zedekiah and had been preaching for him to surrender to the Chaldean armies. As to the death of Zedekiah, Jeremiah predicts that Zedekiah will be "delivered into the hand of the king of Babylon and shall speak with him mouth to mouth and <u>his eyes shall behold his eyes</u>" (4 cf. 34:3). This prophecy seemed to Zedekiah contradictory to what the prophet Ezekiel had been prophesying from the province of Chebar. Ezekiel had prophesied that Zedekiah will be taken to Babylon to the land of the Chaldeans, <u>yet shall he not see it, though he shall die there</u>" (Ezek. 12:13). These two seemingly contradictory statements are solved in an amazing turn of events where Zedekiah flees Jerusalem with his family, but is overtaken by the Nebuzaradan captain of the guard and meets up with Nebuchadnezzar at Riblah. There Zedekiah speaks to Nebuchadnezzar mouth to mouth and eye to eye. Then Nebuchadnezzar has Zedekiah's sons killed before his eyes. Nebuchadnezzar then has Zedekiah's eyes plucked out and then he is taken into Babylon where he dies (Jer. 39:1-7 cf. 2 Kings 4-7) fulfilling both Jeremiah's and Ezekiel's prophesies. Zedekiah did talk to Nebuchadnezzar and behold each other's eyes, but then was blinded and taken into Babylon a city of which he did not see.

And Jeremiah said, The word of the LORD came unto me, saying, Behold, Hanameel the son of Shallum thine uncle shall come unto thee, saying, Buy thee my field that is in Anathoth: for the right of redemption is thine to buy it. So Hanameel mine uncle's son came to me in the court of the prison according to the word of the LORD, and said unto me, Buy my field, I pray thee, that is in Anathoth, which is in the country of Benjamin: for the right of inheritance is thine, and the redemption is thine; buy it for thyself. Then I knew that this was the word of the LORD. And I bought the field of Hanameel my uncle's son, that was in Anathoth, and weighed him the money, even seventeen shekels of silver. And I subscribed the evidence, and sealed it, and took witnesses, and weighed him the money in the balances. So I took the evidence of the purchase, both that which was sealed according to the law and custom, and that which was open: And I gave the evidence of the purchase unto Baruch the son of Neriah, the son of Maaseiah, in the sight of Hanameel mine uncle's son, and in the presence of the witnesses that subscribed the book of the purchase, before all the Jews that sat in the court of the prison. (Jeremiah 32:6-12)

The Purchase of Land (6-12): While Jeremiah is in the court of the prison the LORD tells him that his uncle's son, Hanameel is going to offer Jeremiah to purchase his field in Jeremiah's home town, Anathoth. This act is done according to Leviticus 25:23-38. Land in Jerusalem was never to be sold, nor was it to leave the tribes' families to whom it was given under the original inheritance[43]; in this case Anathoth is in the land of Benjamin (8). Jeremiah had the right of redemption: he had the right to the land, he was of the tribe of Benjamin. He was also able to redeem it, financially he was able and he was willing to redeem it. Jeremiah buys the land from Hanameel and follows the prescribed manner of sale: The price is agreed on, and the silver weighed in the balances. A contract or deed of sale is drawn up, to which both parties agree. Witnesses are brought forward to see it signed and sealed; for the contract was both subscribed and sealed. A duplicate of the deed was drawn, which was not to be sealed, but to lie open for the inspection of those concerned in some public place where it might be safe and always to be seen. However in this case both copies are placed into an earthen vessel due to the fact the city it going to be destroyed. They then subscribed the book of the purchase, perhaps a town book, or register, where such purchases were entered. Baruch was a scribe by

---

[43] God told the Israelites that they were not the actual owners of the land, for it belonged to the LORD; they were simply stewards of it.

profession; and the deeds were delivered into his hands, before witnesses, to be preserved. (9-12).

And I charged Baruch before them, saying, Thus saith the LORD of hosts, the God of Israel; Take these evidences, this evidence of the purchase, both which is sealed, and this evidence which is open; and put them in an earthen vessel, that they may continue many days. For thus saith the LORD of hosts, the God of Israel; Houses and fields and vineyards shall be possessed again in this land. (Jeremiah 32:13-15)

The Purpose of this Act (13-15): This act is done to show that the LORD will bring them back into the land one day: "For thus saith the LORD of hosts, the God of Israel; Houses and fields and vineyards shall be possessed again in this land" (15). This is the whole point of this chapter and the reason that Jeremiah is told to purchase the land of Anathoth, in the land of Benjamin; for the LORD will gather again His people and establish them safely in the land and they will take witness, the title deed to their respective properties (See vs. 44).

Now when I had delivered the evidence of the purchase unto Baruch the son of Neriah, I prayed unto the LORD, saying, Ah Lord GOD! behold, thou hast made the heaven and the earth by thy great power and stretched out arm, and there is nothing too hard for thee: Thou shewest lovingkindness unto thousands, and recompensest the iniquity of the fathers into the bosom of their children after them: the Great, the Mighty God, the LORD of hosts, is his name, Great in counsel, and mighty in work: for thine eyes are open upon all the ways of the sons of men: to give every one according to his ways, and according to the fruit of his doings: Which hast set signs and wonders in the land of Egypt, even unto this day, and in Israel, and among other men; and hast made thee a name, as at this day; And hast brought forth thy people Israel out of the land of Egypt with signs, and with wonders, and with a strong hand, and with a stretched out arm, and with great terror; And hast given them this land, which thou didst swear to their fathers to give them, a land flowing with milk and honey; And they came in, and possessed it; but they obeyed not thy voice, neither walked in thy law; they have done nothing of all that thou commandedst them to do: therefore thou hast caused all this evil to come upon them: Behold the mounts, they are come unto the city to take it; and the city is given into the hand of the Chaldeans, that fight against it, because of the sword, and of the famine, and of the pestilence: and what thou hast spoken is come to pass; and, behold, thou seest it. And thou hast said unto me, O Lord GOD, Buy thee the field for money, and take witnesses; for the city is given into the hand of the Chaldeans. (Jeremiah 32:16-25)

The Prayer of Jeremiah (16-25): Upon delivering the evidence of the purchase of the land to Baruch, Jeremiah prayed unto the LORD. Jeremiah's prayer starts out with the statement, *"Ah Lord GOD! behold, thou hast made the heaven and the earth by thy great power and stretched out arm, and <u>there is nothing too hard for thee</u>"* (17). And his prayer ends with, *"And thou hast said unto me, O Lord GOD, Buy thee the field for money, and take witnesses; for the city is given into the hand of the Chaldeans"* (25). What Jeremiah is emphasizing is the land given to His people (18-22), and how, because of disobedience they are now being removed from it (23-24). Yet the LORD still told Jeremiah to buy the field in the land of Benjamin (25). Thus, God is the faithful One who will see to it that His people inherit their land one day! What follows in verses 36-44 is the faithfulness of God in doing this very thing.

Then came the word of the LORD unto Jeremiah, saying, Behold, I am the LORD, the God of all flesh: is there any thing too hard for me? Therefore thus saith the LORD; Behold, I will give this city into the hand of the Chaldeans, and into the hand of Nebuchadrezzar king of Babylon, and he shall take it: And the Chaldeans, that fight against this city, shall come and set fire on this city, and burn it with the houses, upon whose roofs they have offered incense unto Baal, and poured out drink offerings unto other gods, to provoke me to anger. For the children of Israel and the children of Judah have

only done evil before me from their youth: for the children of Israel have only provoked me to anger with the work of their hands, saith the LORD. For this city hath been to me as a provocation of mine anger and of my fury from the day that they built it even unto this day; that I should remove it from before my face, Because of all the evil of the children of Israel and of the children of Judah, which they have done to provoke me to anger, they, their kings, their princes, their priests, and their prophets, and the men of Judah, and the inhabitants of Jerusalem. And they have turned unto me the back, and not the face: though I taught them, rising up early and teaching them, yet they have not hearkened to receive instruction. But they set their abominations in the house, which is called by my name, to defile it. And they built the high places of Baal, which are in the valley of the son of Hinnom, to cause their sons and their daughters to pass through the fire unto Molech; which I commanded them not, neither came it into my mind, that they should do this abomination, to cause Judah to sin. (Jeremiah 32:26-35)

Rehearsal of the Evil of the Children of Israel and Judah (26-35): The LORD will start out this section with, "Behold, I am the LORD, the God of all flesh: is there anything too hard for me?" (27). This statement, lining up with verse 17 of Jeremiah, is a reference to the LORD being able to bring them back into the land, as is stated in verses 36-44. However prior to that promise, the LORD recounts the evil of both Israel and Judah (30, 32).

And now therefore thus saith the LORD, the God of Israel, concerning this city, whereof ye say, It shall be delivered into the hand of the king of Babylon by the sword, and by the famine, and by the pestilence; Behold, I will gather them out of all countries, whither I have driven them in mine anger, and in my fury, and in great wrath; and I will bring them again unto this place, and I will cause them to dwell safely: And they shall be my people, and I will be their God: And I will give them one heart, and one way, that they may fear me for ever, for the good of them, and of their children after them: And I will make an everlasting covenant with them, that I will not turn away from them, to do them good; but I will put my fear in their hearts, that they shall not depart from me. Yea, I will rejoice over them to do them good, and I will plant them in this land assuredly with my whole heart and with my whole soul. For thus saith the LORD; Like as I have brought all this great evil upon this people, so will I bring upon them all the good that I have promised them. And fields shall be bought in this land, whereof ye say, It is desolate without man or beast; it is given into the hand of the Chaldeans. Men shall buy fields for money, and subscribe evidences, and seal them, and take witnesses in the land of Benjamin, and in the places about

Jerusalem, and in the cities of Judah, and in the cities of the mountains, and in the cities of the valley, and in the cities of the south: for I will cause their captivity to return, saith the LORD. (Jeremiah 32:36-44)

I Will Cause the Captivity to Return (36-44): This section ends with the reality that nothing is too hard for the LORD! The LORD reconfirms the New Covenant through Jeremiah to His people. Once again this is not anything the LORD has already accomplished, for it will only be accomplished once all Israel and all Judah is returned to the land. They will have one heart and one way before the LORD, "forever" (39). Once again this is the sum of all things pertaining to this chapter and why it is that Jeremiah is told to purchase the land of Anathoth in the country of Benjamin (vs. 8 cf. vs. 44).

CHAPTER THIRTY-THREE
Confirmation of the Faithfulness of God

Moreover the word of the LORD came unto Jeremiah the second time, while he was yet shut up in the court of the prison, saying, Thus saith the LORD the maker thereof, the LORD that formed it, to establish it; the LORD is his name; Call unto me, and I will answer thee, and shew thee great and mighty things, which thou knowest not. For thus saith the LORD, the God of Israel, concerning the houses of this city, and concerning the houses of the kings of Judah, which are thrown down by the mounts, and by the sword; They come to fight with the Chaldeans, but it is to fill them with the dead bodies of men, whom I have slain in mine anger and in my fury, and for all whose wickedness I have hid my face from this city. Behold, I will bring it health and cure, and I will cure them, and will reveal unto them the abundance of peace and truth. And I will cause the captivity of Judah and the captivity of Israel to return, and will build them, as at the first.

And I will cleanse them from all their iniquity, whereby they have sinned against me; and I will pardon all their iniquities, whereby they have sinned, and whereby they have transgressed against me. (Jeremiah 33:1-8)

Great and Mighty Things (1-8): In this chapter Jeremiah is still shut up in prison as in the previous chapter (1). This chapter is going to confirm the faithfulness of God in restoring both Judah and Israel back into the land. As has been mentioned, this is more than a fulfillment of the return of a remnant under Ezra and Nehemiah but is at a time yet future in which they will have their iniquities dealt with and begin to function at the capacity for which God originally created them (Ex. 19:5,6). The LORD is accomplishing this for His people in the "great and mighty things..." which the LORD will show Jeremiah and what follows in the remainder of this chapter (3). Once again the reconfirmation of the issues pertaining to the New Covenant is reiterated in verses 7 & 8 (cf. Jer. 31; Ezek. 36:26). Notice as well that it is both the captivity of Judah and of Israel that is in view, no lost tribes here!

And it shall be to me a name of joy, a praise and an honour before all the nations of the earth, which shall hear all the good that I do unto them: and they shall fear and tremble for all the goodness and for

all the prosperity that I procure unto it. Thus saith the LORD; Again there shall be heard in this place, which ye say shall be desolate without man and without beast, even in the cities of Judah, and in the streets of Jerusalem, that are desolate, without man, and without inhabitant, and without beast, The voice of joy, and the voice of gladness, the voice of the bridegroom, and the voice of the bride, the voice of them that shall say, Praise the LORD of hosts: for the LORD is good; for his mercy endureth for ever: and of them that shall bring the sacrifice of praise into the house of the LORD. For I will cause to return the captivity of the land, as at the first, saith the LORD. Thus saith the LORD of hosts; Again in this place, which is desolate without man and without beast, and in all the cities thereof, shall be an habitation of shepherds causing their flocks to lie down. In the cities of the mountains, in the cities of the vale, and in the cities of the south, and in the land of Benjamin, and in the places about Jerusalem, and in the cities of Judah, shall the flocks pass again under the hands of him that telleth them, saith the LORD. Behold, the days come, saith the LORD, that I will perform that good thing which I have promised unto the house of Israel and to the house of Judah. (Jeremiah 33:9-14)

The Goodness of the Land Restored (9-14): Again, this entire chapter is dealing with the "great and mighty things" that the LORD will accomplish once He comes to gather His people both Israel and Judah back into the land and deal with them according to the New Covenant. Jerusalem and its people that are about to be desolated are going to be glorious once again. They will be unto the LORD a name of joy, and praise and honor before all the nations, for the goodness and prosperity that the LORD will procure unto it (9 cf. Deut. 28:13, 14). Within the walls of Jerusalem and throughout the cities of Judah will be restored the voice of joy, the voice of gladness, the voice of the bridegroom, and the voice of the bride, the voice of them that shall say, "Praise the LORD of hosts" shall bring the sacrifice of praise into the house of the LORD (11). And Jerusalem and the cities of Judah will be a place for the shepherds to tend their flocks (12-13). The LORD tells Jeremiah that these days described will come as the LORD has promised to the house of Israel and the house of Judah (14).

In those days, and at that time, will I cause the Branch of righteousness to grow up unto David; and he shall execute judgment and righteousness in the land. In those days shall Judah be saved, and Jerusalem shall dwell safely: and this is the name wherewith she shall be called, The LORD our righteousness. For thus saith the LORD; David shall never want a man to sit upon the throne of the house of Israel; Neither shall the priests the Levites want a man before me to offer burnt offerings, and to

kindle meat offerings, and to do sacrifice continually. (Jeremiah 33:15-18)

The Continuation of the Davidic Line and the Unchanging Priesthood (15-18): These verses are to take place "in those days and at that time" (15) in which this chapter is dealing. A time when God will re-gather both Israel and Judah into the land and bless them according to God's Covenant. The LORD Jesus Christ is the Branch of David the Stem of Jesse (Isaiah 11:1). The context of these passages and those in Zechariah (Zech. 6:12) show that the time of their fulfilment is the establishment of the Kingdom in which the Branch will execute judgment and righteousness in the land (15). He will also deliver Judah and cause Jerusalem to dwell safely (16). Verse 17 is a confirmation of the Davidic Covenant, the promise that the Davidic line will never be broken. The LORD also confirms that the tribe of Levi will continue its service stating, "neither shall the priests and the Levites want a man before me to offer burnt offerings and to kindle meat offering and to do sacrifice continually" (18).

And the word of the LORD came unto Jeremiah, saying, Thus saith the LORD; If ye can break my covenant of the day, and my covenant of the night, and that there should not be day and night in their season; Then may also my covenant be broken with

David my servant, that he should not have a son to reign upon his throne; and with the Levites the priests, my ministers. As the host of heaven cannot be numbered, neither the sand of the sea measured: so will I multiply the seed of David my servant, and the Levites that minister unto me. Moreover the word of the LORD came to Jeremiah, saying, Considerest thou not what this people have spoken, saying, The two families which the LORD hath chosen, he hath even cast them off? thus they have despised my people, that they should be no more a nation before them. Thus saith the LORD; If my covenant be not with day and night, and if I have not appointed the ordinances of heaven and earth; Then will I cast away the seed of Jacob, and David my servant, so that I will not take any of his seed to be rulers over the seed of Abraham, Isaac, and Jacob: for I will cause their captivity to return, and have mercy on them. (Jeremiah 33:19-26)

The Everlasting Covenant of the LORD (19-26): In this portion the LORD is reconfirming the unchanging covenant promises. We have seen this confirmation by the LORD in Jeremiah 31:35-37. The inability of man to directly or indirectly thwart the Covenant Promises of God is seen in the statement: "If ye can break my covenant of the day, and my covenant of the night, and that there should not be day and night in their season; then may also my covenant be broken with David, my servant..." (20, 21). Jeremiah is told not to consider what the people have spoken, for they say, "The two families which the LORD hath chosen, he hath even cast them off ... that they should be no more a nation" (24). The people are saying these things because this is what it would seem the LORD is doing: the Babylonian armies are coming to take away Judah; with the Assyrian armies having taken away Israel over a hundred years previous. The LORD will see to it, however that the seed of Jacob is not cast away (26).

CHAPTER THIRTY-FOUR
Proclaiming Liberty

The word which came unto Jeremiah from the LORD, when Nebuchadnezzar king of Babylon, and all his army, and all the kingdoms of the earth of his dominion, and all the people, fought against Jerusalem, and against all the cities thereof, saying, Thus saith the LORD, the God of Israel; Go and speak to Zedekiah king of Judah, and tell him, Thus saith the LORD; Behold, I will give this city into the hand of the king of Babylon, and he shall burn it with fire: And thou shalt not escape out of his hand, but shalt surely be taken, and delivered into his hand; and thine eyes shall behold the eyes of the king of Babylon, and he shall speak with thee mouth to mouth, and thou shalt go to Babylon. Yet hear the word of the LORD, O Zedekiah king of Judah; Thus saith the LORD of thee, Thou shalt not die by the sword: But thou shalt die in peace: and with the burnings of thy fathers, the former kings which were before thee, so shall they burn odours for thee; and they will lament thee, saying, Ah lord! for I have pronounced the word, saith the LORD.

Then Jeremiah the prophet spake all these words unto Zedekiah king of Judah in Jerusalem, When the king of Babylon's army fought against Jerusalem, and against all the cities of Judah that were left, against Lachish, and against Azekah: for these defenced cities remained of the cities of Judah. (Jeremiah 34:1-7)

The Death of Zedekiah Revisited (1-7): The armies of Babylon have surrounded the walls of Jerusalem. Nebuchadnezzar's armies are also fighting against the final hold outs of the cities of Judah, Lachish to Azekah (1 cf. 7). In the backdrop of this turbulent time Jeremiah is told to pronounce to King Zedekiah the demise he will encounter (2-6). [44]

This is the word that came unto Jeremiah from the LORD, after that the king Zedekiah had made a covenant with all the people which were at Jerusalem, to proclaim liberty unto them; That every man should let his manservant, and every man his maidservant, being an Hebrew or an Hebrewess, go free; that none should serve himself of them, to wit, of a Jew his brother. Now when all the princes, and all the people, which had entered into the covenant, heard that every one should let his manservant, and every one his maidservant, go

---

[44] We have seen this prophetic announcement before in Jeremiah chapter 32:4, 5 see notes.

free, that none should serve themselves of them any more, then they obeyed, and let them go. But afterward they turned, and caused the servants and the handmaids, whom they had let go free, to return, and brought them into subjection for servants and for handmaids. (Jeremiah 34:8-11)

Business as Usual (8-11): These verses show the wickedness of the heart of the people that the LORD had been putting up with for years (490 years at least), and what will lead to their ultimate demise. Zedekiah makes a covenant with all the people to proclaim liberty throughout the land. This act is really done as a desperate act of repentance. Zedekiah is attempting to get the people to adhere to the Law of God in respect to the treatment of their hired servants. According to the Law every seven years the indentured servant had an opportunity to go free (Deut. 15:12-18). However all indentured servants could not indenture themselves beyond the year of Jubilee[45]. Zedekiah is proclaiming liberty unto the people, thus they are to set all their indentured servants free (8-9 cf. Lev. 25:10). The people adhere to this request at first, however as has been their nature since the day the LORD delivered them from Egypt they break their covenant promise and take to them servants (10-11). The historical events surrounding the people's response to Zedekiah's proclamation of

---

[45] Every seventh year was a Sabbath year. After seven Sabbaths or forty-nine years was a Jubilee year.

Liberty is as follows: The Babylonian army was encamped around Jerusalem during the time that Zedekiah makes the proclamation of Liberty. Once the people obey the proclamation the LORD sees to it that Babylon pack up their tents and head out to deal with Pharaoh Neco. Upon seeing the Babylonians leave the inhabitance of Jerusalem renege on their covenant. This hypocrisy is a reproach to God and therefore the Babylonians come back and continue their campaign against Jerusalem. See verses 21 & 22.

Therefore the word of the LORD came to Jeremiah from the LORD, saying, Thus saith the LORD, the God of Israel; I made a covenant with your fathers in the day that I brought them forth out of the land of Egypt, out of the house of bondmen, saying, At the end of seven years let ye go every man his brother an Hebrew, which hath been sold unto thee; and when he hath served thee six years, thou shalt let him go free from thee: but your fathers hearkened not unto me, neither inclined their ear. And ye were now turned, and had done right in my sight, in proclaiming liberty every man to his neighbour; and ye had made a covenant before me in the house which is called by my name: But ye turned and polluted my name, and caused every man his servant, and every man his handmaid, whom ye had set at liberty at their pleasure, to return, and brought them into subjection, to be unto you for servants and for handmaids. Therefore thus

saith the LORD; Ye have not hearkened unto me, in proclaiming liberty, every one to his brother, and every man to his neighbour: behold, I proclaim a liberty for you, saith the LORD, to the sword, to the pestilence, and to the famine; and I will make you to be removed into all the kingdoms of the earth. And I will give the men that have transgressed my covenant, which have not performed the words of the covenant which they had made before me, when they cut the calf in twain, and passed between the parts thereof, The princes of Judah, and the princes of Jerusalem, the eunuchs, and the priests, and all the people of the land, which passed between the parts of the calf; I will even give them into the hand of their enemies, and into the hand of them that seek their life: and their dead bodies shall be for meat unto the fowls of the heaven, and to the beasts of the earth. And Zedekiah king of Judah and his princes will I give into the hand of their enemies, and into the hand of them that seek their life, and into the hand of the king of Babylon's army, which are gone up from you. Behold, I will command, saith the LORD, and cause them to return to this city; and they shall fight against it, and take it, and burn it with fire: and I will make the cities of Judah a desolation without an inhabitant. (Jeremiah 34:12-22)

The Long History of Rebellion (12-22): Jeremiah brings Zedekiah and the people all the way back to the time in which the Law Covenant was given that dealt with this issue of servants (12-14 cf. Ex. 21:1-11). Jeremiah shows that from the very beginning their fathers broke the Covenant with God (14). And though they did adhere to the request of Zedekiah for a time in proclaiming liberty (15); they quickly turned and rebelled just as their fathers had done (16-17). The results of this disobedience is judgment of the sword, famine and pestilence and Babylonian captivity (17).

An interesting thing Jeremiah does in verses 18-19 is make a comparison between the cutting of the animal, and the nation passing through those pieces (see Gen. 15:10, 17), to what the LORD is going to allow to happen to the people of Jerusalem at the hands of Nebuchadnezzar's armies: they will be cut to pieces and made food for the fowls of the air (20). Zedekiah and the princes will also suffer the wrath for their part in this disobedience. Verses 21 & 22 show how the Babylonian army left its campaign against Jerusalem following Zedekiah's proclamation of liberty; for the king of Babylon was "gone up from them" (21). However following their failure to uphold the covenant, God causes the Babylonian army to "return to this city..." (22).

CHAPTER THIRTY-FIVE
The House of Jonadab

The word which came unto Jeremiah from the LORD in the days of Jehoiakim the son of Josiah king of Judah, saying, Go unto the house of the Rechabites, and speak unto them, and bring them into the house of the LORD, into one of the chambers, and give them wine to drink. Then I took Jaazaniah the son of Jeremiah, the son of Habaziniah, and his brethren, and all his sons, and the whole house of the Rechabites; And I brought them into the house of the LORD, into the chamber of the sons of Hanan, the son of Igdaliah, a man of God, which was by the chamber of the princes, which was above the chamber of Maaseiah the son of Shallum, the keeper of the door: And I set before the sons of the house of the Rechabites pots full of wine, and cups, and I said unto them, Drink ye wine. But they said, We will drink no wine: for Jonadab the son of Rechab our father commanded us, saying, Ye shall drink no wine, neither ye, nor your sons for ever: Neither shall ye build house, nor sow seed, nor plant vineyard, nor have any: but all your days ye shall dwell in tents; that ye may live many days in the land where ye be strangers. Thus have we obeyed the voice of Jonadab the son of Rechab our father in all that he hath charged us, to drink no wine all our days, we, our wives, our sons, nor our daughters; Nor to build houses for us to dwell in: neither have we vineyard, nor field, nor seed: But we have dwelt in tents, and have obeyed, and done according to all that Jonadab our father commanded us. But it came to pass, when Nebuchadrezzar king of Babylon came up into the land, that we said, Come, and let us go to Jerusalem for fear of the army of the Chaldeans, and for fear of the army of the Syrians: so we dwell at Jerusalem. (Jeremiah 35:1-11)

Tradition Over the Word of the LORD (1-11): This chapter takes place during the reign of Josiah king of Judah. Jeremiah is told to go unto the house of Rechabites and set wine before them to drink (2-5). The Rechabites however are faithful in not drinking the wine, for they say, "Jonadab the son of Rechab our father commanded us, saying, Ye shall drink no wine, neither ye nor your sons for ever" (6). The emphasis in this first section is the faithfulness of Jonadab to the words of his family in not doing the things described in this section (6 – 10). In the following verses we see the reason for this symbolic act that Jeremiah was to perform. The house of Jonadab was faithful in following the words of their fathers but the House of Israel and the house of Judah were not faithful in following the words of their Father, by the mouth of Jeremiah; this is the lesson that the LORD is communicating.

Then came the word of the LORD unto Jeremiah, saying, Thus saith the LORD of hosts, the God of Israel; Go and tell the men of Judah and the inhabitants of Jerusalem, Will ye not receive instruction to hearken to my words? saith the LORD. The words of Jonadab the son of Rechab, that he commanded his sons not to drink wine, are performed; for unto this day they drink none, but obey their father's commandment: notwithstanding I have spoken unto you, rising early and speaking; but ye hearkened not unto me. I have sent also unto you all my servants the prophets, rising up early and sending them, saying, Return ye now every man from his evil way, and amend your doings, and go not after other gods to serve them, and ye shall dwell in the land which I have given to you and to your fathers: but ye have not inclined your ear, nor hearkened unto me. Because the sons of Jonadab the son of Rechab have performed the commandment of their father, which he commanded them; but this people hath not hearkened unto me: Therefore thus saith the LORD God of hosts, the God of Israel; Behold, I will bring upon Judah and upon all the inhabitants of Jerusalem all the evil that I have pronounced against them: because I have spoken unto them, but they have not heard; and I have called unto them, but they have not answered. (Jeremiah 35:12-17)

But Ye Hearkened Not (12-17): The truth that is communicated through Jeremiah's symbolic act is brought out in these verses. This portion of Scripture is not so much a commentary on wine but rather the reality that the house of Jonadab and their faithfulness in obeying the voice of the fathers; Israel and Judah however have not obeyed the voice of their Father (13). Notice this emphasis in the following verses: "... but ye hearkened not unto me." (14); "but ye have not inclined your ear nor harkened unto me." (15); "...but this people hath not hearkened unto me." (16). "... but they have not answered." (17).

And Jeremiah said unto the house of the Rechabites, Thus saith the LORD of hosts, the God of Israel; Because ye have obeyed the commandment of Jonadab your father, and kept all his precepts, and done according unto all that he hath commanded you: Therefore thus saith the LORD of hosts, the God of Israel; Jonadab the son of Rechab shall not want a man to stand before me for ever. (Jeremiah 35:18-19)

Reward for Faithfulness to the House of Jonadab (18-19): Not a lot of commentary to add to this; the LORD will see to it that the house of Jonadab will not cease to stand before Him forever.

CHAPTER THIRTY-SIX
A Roll of a Book

And it came to pass in the fourth year of Jehoiakim the son of Josiah king of Judah, that this word came unto Jeremiah from the LORD, saying, Take thee a roll of a book, and write therein all the words that I have spoken unto thee against Israel, and against Judah, and against all the nations, from the day I spake unto thee, from the days of Josiah, even unto this day. It may be that the house of Judah will hear all the evil which I purpose to do unto them; that they may return every man from his evil way; that I may forgive their iniquity and their sin. Then Jeremiah called Baruch the son of Neriah: and Baruch wrote from the mouth of Jeremiah all the words of the LORD, which he had spoken unto him, upon a roll of a book. And Jeremiah commanded Baruch, saying, I am shut up; I cannot go into the house of the LORD: Therefore go thou, and read in the roll, which thou hast written from my mouth, the words of the LORD in the ears of the people in the LORD'S house upon the fasting day: and also thou shalt read them in the ears of all Judah that come out of their cities. It may be they will present their supplication before the LORD, and will return every one from his evil way: for great is the anger and the fury that the LORD hath pronounced against this people. And Baruch the son of Neriah did according to all that Jeremiah the prophet commanded him, reading in the book the words of the LORD in the LORD'S house. And it came to pass in the fifth year of Jehoiakim the son of Josiah king of Judah, in the ninth month, that they proclaimed a fast before the LORD to all the people in Jerusalem, and to all the people that came from the cities of Judah unto Jerusalem. Then read Baruch in the book the words of Jeremiah in the house of the LORD, in the chamber of Gemariah the son of Shaphan the scribe, in the higher court, at the entry of the new gate of the LORD'S house, in the ears of all the people. (Jeremiah 36:1-10)

The Roll of a Book (1-10): The events of this section happen during the reign of Jehoiakim king of Judah. Jeremiah is told to write in a roll of a book all the words the LORD has spoken to Jeremiah concerning Israel, Judah and the cities from the beginning of his ministry (The reign of Josiah king of Judah) unto this day (The reign of Jehoiakim).
What is in this "roll of a book" is all that the LORD purposes to do unto them if they do not turn from their wickedness. Once again the LORD extends his arm of mercy to them desiring them to repent so He can forgive their iniquity and sin (3).

Jeremiah will dictate all that the LORD has spoken to him to his scribe, Baruch[46] and it is written down in a roll of a book (4).

Jeremiah is in prison and is unable to go and read the things he has dictated in the house of the LORD (5). Therefore, Jeremiah sends Baruch to go to the house of the LORD on the fasting day to read all the things spoken by the mouth of Jeremiah, a day that Jeremiah's message would make its greatest impact (5-6). The desire is that the people will hear and repent and turn back to the LORD (7). Notice when the prophet is not able to proclaim the words of the LORD in person, he has the words written down and others proclaim them and they have all the authority as if the prophet himself was proclaiming them (see 2 Tim. 2:9).

Baruch does what is requested of him, reading the words of Jeremiah from the roll of the book in the house of the LORD (8). It would seem from these passages that Baruch reads Jeremiah's message each fast day, for in the "fifth year of the ninth month" he reads again from the book of Jeremiah at the time when all the people proclaim a fast (9). Baruch reads the book of Jeremiah in the chamber of Gemariah the son of Shaphan the scribe in the higher court, at the entering of the new gate of the LORD'S house (10). This will draw added attention from rulers of

---

[46] Baruch is the one also that did record the purchase of the land back in chapter 32:16. Chapter 45 deals with Baruch's lamenting over the events surrounding this chapter.

Jerusalem that leads to the events unfolding in the rest of this chapter.

When Michaiah the son of Gemariah, the son of Shaphan, had heard out of the book all the words of the LORD, Then he went down into the king's house, into the scribe's chamber: and, lo, all the princes sat there, even Elishama the scribe, and Delaiah the son of Shemaiah, and Elnathan the son of Achbor, and Gemariah the son of Shaphan, and Zedekiah the son of Hananiah, and all the princes. Then Michaiah declared unto them all the words that he had heard, when Baruch read the book in the ears of the people. Therefore all the princes sent Jehudi the son of Nethaniah, the son of Shelemiah, the son of Cushi, unto Baruch, saying, Take in thine hand the roll wherein thou hast read in the ears of the people, and come. So Baruch the son of Neriah took the roll in his hand, and came unto them. And they said unto him, Sit down now, and read it in our ears. So Baruch read it in their ears. Now it came to pass, when they had heard all the words, they were afraid both one and other, and said unto Baruch, We will surely tell the king of all these words. And they asked Baruch, saying, Tell us now, How didst thou write all these words at his mouth? Then Baruch answered them, He pronounced all these words unto me with his mouth, and I wrote them with ink in the book. Then said the princes unto Baruch, Go, hide thee, thou and Jeremiah; and let no man know where ye be. (Jeremiah 36:11-19)

The Book Read before the Princes (11-18): Michaiah upon hearing all the words of Baruch goes down to the king's house, into the scribe's chamber, where all the princes sat (11-12). Michaiah then declares all the words that he heard when Baruch read the book in the ears of the people (13). The princes then sent for Baruch and the roll from which he read (14-15). Following Baruch's reading the princes feared for the words that Baruch read, saying, "We will surely tell the king all these words" (16).

The words in the book are words of all the evil that the LORD will do against Israel and Judah and the cities round about. The princes tell Baruch to hide himself and Jeremiah so that no man can find them (19). The LORD will be the one to hide these men (26).

And they went in to the king into the court, but they laid up the roll in the chamber of Elishama the scribe, and told all the words in the ears of the king. So the king sent Jehudi to fetch the roll: and he took it out of Elishama the scribe's chamber. And Jehudi read it in the ears of the king, and in the ears of all the princes which stood beside the king. Now the king sat in the winterhouse in the ninth month: and there was a fire on the hearth burning before him. And it came to pass, that when Jehudi had read three or four leaves, he cut it with the penknife, and

cast it into the fire that was on the hearth, until all the roll was consumed in the fire that was on the hearth. Yet they were not afraid, nor rent their garments, neither the king, nor any of his servants that heard all these words. Nevertheless Elnathan and Delaiah and Gemariah had made intercession to the king that he would not burn the roll: but he would not hear them. But the king commanded Jerahmeel the son of Hammelech, and Seraiah the son of Azriel, and Shelemiah the son of Abdeel, to take Baruch the scribe and Jeremiah the prophet: but the LORD hid them. (Jeremiah 36:20-26)

The Reading of the Book before Jehoiakim (20-26): The princes go before the king and rehearse what was written in the book (20). Jehoiakim commands that Jehudi fetch the roll from Elishama the scribe's chamber and have it read before him and the princes (21). Upon hearing three or four of the leaves of the book, Jehoiakim and his servants were not afraid nor rent their garments but has the roll of the book cut with a penknife and burnt in the fire that was on the hearth, disregarding the pleading of several of his princes (22-25). Jehoiakim also sought to take Jeremiah and Baruch but, "the LORD hid them" (26). All this is done because contained in the roll of the book of Jeremiah is pronouncements of coming judgments specifically that the king of Babylon shall come and destroy this land, and shall cause to cease man and beast (29).

Then the word of the LORD came to Jeremiah, after that the king had burned the roll, and the words which Baruch wrote at the mouth of Jeremiah, saying, Take thee again another roll, and write in it all the former words that were in the first roll, which Jehoiakim the king of Judah hath burned. And thou shalt say to Jehoiakim king of Judah, Thus saith the LORD; Thou hast burned this roll, saying, Why hast thou written therein, saying, The king of Babylon shall certainly come and destroy this land, and shall cause to cease from thence man and beast? Therefore thus saith the LORD of Jehoiakim king of Judah; He shall have none to sit upon the throne of David: and his dead body shall be cast out in the day to the heat, and in the night to the frost. And I will punish him and his seed and his servants for their iniquity; and I will bring upon them, and upon the inhabitants of Jerusalem, and upon the men of Judah, all the evil that I have pronounced against them; but they hearkened not. Then took Jeremiah another roll, and gave it to Baruch the scribe, the son of Neriah; who wrote therein from the mouth of Jeremiah all the words of the book which Jehoiakim king of Judah had burned in the fire: and there were added besides unto them many like words. (Jeremiah 36:27-32)

Write Again the Words of Jeremiah (27-32): The words of the LORD come to Jeremiah telling him to write again all the words that were in the roll that Jehoiakim had burned (27-28). The reason for the hatred on king Jehoiakim's part is due in part that the roll predicted that the king of Babylon would take the city (29). This indeed does take place just as the word of the LORD said, for they did not repent and therefore judgment came (24). Jeremiah also declares judgment unto Jehoiakim for his burning of the roll, pronouncing that Jehoiakim king of Judah, "will have none to sit upon the throne of David and his dead body shall be cast out in the day to the heat and in the night to the frost". All the judgment that is pronounced in the book of the roll by Jeremiah will come to pass, for the first siege against Jerusalem happens during his reign (29-31 cf. 2 Kings 24:1-4). The LORD added besides the original words that were first written in the roll of the book of Jeremiah, "many like words" (32).

CHAPTER THIRTY-SEVEN
Jeremiah's Imprisonment

And king Zedekiah the son of Josiah reigned instead of Coniah the son of Jehoiakim, whom Nebuchadrezzar king of Babylon made king in the land of Judah. But neither he, nor his servants, nor the people of the land, did hearken unto the words of the LORD, which he spake by the prophet Jeremiah. And Zedekiah the king sent Jehucal the son of Shelemiah and Zephaniah the son of Maaseiah the priest to the prophet Jeremiah, saying, Pray now unto the LORD our God for us. Now Jeremiah came in and went out among the people: for they had not put him into prison. Then Pharaoh's army was come forth out of Egypt: and when the Chaldeans that besieged Jerusalem heard tidings of them, they departed from Jerusalem. (Jeremiah 37:1-5)

The Rebellious Puppet King Zedekiah (1-5): Zedekiah is placed on the throne by Babylon and therefore was expected to be loyal to king Nebuchadnezzar (2 Kings 24:17). However, Zedekiah rebels against the king Nebuchadnezzar and makes alliance with Pharaoh (Pharaoh Hophra) just as Israel had done in hope to deliver them from the Assyrian armies (2 Chron. 36:12-13; 2 Kings 24:20; Isa. 36:6).

Then came the word of the LORD unto the prophet Jeremiah, saying, Thus saith the LORD, the God of Israel; Thus shall ye say to the king of Judah, that sent you unto me to inquire of me; Behold, Pharaoh's army, which is come forth to help you, shall return to Egypt into their own land. And the Chaldeans shall come again, and fight against this city, and take it, and burn it with fire. Thus saith the LORD; Deceive not yourselves, saying, The Chaldeans shall surely depart from us: for they shall not depart. For though ye had smitten the whole army of the Chaldeans that fight against you, and there remained but wounded men among them, yet should they rise up every man in his tent, and burn this city with fire. (Jeremiah 37:6-10)

Deceived Alliances (6-10): Zedekiah sends for Jeremiah to inquire of the LORD concerning Pharaoh's armies coming to help Zedekiah resist the Babylonian armies (6). The LORD'S response from the mouth of Jeremiah is not favorable; for Jeremiah tells Zedekiah that "the Chaldeans shall come again, and fight against this city, and take it, and burn it with fire" (8). Zedekiah should not be deceived in trusting alliances made with Egypt to stop the

Babylonian campaign, for though they have withdrawn for a time they will come again and burn this city to the ground (10). This event is literally fulfilled (Jer. 39:8).

And it came to pass, that when the army of the Chaldeans was broken up from Jerusalem for fear of Pharaoh's army, Then Jeremiah went forth out of Jerusalem to go into the land of Benjamin, to separate himself thence in the midst of the people. And when he was in the gate of Benjamin, a captain of the ward was there, whose name was Irijah, the son of Shelemiah, the son of Hananiah; and he took Jeremiah the prophet, saying, Thou fallest away to the Chaldeans. Then said Jeremiah, It is false; I fall not away to the Chaldeans. But he hearkened not to him: so Irijah took Jeremiah, and brought him to the princes. Wherefore the princes were wroth with Jeremiah, and smote him, and put him in prison in the house of Jonathan the scribe: for they had made that the prison. (Jeremiah 37:11-15)

The Imprisonment of Jeremiah (11-15): Jeremiah flees to the land of Benjamin seeking to separate himself from the midst of the people, Benjamin being Jeremiah's home town, Anathoth (12). Coming to the gate of Benjamin Jeremiah is accused of trying to flee to the Chaldeans (14). This is due to the fact that Jeremiah is known throughout Jerusalem for his prophesying to the people to submit to the armies of the Chaldeans and they shall live. Jeremiah is looked at as pro-Babylonian. Jeremiah is beaten and placed in a make shift prison of sorts in the house of Jonathan the scribe (15).

When Jeremiah was entered into the dungeon, and into the cabins, and Jeremiah had remained there many days; Then Zedekiah the king sent, and took him out: and the king asked him secretly in his house, and said, Is there any word from the LORD? And Jeremiah said, There is: for, said he, thou shalt be delivered into the hand of the king of Babylon. Moreover Jeremiah said unto king Zedekiah, What have I offended against thee, or against thy servants, or against this people, that ye have put me in prison? Where are now your prophets which prophesied unto you, saying, The king of Babylon shall not come against you, nor against this land? Therefore hear now, I pray thee, O my lord the king: let my supplication, I pray thee, be accepted before thee; that thou cause me not to return to the house of Jonathan the scribe, lest I die there. Then Zedekiah the king commanded that they should commit Jeremiah into the court of the prison, and that they should give him daily a piece of bread out of the bakers' street, until all the bread in the city were spent. Thus Jeremiah remained in the court of the prison. (Jeremiah 37:16-21)

The Unwavering Words of Jeremiah (16-21): Jeremiah having spent sometime in the prison house of Jonathan the scribe is taken out privately by King Zedekiah to see if there is any word from the LORD (17). Jeremiah is undaunted by his imprisonment and proclaims the truth from God's word, stating once again that Zedekiah will be taken and given into the hands of the king of Babylon (17). Not only is Jeremiah undaunted in proclaiming the truth of judgment to Zedekiah but rebukes Zedekiah by saying, "Where are now your prophets which prophesied unto you, saying, The King of Babylon shall not come against you, nor against this land?" (18-19). Jeremiah is basically saying, those prophets have lied to you and I have told you the truth, yet I'm in prison! Jeremiah uses this argument in attempts to not go back into the prison house of Jonathan the scribe (20 cf. 38:26). Zedekiah harkens to Jeremiah, is taken and placed in the court of the prison, and is given daily portion of bread until all the bread is spent in the city (famine will take hold of the city).

CHAPTER THIRTY-EIGHT
Rescued From the Mire

Then Shephatiah the son of Mattan, and Gedaliah the son of Pashur, and Jucal the son of Shelemiah, and Pashur the son of Malchiah, heard the words that Jeremiah had spoken unto all the people, saying, Thus saith the LORD, He that remaineth in this city shall die by the sword, by the famine, and by the pestilence: but he that goeth forth to the Chaldeans shall live; for he shall have his life for a prey, and shall live. Thus saith the LORD, This city shall surely be given into the hand of the king of Babylon's army, which shall take it. Therefore the princes said unto the king, We beseech thee, let this man be put to death: for thus he weakeneth the hands of the men of war that remain in this city, and the hands of all the people, in speaking such words unto them: for this man seeketh not the welfare of this people, but the hurt. Then Zedekiah the king said, Behold, he is in your hand: for the king is not he that can do any thing against you. Then took they Jeremiah, and cast him into the dungeon of Malchiah the son of Hammelech, that was in the court of the prison: and they let down Jeremiah with cords. And in the dungeon there was no water, but mire: so Jeremiah sunk in the mire. (Jeremiah 38:1-6)

Jeremiah Imprisoned, Sinking in the Mire (1-6): Once again the leadership is against Jeremiah for the words he is speaking to the people, telling them, "He that goeth forth to the Chaldeans shall live..." (2). If these words were not of the LORD they would seem at the least discouraging in a time of war. However these are the words of the LORD Jeremiah is speaking; and truth it is, for if they resist and rebel against these words they shall "die by the sword, by the famine and by the pestilence..." (2).

Convinced that Jeremiah is weakening the fight of the people, the leadership seeks Jeremiah's life (4). Zedekiah, allows these men to take Jeremiah and they let him down into the dungeon of Malchiah, where there was no water but rather Jeremiah sank into the mire (6 cf. 1). Surely Jeremiah's fate would have been sealed if God had not promised to preserve His life (Jer. 1:18, 19).

Now when Ebedmelech the Ethiopian, one of the eunuchs which was in the king's house, heard that they had put Jeremiah in the dungeon; the king then sitting in the gate of Benjamin; Ebedmelech went forth out of the king's house, and spake to the king,

saying, My lord the king, these men have done evil in all that they have done to Jeremiah the prophet, whom they have cast into the dungeon; and he is like to die for hunger in the place where he is: for there is no more bread in the city. Then the king commanded Ebedmelech the Ethiopian, saying, Take from hence thirty men with thee, and take up Jeremiah the prophet out of the dungeon, before he die. So Ebedmelech took the men with him, and went into the house of the king under the treasury, and took thence old cast clouts and old rotten rags, and let them down by cords into the dungeon to Jeremiah. And Ebedmelech the Ethiopian said unto Jeremiah, Put now these old cast clouts and rotten rags under thine armholes under the cords. And Jeremiah did so. So they drew up Jeremiah with cords, and took him up out of the dungeon: and Jeremiah remained in the court of the prison. (Jeremiah 38:7-13)

Ebedmelech the Ethiopian (7-13): The LORD raises up Ebedmelech an Ethiopian to intercede on behalf of Jeremiah, desiring of Zedekiah to come to Jeremiah's rescue. Ebedmelech tells of Jeremiah's plight being in the dungeon, having no food he is likely to die (7-9). Zedekiah gives the command to Ebedmelech to take thirty men and get Jeremiah out of the dungeon before he die (10). The thirty men go and draw up Jeremiah out of the dungeon using old cloths and rags (11-13). Jeremiah however will remain in prison until the Babylonians take the city (vs. 28 cf. 39:14).

Because of the mercy shown towards Jeremiah by Ebedmelech God will see to it that he is spared once the city if invaded (Jer. 39:15-18).

Then Zedekiah the king sent, and took Jeremiah the prophet unto him into the third entry that is in the house of the LORD: and the king said unto Jeremiah, I will ask thee a thing; hide nothing from me. Then Jeremiah said unto Zedekiah, If I declare it unto thee, wilt thou not surely put me to death? and if I give thee counsel, wilt thou not hearken unto me? So Zedekiah the king sware secretly unto Jeremiah, saying, As the LORD liveth, that made us this soul, I will not put thee to death, neither will I give thee into the hand of these men that seek thy life. Then said Jeremiah unto Zedekiah, Thus saith the LORD, the God of hosts, the God of Israel; If thou wilt assuredly go forth unto the king of Babylon's princes, then thy soul shall live, and this city shall not be burned with fire; and thou shalt live, and thine house: But if thou wilt not go forth to the king of Babylon's princes, then shall this city be given into the hand of the Chaldeans, and they shall burn it with fire, and thou shalt not escape out of their hand. And Zedekiah the king said unto Jeremiah, I am afraid of the Jews that are fallen to the Chaldeans, lest they deliver me into their hand, and they mock me. But Jeremiah said, they shall not deliver thee. Obey, I beseech thee, the voice of the LORD, which I speak unto thee: so it shall be well unto thee, and thy soul shall live. But if thou refuse to go forth, this is the word that the LORD hath shewed me: And, behold, all the women that are left in the king of Judah's house shall be brought forth to the king of Babylon's princes, and those women shall say, Thy friends have set thee on, and have prevailed against thee: thy feet are sunk in the mire, and they are turned away back. So they shall bring out all thy wives and thy children to the Chaldeans: and thou shalt not escape out of their hand, but shalt be taken by the hand of the king of Babylon: and thou shalt cause this city to be burned with fire. (Jeremiah 38:14-23)

Final Word to Zedekiah (14-23): Zedekiah privately seeks the word of the LORD concerning his fate from the mouth of Jeremiah (14). If Jeremiah tells the word of the LORD to Zedekiah he is concerned that Zedekiah will either have him killed or not take heed to the word of the LORD, by the mouth of Jeremiah (15). Zedekiah, secretly promises to Jeremiah that he will not put him to death, nor will he give him into the hands of the men that seek his life (16). Notice Zedekiah does not commit to obeying his words. The words of the LORD by the mouth of Jeremiah are the same they have been for upwards of 40 years of ministry, surrender to the princes of the king of Babylon and live; if not this city will be burned to the ground and you shall die (17-18)[47].

---

[47] Zedekiah does not listen and his house of the city is burn with fire (39:8).

Zedekiah's reason he gives for not surrendering is that the Jews that have already surrendered to Nebuchadnezzar's forces will mock him (19 cf. 39:9). Jeremiah pleads with Zedekiah to obey the voice of the LORD and it shall go well with him just as the LORD hath promised. However, if Zedekiah refuses to obey the voice of the LORD then even the women that are left in the king's house shall mock him and the city shall be burnt with fire (21-23).

Then said Zedekiah unto Jeremiah, Let no man know of these words, and thou shalt not die. But if the princes hear that I have talked with thee, and they come unto thee, and say unto thee, Declare unto us now what thou hast said unto the king, hide it not from us, and we will not put thee to death; also what the king said unto thee: Then thou shalt say unto them, I presented my supplication before the king, that he would not cause me to return to Jonathan's house, to die there. Then came all the princes unto Jeremiah, and asked him: and he told them according to all these words that the king had commanded. So they left off speaking with him; for the matter was not perceived. So Jeremiah abode in the court of the prison until the day that Jerusalem was taken: and he was there when Jerusalem was taken. (Jeremiah 38:24-28)

A Secret For the King (24-28): Zedekiah is set in his ways, and will not listen to the voice of the LORD by

Jeremiah. Therefore the fate of him and the city is sealed (25). Zedekiah asks Jeremiah to not tell all the words that Jeremiah has told Zedekiah but only the request that Jeremiah made regarding not being left in the prison in Jonathan's house (26 cf. 37:15). Jeremiah holds up his end of the deal as did Zedekiah and Jeremiah remained in the prison house until the day the city was taken (28).

CHAPTER THIRTY-NINE
The Fall of Jerusalem

In the ninth year of Zedekiah king of Judah, in the tenth month, came Nebuchadrezzar king of Babylon and all his army against Jerusalem, and they besieged it. And in the eleventh year of Zedekiah, in the fourth month, the ninth day of the month, the city was broken up. And all the princes of the king of Babylon came in, and sat in the middle gate, even Nergalsharezer, Samgarnebo, Sarsechim, Rabsaris, Nergalsharezer, Rabmag, with all the residue of the princes of the king of Babylon. (Jeremiah 39:1-3)

The Fall of Jerusalem (1-3): The fall of Jerusalem that has been predicted throughout the book of Jeremiah is now come to pass. This date is very important in history and is recorded four times (here and Jer. 52; 2 Kings 25; 2 Chron. 36).

And it came to pass, that when Zedekiah the king of Judah saw them, and all the men of war, then they fled, and went forth out of the city by night, by the way of the king's garden, by the gate betwixt the two walls: and he went out the way of the plain. But the Chaldeans' army pursued after them, and overtook Zedekiah in the plains of Jericho: and when they had taken him, they brought him up to Nebuchadnezzar king of Babylon to Riblah in the land of Hamath, where he gave judgment upon him. Then the king of Babylon slew the sons of Zedekiah in Riblah before his eyes: also the king of Babylon slew all the nobles of Judah. Moreover he put out Zedekiah's eyes, and bound him with chains, to carry him to Babylon. (Jeremiah 39:4-7)

The Events Surrounding the Capture of Zedekiah (4-7): The events surrounding the capture of Zedekiah are an amazing fulfillment of Bible prophecy. Two contemporary prophets had predicted the events surrounding the capture of Zedekiah, Jeremiah and Ezekiel. However, Zedekiah perceived that these two prophets' prophecies concerning his capture contradicted one another (Jeremiah 32:4 cf. Ezekiel 12:13). However, both these verses are fulfilled in the events that unfold surrounding the capture of Zedekiah as is recorded here (Jer. 4-7) and by Flavius Josephus:

FLAVIUS JOSEPHUS, ANTIQUITIES
BOOK 10, CHAPTER 7

Now Zedekiah was twenty-and-one years old when he took the government and has the same mother with his brother Jehoiachin, but was a despiser of justice and of his duty, for truly those of the same age with him were wicked about him and the whole multitude did what unjust and insolent things they pleased.

... for which reason the prophet Jeremiah came often to him, and protested to him, and insisted that he must leave off his impieties and transgressions and take care of what was right, neither giver ear to the rulers (among whom were wicked men) nor give credit to their false prophets who deluded them, as if the king of Babylon would make no more war against him, and as if the Egyptians would make war against him, and conquer him, since what they said was not true; and the events would not prove such.

Now as Zedekiah himself, while he heard the prophet speak, he believed him, and agreed to everything as true, and supposed it was for his advantage; but then his friends perverted him, and dissuaded him from what the prophet advised, and obliged him to do what they pleased.

Ezekiel also foretold in Babylon what calamities were coming upon, which when he heard he sent accounts of them unto Jerusalem; but Zedekiah did not believe their prophecies, for the reason following – it happed that the two prophets agreed with one another in what they said as in all other things, that the city should be taken, and Zedekiah himself should be taken captive;

but Ezekiel disagreed with him, and said that Zedekiah should not see Babylon; while Jeremiah said to him, that the king of Babylon should carry him away thither in bonds.

... and because they did not both say the same thing as to this circumstance, he disbelieved what they both appeared to agree in, and condemned them as not speaking truth therein, although all the things foretold him did come to pass according to their prophecies, as we shall show upon a fitter opportunity.

FLAVIUS JOSEPHUS, ANTIQUITIES
BOOK 10, CHAPTER 8

Now the city was taken on the ninth day of the fourth month, in the eleventh year of the reign of Zedekiah. They were indeed only generals of the king of Babylon, to whom Nebuchadnezzar committed the care of the siege, for he abode himself in the city of Ribliah.

... and when the city was taken about midnight, and the enemy's generals were entered into the temple, and when Zedekiah was sensible of it, he took his wives and children, and his captains and friends and with them fled out of the city; through the fortified ditch and through the desert;

... and when certain of the deserters had informed the Babylonians of this at break of day, they made haste to pursue after Zedekiah, and overtook him not far from Jericho, and encamped him about. But for those friends and captains of Zedekiah who had fled out of the city with him, when they saw their enemies near

them they left him and dispersed themselves, some one way and some another, and everyone resolved to save themselves.

… so the enemy took Zedekiah alive, when he was deserted by all but a few, with his children and his wives, and brought him to the king. When he was come, Nebuchadnezzar began to call him a wicked wretch, and convent-breaker, and one that had forgotten his former words, when he promised to keep the country for him.

He also reproached him for his ingratitude, that when he had received the kingdom from him, who had taken it from Jehoiachin, and given it him, he had made use of the power he gave him against him that gave it: "but" said he, "God is great, who hateth that conduct of thine, hath brought thee under us"

And when he had used these words to Zedekiah, he commanded his sons and his friends to be slain, while Zedekiah and the rest of the captains looked on; after which he put out the eyes of Zedekiah, and bound him and carried him to Babylon.

And these things happened to him, as Jeremiah and Ezekiel had foretold to him, that he should be caught, and brought before the king of Babylon, and should speak to him face to face, and should see his eyes with his own eyes; and thus far did Jeremiah prophecy. But he was also made blind, and brought to Babylon but did not see it, according to the prediction of Ezekiel.

Thus, the amazing fulfilment of this seeming discrepancy is that upon Zedekiah's fleeing from the

Babylonian armies invading Jerusalem he is captured by Nebuchadnezzar's armies. At the city of Riblah Nebuchadnezzar slew the sons of Zedekiah and then took out the eyes of Zedekiah. Zedekiah was then taken into Babylon fulfilling all prophecies concerning Zedekiah.

And the Chaldeans burned the king's house, and the houses of the people, with fire, and brake down the walls of Jerusalem. Then Nebuzaradan the captain of the guard carried away captive into Babylon the remnant of the people that remained in the city, and those that fell away, that fell to him, with the rest of the people that remained. But Nebuzaradan the captain of the guard left of the poor of the people, which had nothing, in the land of Judah, and gave them vineyards and fields at the same time. (Jeremiah 39:8-10)

The Dispersal of the People (8-10): Nebuchadnezzar's armies do as God had predicted by the mouth of Jeremiah (Jer. 37:10) and burns the King's house and the houses of the people and broke down the walls of Jerusalem (8). Then Nebuchadnezzar's armies took away to Babylon all the remnant of the people that remained in Jerusalem and those that had surrendered during the siege (9). The only ones to remain are the poor of the poor to till the land (10). It is this people group that will become the Samaritans.

Now Nebuchadrezzar king of Babylon gave charge concerning Jeremiah to Nebuzaradan the captain of the guard, saying, Take him, and look well to him, and do him no harm; but do unto him even as he shall say unto thee. So Nebuzaradan the captain of the guard sent, and Nebushasban, Rabsaris, and Nergalsharezer, Rabmag, and all the king of Babylon's princes; Even they sent, and took Jeremiah out of the court of the prison, and committed him unto Gedaliah the son of Ahikam the son of Shaphan, that he should carry him home: so he dwelt among the people. (Jeremiah 39:11-14)

The Mercy to Jeremiah by the Hand of Nebuchadnezzar (11-14): Nebuchadnezzar gave charge concerning Jeremiah to not hurt him and released him from prison. They were also instructed to give him freedom to choose his own dwelling place (11-13). Jeremiah's decision is to remain in the land under the leadership of Gedaliah (14). It is Gedaliah that is placed governor over the land (see chapters 40-44). The details of the activities surrounding this is covered in the following chapter.

Now the word of the LORD came unto Jeremiah, while he was shut up in the court of the prison, saying, Go and speak to Ebedmelech the Ethiopian, saying, Thus saith the LORD of hosts, the God of Israel; Behold, I will bring my words upon this city for evil, and not for good; and they shall be accomplished in that day before thee. But I will deliver thee in that day, saith the LORD: and thou shalt not be given into the hand of the men of whom thou art afraid. For I will surely deliver thee, and thou shalt not fall by the sword, but thy life shall be for a prey unto thee: because thou hast put thy trust in me, saith the LORD. (Jeremiah 39:15-18)

The Mercy Shown to Ebedmelech (15-18): The LORD rewards Ebedmelech for his harkening to the words of the LORD in pleading for the deliverance of Jeremiah from the pit (Jer. 38:7-13). The reward the LORD gives Ebedmelech is that the LORD will deliver him from the armies of the Chaldeans, he shall live (17-18).

CHAPTER FORTY
Governor Gedalilah

The word that came to Jeremiah from the LORD, after that Nebuzaradan the captain of the guard had let him go from Ramah, when he had taken him being bound in chains among all that were carried away captive of Jerusalem and Judah, which were carried away captive unto Babylon. And the captain of the guard took Jeremiah, and said unto him, The LORD thy God hath pronounced this evil upon this place. Now the LORD hath brought it, and done according as he hath said: because ye have sinned against the LORD, and have not obeyed his voice, therefore this thing is come upon you. And now, behold, I loose thee this day from the chains which were upon thine hand. If it seem good unto thee to come with me into Babylon, come; and I will look well unto thee: but if it seem ill unto thee to come with me into Babylon, forbear: behold, all the land is before thee: whither it seemeth good and convenient for thee to go, thither go. Now while he was not yet gone back, he said, Go back also to Gedaliah the son of Ahikam the son of Shaphan, whom the king of Babylon hath made governor over the cities of Judah, and dwell with him among the people: or go wheresoever it seemeth convenient unto thee to go. So the captain of the guard gave him victuals and a reward, and let him go. Then went Jeremiah unto Gedaliah the son of Ahikam to Mizpah; and dwelt with him among the people that were left in the land. (Jeremiah 40:1-6)

Jeremiah and Gedaliah (1-6): Chapters 40-44 describe a series of events that occur after the fall of Jerusalem with chapters 40-42 dealing with events occurring in Judah covering the details of Gedaliah and Jeremiah. Chapters 43-44 detailing the flight of Jeremiah to Egypt.

Jeremiah in this chapter is treated favorably by Nebuzaradan, a sub-governor of Babylon in the region. As stated in the previous chapter, Jeremiah by the order of Nebuchadnezzar is not allowed to be hurt and is given the decision to choose if he would like to come into Babylon and live in health and wealth or stay in the land. Jeremiah chooses to stay in the land with the poor remnant left to till the land. Jeremiah is given food and provisions and settles in Mizpah under Gedaliah. Gedaliah is governor of the land setup by Nebuchadnezzar (7).

Now when all the captains of the forces which were in the fields, even they and their men, heard that the

king of Babylon had made Gedaliah the son of Ahikam governor in the land, and had committed unto him men, and women, and children, and of the poor of the land, of them that were not carried away captive to Babylon; Then they came to Gedaliah to Mizpah, even Ishmael the son of Nethaniah, and Johanan and Jonathan the sons of Kareah, and Seraiah the son of Tanhumeth, and the sons of Ephai the Netophathite, and Jezaniah the son of a Maachathite, they and their men. And Gedaliah the son of Ahikam the son of Shaphan sware unto them and to their men, saying, Fear not to serve the Chaldeans: dwell in the land, and serve the king of Babylon, and it shall be well with you. As for me, behold, I will dwell at Mizpah to serve the Chaldeans, which will come unto us: but ye, gather ye wine, and summer fruits, and oil, and put them in your vessels, and dwell in your cities that ye have taken. Likewise when all the Jews that were in Moab, and among the Ammonites, and in Edom, and that were in all the countries, heard that the king of Babylon had left a remnant of Judah, and that he had set over them Gedaliah the son of Ahikam the son of Shaphan; Even all the Jews returned out of all places whither they were driven, and came to the land of Judah, to Gedaliah, unto Mizpah, and gathered wine and summer fruits very much. (Jeremiah 40:7-12)

The Dispersed of the Land and Gedaliah their Governor (7-12): Gedaliah is placed as governor of the land of Mizpah[48] by the king of Babylon (7). Once the people that had not been carried away captive heard that Gedaliah was governor of the land, joined themselves unto him. Gedaliah tells this remnant of people to serve the Chaldeans, the Babylonians and it shall be well with them (7-10). The Jews also that had been scattered throughout Moab, Edom and Ammon, returned, having heard of Gedaliah being set up in the land as governor (11-12).

Moreover Johanan the son of Kareah, and all the captains of the forces that were in the fields, came to Gedaliah to Mizpah, And said unto him, Dost thou certainly know that Baalis the king of the Ammonites hath sent Ishmael the son of Nethaniah to slay thee? But Gedaliah the son of Ahikam believed them not. Then Johanan the son of Kareah spake to Gedaliah in Mizpah secretly, saying, Let me go, I pray thee, and I will slay Ishmael the son of Nethaniah, and no man shall know it: wherefore should he slay thee, that all the Jews which are gathered unto thee should be scattered, and the remnant in Judah perish? But Gedaliah the son of Ahikam said unto Johanan the son of Kareah, Thou shalt not do this thing: for thou speakest falsely of Ishmael. (Jeremiah 40:13-16)

---

[48] Mizpah is located north of Jerusalem in the land of Benjamin.

Plot to Kill Gedadiah (13-16): Gedadiah is told by Johanan and all the captains in the field that Baalis King of the Ammonites has sent Ishmael to kill him (13-14). Johanan offers to kill Ishmael secretly but Gedaliah does not believe Johanan (15-16).

CHAPTER FORTY-ONE
Murder of Gedalilah

Now it came to pass in the seventh month, that Ishmael the son of Nethaniah the son of Elishama, of the seed royal, and the princes of the king, even ten men with him, came unto Gedaliah the son of Ahikam to Mizpah; and there they did eat bread together in Mizpah. Then arose Ishmael the son of Nethaniah, and the ten men that were with him, and smote Gedaliah the son of Ahikam the son of Shaphan with the sword, and slew him, whom the king of Babylon had made governor over the land. Ishmael also slew all the Jews that were with him, even with Gedaliah, at Mizpah, and the Chaldeans that were found there, and the men of war. And it came to pass the second day after he had slain Gedaliah, and no man knew it, That there came certain from Shechem, from Shiloh, and from Samaria, even fourscore men, having their beards shaven, and their clothes rent, and having cut themselves, with offerings and incense in their hand, to bring them to the house of the LORD. And Ishmael the son of Nethaniah went forth from

Mizpah to meet them, weeping all along as he went: and it came to pass, as he met them, he said unto them, Come to Gedaliah the son of Ahikam. And it was so, when they came into the midst of the city, that Ishmael the son of Nethaniah slew them, and cast them into the midst of the pit, he, and the men that were with him. But ten men were found among them that said unto Ishmael, Slay us not: for we have treasures in the field, of wheat, and of barley, and of oil, and of honey. So he forbare, and slew them not among their brethren. Now the pit wherein Ishmael had cast all the dead bodies of the men, whom he had slain because of Gedaliah, was it which Asa the king had made for fear of Baasha king of Israel: and Ishmael the son of Nethaniah filled it with them that were slain. Then Ishmael carried away captive all the residue of the people that were in Mizpah, even the king's daughters, and all the people that remained in Mizpah, whom Nebuzaradan the captain of the guard had committed to Gedaliah the son of Ahikam: and Ishmael the son of Nethaniah carried them away captive, and departed to go over to the Ammonites. (Jeremiah 41:1-10)

The Wicked Acts of Ishmael (1-10): As is stated in the previous chapter Gedaliah did not believe those who tried to tell him of the plot of Baalis, King of the Ammonites in sending Ishmael to kill him (40:13-16). So we see Ishmael with ten men being invited to eat bread with Gedaliah in Mizpah (1). The table they shared in breaking of bread ends with blood shed. Ishmael and his men kill Gedaliah and all the men that were with him (2-3). Ishmael and his men killed all Gedaliah's staff some of which were Chaldeans, men whom the King of Babylon left in the land to assist Gedaliah in establishing the government. Ishmael and his men also killed all the men of war that were in Mizpah, showing that Ishmael and his men were skilled in warfare: they were skilled assassins (3). Two days after the slaughter eighty men came to Mizpah to worship (5). Ishmael and his ten men seeking to keep the slaughter of Gedalaih secret, come out to the party feigning themselves to be weeping and in mourning to draw these 80 men into the city (6). Once these eighty men are in the city Ishmael and his men slay them and cast them into the pit, a water cistern made by King Asa in Mizpah (vs. 9 cf. I Kings 15:16-22, 2 Chron. 16:6). Again, these men were well trained assassins, 10 men killing seventy. Ishmael and his men did leave ten men of the eighty alive because they promised them food, a great commodity during this time of famine (8). Ishmael then sets out with all the residue of the city, back to the mastermind of the conspiracy, Baalis, king of the Ammonites (10).

But when Johanan the son of Kareah, and all the captains of the forces that were with him, heard of all the evil that Ishmael the son of Nethaniah had

done, Then they took all the men, and went to fight with Ishmael the son of Nethaniah, and found him by the great waters that are in Gibeon. Now it came to pass, that when all the people which were with Ishmael saw Johanan the son of Kareah, and all the captains of the forces that were with him, then they were glad. So all the people that Ishmael had carried away captive from Mizpah cast about and returned, and went unto Johanan the son of Kareah. But Ishmael the son of Nethaniah escaped from Johanan with eight men, and went to the Ammonites. Then took Johanan the son of Kareah, and all the captains of the forces that were with him, all the remnant of the people whom he had recovered from Ishmael the son of Nethaniah, from Mizpah, after that he had slain Gedaliah the son of Ahikam, even mighty men of war, and the women, and the children, and the eunuchs, whom he had brought again from Gibeon: And they departed, and dwelt in the habitation of Chimham, which is by Bethlehem, to go to enter into Egypt, Because of the Chaldeans: for they were afraid of them, because Ishmael the son of Nethaniah had slain Gedaliah the son of Ahikam, whom the king of Babylon made governor in the land. (Jeremiah 41:11-18)

Deliverance by Johanan (11-18): Ishmael and his men are taking the residue of the town of Mispah back to the king of Ammon when Johanan and all his company get wind of all the evil that Ishmael had done (11). Johanan and all his men go out to Gibeon to fight Ishmael (12). The "great waters that are in Gibeon" is the pool or well at Gibeon (2 Sam. 2:13). As Johanan approached Ishmael and his men, and all the people that he had led out of the city of Mizpah saw Johanan and his armies retreated from Ishmael and his men to join Johanan (13-14). Seeing all the people of the city flee from him, Ishmael flees to the one who commissioned him, Baalis, king of the Ammonites (15). At Gibeon all the people that had joined Johanan depart to Chimham which is by Bethlehem to flee to Egypt for fear of the Chaldeans, for they were afraid what the retaliation would be from the Chaldeans once they heard of the killing of Gedaliah and the officers whom the king of Babylon had set up (17-18).

CHAPTER FORTY-TWO
The Rebellion of the Remnant (Part One)

Then all the captains of the forces, and Johanan the son of Kareah, and Jezaniah the son of Hoshaiah, and all the people from the least even unto the greatest, came near, And said unto Jeremiah the prophet, Let, we beseech thee, our supplication be accepted before thee, and pray for us unto the LORD thy God, even for all this remnant; (for we are left but a few of many, as thine eyes do behold us:) That the LORD thy God may shew us the way wherein we may walk, and the thing that we may do. Then Jeremiah the prophet said unto them, I have heard you; behold, I will pray unto the LORD your God according to your words; and it shall come to pass, that whatsoever thing the LORD shall answer you, I will declare it unto you; I will keep nothing back from you. Then they said to Jeremiah, The LORD be a true and faithful witness between us, if we do not even according to all things for the which the LORD thy God shall send thee to us.

Whether it be good, or whether it be evil, we will obey the voice of the LORD our God, to whom we send thee; that it may be well with us, when we obey the voice of the LORD our God. (Jeremiah 42:1-6)

The Request of the People (1-6): The people that remained under the leadership of Johanan requested Jeremiah to pray to the LORD on their behalf that they would walk in all the ways of the LORD (1-3). This supplication on behalf of the people is a false desire (vs. 20). They have deceived themselves in believing they want the will of the LORD, but in reality they want the LORD to bless them in their choice to go into Egypt (vs. 6 cf. 13-14). Chapters 42-44 deal with all the events surrounding the desire of the people to dwell in Egypt.

And it came to pass after ten days, that the word of the LORD came unto Jeremiah. Then called he Johanan the son of Kareah, and all the captains of the forces which were with him, and all the people from the least even to the greatest, And said unto them, Thus saith the LORD, the God of Israel, unto whom ye sent me to present your supplication before him; If ye will still abide in this land, then will I build you, and not pull you down, and I will plant you, and not pluck you up: for I repent me of the evil that I have done unto you. Be not afraid of the king of Babylon, of whom ye are afraid; be not afraid of him, saith the LORD: for I am with you to save you, and to deliver you from his hand. And I will shew mercies unto you, that he may have mercy upon you, and cause you to return to your own land. But if ye say, We will not dwell in this land, neither obey the voice of the LORD your God, Saying, No; but we will go into the land of Egypt, where we shall see no war, nor hear the sound of the trumpet, nor have hunger of bread; and there will we dwell: And now therefore hear the word of the LORD, ye remnant of Judah; Thus saith the LORD of hosts, the God of Israel; If ye wholly set your faces to enter into Egypt, and go to sojourn there; Then it shall come to pass, that the sword, which ye feared, shall overtake you there in the land of Egypt, and the famine, whereof ye were afraid, shall follow close after you there in Egypt; and there ye shall die. So shall it be with all the men that set their faces to go into Egypt to sojourn there; they shall die by the sword, by the famine, and by the pestilence: and none of them shall remain or escape from the evil that I will bring upon them. For thus saith the LORD of hosts, the God of Israel; As mine anger and my fury hath been poured forth upon the inhabitants of Jerusalem; so shall my fury be poured forth upon you, when ye shall enter into Egypt: and ye shall be an execration, and an astonishment, and a curse, and a reproach; and ye shall see this place no more. (Jeremiah 42:7-18)

The Answer of the LORD (7-18): The LORD responds after 10 days to the supplication of the people by the prayer of Jeremiah. The answer from the LORD is that they are not to go into Egypt. They are called to abide in the land God has given them and they are not to be afraid of the king of Babylon (this is the reason for their desire to retreat to Egypt) (10-12). The warning against them for not obeying the word of the LORD, (which they vowed to obey vs. 6) is that the LORD will see to it that the king of Babylon will come down to Egypt and all the things they are afraid of happening to them if they stay in the land will befall them in the land of Egypt (13-18).

The LORD hath said concerning you, O ye remnant of Judah; Go ye not into Egypt: know certainly that I have admonished you this day. For ye dissembled in your hearts, when ye sent me unto the LORD your God, saying, Pray for us unto the LORD our God; and according unto all that the LORD our God shall say, so declare unto us, and we will do it. And now I have this day declared it to you; but ye have not obeyed the voice of the LORD your God, nor any thing for the which he hath sent me unto you. Now therefore know certainly that ye shall die by the sword, by the famine, and by the pestilence, in the place whither ye desire to go and to sojourn. (Jeremiah 42:19-22)

The Heart of the People (19-22): Despite the words of the LORD the people's heart is dissembled, it is already moving to Egypt (20). The people refuse to obey the voice of the LORD and so Jeremiah pronounces, "Now therefore know certainly that ye shall die by the sword, famine and by the pestilence, in the place whither ye desire to go and to sojourn." (22).

CHAPTER FORTY-THREE
The Rebellion of the Remnant (Part Two)

And it came to pass, that when Jeremiah had made an end of speaking unto all the people all the words of the LORD their God, for which the LORD their God had sent him to them, even all these words, Then spake Azariah the son of Hoshaiah, and Johanan the son of Kareah, and all the proud men, saying unto Jeremiah, Thou speakest falsely: the LORD our God hath not sent thee to say, Go not into Egypt to sojourn there: But Baruch the son of Neriah setteth thee on against us, for to deliver us into the hand of the Chaldeans, that they might put us to death, and carry us away captives into Babylon. So Johanan the son of Kareah, and all the captains of the forces, and all the people, obeyed not the voice of the LORD, to dwell in the land of Judah. But Johanan the son of Kareah, and all the captains of the forces, took all the remnant of Judah, that were returned from all nations, whither they had been driven, to dwell in the land of Judah; Even men, and women, and children, and the king's daughters, and every person that Nebuzaradan the captain of the guard had left with Gedaliah the son of Ahikam the son of Shaphan, and Jeremiah the prophet, and Baruch the son of Neriah. So they came into the land of Egypt: for they obeyed not the voice of the LORD: thus came they even to Tahpanhes. (Jeremiah 43:1-7)

Johanan and His Disobedience (1-7): Azariah and Johanan speak against Jeremiah concerning the words of the LORD, telling them not to go into Egypt (2). Johanan and his men charge Baruch of manipulating Jeremiah against Johanan and his men in the hope they might be put to death (3). So contrary to the promise the people made to obey the words of the LORD (42:6); they rebel against the words of the LORD by the mouth of Jeremiah (4). Johanan and his men take all the remnant of Judah into the land of Egypt to the land of Tahpanhes in direct disobedience to the LORD (5-7). Jeremiah and Baruch also are taken into Egypt as well, apparently as prisoners (8).

Then came the word of the LORD unto Jeremiah in Tahpanhes, saying, Take great stones in thine hand, and hide them in the clay in the brickkiln, which is at the entry of Pharaoh's house in Tahpanhes, in the sight of the men of Judah; And say unto them, Thus saith the LORD of hosts, the God of Israel; Behold, I will send and take Nebuchadrezzar the king of

Babylon, my servant, and will set his throne upon these stones that I have hid; and he shall spread his royal pavilion over them. And when he cometh, he shall smite the land of Egypt, and deliver such as are for death to death; and such as are for captivity to captivity; and such as are for the sword to the sword. And I will kindle a fire in the houses of the gods of Egypt; and he shall burn them, and carry them away captives: and he shall array himself with the land of Egypt, as a shepherd putteth on his garment; and he shall go forth from thence in peace. He shall break also the images of Bethshemesh, that is in the land of Egypt; and the houses of the gods of the Egyptians shall he burn with fire. (Jeremiah 43:8-13)

The Word of God Concerning Egypt (8-13): Jeremiah is told to do a symbolic act of hiding great stones in the entry of Pharaoh's house in Tahpanhes (8-9). This act was done in the sight of Judah (9). Then Jeremiah told all the people of Israel that were in Egypt that Babylon will come into Egypt and will set his throne over these great stones, establishing his royal pavilion over them (10). Jeremiah also tells them that when Nebuchadnezzar comes he will smite the land of Egypt and take some captive and others will die by the sword (11). He will also kindle a fire in the house of the gods of Egypt, break their images to pieces and take them captive as well (12-13).

CHAPTER FORTY-FOUR
The Rebellion of the Remnant (Part Three)

The word that came to Jeremiah concerning all the Jews which dwell in the land of Egypt, which dwell at Migdol, and at Tahpanhes, and at Noph, and in the country of Pathros, saying, Thus saith the LORD of hosts, the God of Israel; Ye have seen all the evil that I have brought upon Jerusalem, and upon all the cities of Judah; and, behold, this day they are a desolation, and no man dwelleth therein, Because of their wickedness which they have committed to provoke me to anger, in that they went to burn incense, and to serve other gods, whom they knew not, neither they, ye, nor your fathers. Howbeit I sent unto you all my servants the prophets, rising early and sending them, saying, Oh, do not this abominable thing that I hate. But they hearkened not, nor inclined their ear to turn from their wickedness, to burn no incense unto other gods. Wherefore my fury and mine anger was poured forth, and was kindled in the cities of Judah and in the streets of Jerusalem; and they are wasted and desolate, as at this day. Therefore now thus saith the LORD, the God of hosts, the God of Israel; Wherefore commit ye this great evil against your souls, to cut off from you man and woman, child and suckling, out of Judah, to leave you none to remain; In that ye provoke me unto wrath with the works of your hands, burning incense unto other gods in the land of Egypt, whither ye be gone to dwell, that ye might cut yourselves off, and that ye might be a curse and a reproach among all the nations of the earth? Have ye forgotten the wickedness of your fathers, and the wickedness of the kings of Judah, and the wickedness of their wives, and your own wickedness, and the wickedness of your wives, which they have committed in the land of Judah, and in the streets of Jerusalem? They are not humbled even unto this day, neither have they feared, nor walked in my law, nor in my statutes, that I set before you and before your fathers. (Jeremiah 44:1-10)

A Historical Rebuke to the Jews in Egypt (1-10): Jeremiah is speaking the words of the LORD to the Jews that are dwelling in the land of Egypt (1). God starts out this historical rebuke reminding them what God allowed Jerusalem to become, wasted and desolate (2, 6). The results of all this judgment on the city of peace is the direct result of their idolatry (3-4, 7-8). The LORD charges his people with four things in verses 9 & 10; forgetting the wickedness of their fathers, refusing to humble themselves, fear God nor walk in His ways.

Therefore thus saith the LORD of hosts, the God of Israel; Behold, I will set my face against you for evil, and to cut off all Judah. And I will take the remnant of Judah, that have set their faces to go into the land of Egypt to sojourn there, and they shall all be consumed, and fall in the land of Egypt; they shall even be consumed by the sword and by the famine: they shall die, from the least even unto the greatest, by the sword and by the famine: and they shall be an execration, and an astonishment, and a curse, and a reproach. For I will punish them that dwell in the land of Egypt, as I have punished Jerusalem, by the sword, by the famine, and by the pestilence: So that none of the remnant of Judah, which are gone into the land of Egypt to sojourn there, shall escape or remain, that they should return into the land of Judah, to the which they have a desire to return to dwell there: for none shall return but such as shall escape. (Jeremiah 44:11-14)

Judgment on the Jews in the Land of Egypt (11-14): The result of their unwillingness to harken to the words of the LORD by the mouth of Jeremiah is that all the Jews in the land of Egypt (who fled there in fear of dying by the hand of Nebuchadnezzar) will die, never to return to their land (12-14).

Then all the men which knew that their wives had burned incense unto other gods, and all the women that stood by, a great multitude, even all the people that dwelt in the land of Egypt, in Pathros, answered Jeremiah, saying, As for the word that thou hast spoken unto us in the name of the LORD, we will not hearken unto thee. But we will certainly do whatsoever thing goeth forth out of our own mouth, to burn incense unto the queen of heaven, and to pour out drink offerings unto her, as we have done, we, and our fathers, our kings, and our princes, in the cities of Judah, and in the streets of Jerusalem: for then had we plenty of victuals, and were well, and saw no evil. But since we left off to burn incense to the queen of heaven, and to pour out drink offerings unto her, we have wanted all things, and have been consumed by the sword and by the famine. And when we burned incense to the queen of heaven, and poured out drink offerings unto her, did we make her cakes to worship her, and pour out drink offerings unto her, without our men? (Jeremiah 44:15-19)

The Response of the People (15-19): What happens next is truly amazing. All the people responded with a brazen, "We will not hearken unto thee" (15-16). The reason for their obstinacy in refusing to obey the word of the LORD is stated in verse 15. The men's wives burned incense to other gods, therefore the men were sympathetic (15). It is one thing to disobey the word of the LORD in spirit and mind but these voiced with their mouths, "We will certainly do whatsoever thing goeth forth out of our own mouth to burn incense unto the queen of heaven..." (17). These brazen individuals explain that when they burned incense unto the queen of heaven they had plenty, but when they cease burning incense to the queen of heaven they were in want of all things and were consumed by the sword (17-18). This kind of reasoning is along the lines of Ecclesiastes 8:11, "because sentence against an evil work is not executed speedily, therefore the heart of the sons of men is fully set in them to do evil."

Then Jeremiah said unto all the people, to the men, and to the women, and to all the people which had given him that answer, saying, The incense that ye burned in the cities of Judah, and in the streets of Jerusalem, ye, and your fathers, your kings, and your princes, and the people of the land, did not the LORD remember them, and came it not into his mind? So that the LORD could no longer bear, because of the evil of your doings, and because of the abominations which ye have committed; therefore is your land a desolation, and an astonishment, and a curse, without an inhabitant, as at this day. Because ye have burned incense, and because ye have sinned against the LORD, and have not obeyed the voice of the LORD, nor walked in his law, nor in his statutes, nor in his testimonies; therefore this evil is happened unto you, as at this

day. Moreover Jeremiah said unto all the people, and to all the women, Hear the word of the LORD, all Judah that are in the land of Egypt: Thus saith the LORD of hosts, the God of Israel, saying; Ye and your wives have both spoken with your mouths, and fulfilled with your hand, saying, We will surely perform our vows that we have vowed, to burn incense to the queen of heaven, and to pour out drink offerings unto her: ye will surely accomplish your vows, and surely perform your vows. Therefore hear ye the word of the LORD, all Judah that dwell in the land of Egypt; Behold, I have sworn by my great name, saith the LORD, that my name shall no more be named in the mouth of any man of Judah in all the land of Egypt, saying, The Lord GOD liveth. Behold, I will watch over them for evil, and not for good: and all the men of Judah that are in the land of Egypt shall be consumed by the sword and by the famine, until there be an end of them. Yet a small number that escape the sword shall return out of the land of Egypt into the land of Judah, and all the remnant of Judah, that are gone into the land of Egypt to sojourn there, shall know whose words shall stand, mine, or theirs. (Jeremiah 44:20-28)

The Words of the LORD Shall Stand (20-28): Jeremiah explains to the Jews in Egypt that all the evil that has befallen them and to Jerusalem is a result of their idolatrous practices (20-23). Thus, their fate is sealed because of the words they have spoken, insisting to maintain their worshiping of the queen of heaven (24-25). Their judgment is that the LORD will see to it that all those of Judah, in the land of Egypt, shall no more mention the LORD's great name. They shall be consumed by the sword, by famine until there be an end of them. (26-27). The LORD always has a remnant, as is seen in verse 28 where He promises to reserve a small number out of Egypt into the land of Judah, Jeremiah would be one of these (28).

And this shall be a sign unto you, saith the LORD, that I will punish you in this place, that ye may know that my words shall surely stand against you for evil: Thus saith the LORD; Behold, I will give Pharaohhophra king of Egypt into the hand of his enemies, and into the hand of them that seek his life; as I gave Zedekiah king of Judah into the hand of Nebuchadrezzar king of Babylon, his enemy, and that sought his life. (Jeremiah 44:29-30)

This Shall be a Sign (29-30): The LORD wants them to understand that when Pharaoh-hophra king of Egypt is taken away captive that all things that the LORD has promised concerning their fate will come to pass. They are to understand that it is the LORD's allowing because of all their evil ways (29-30).

CHAPTER FORTY-FIVE
The Word of God to Baruch

The word that Jeremiah the prophet spake unto Baruch the sokn of Neriah, when he had written these words in a book at the mouth of Jeremiah, in the fourth year of Jehoiakim the son of Josiah king of Judah, saying, Thus saith the LORD, the God of Israel, unto thee, O Baruch; Thou didst say, Woe is me now! for the LORD hath added grief to my sorrow; I fainted in my sighing, and I find no rest. Thus shalt thou say unto him, The LORD saith thus; Behold, that which I have built will I break down, and that which I have planted I will pluck up, even this whole land. And seekest thou great things for thyself? seek them not: for, behold, I will bring evil upon all flesh, saith the LORD: but thy life will I give unto thee for a prey in all places whither thou goest. (Jeremiah 45:1-5)

The Word of God to Baruch (1-5): This chapter transpires during the events of chapter 36 when Baruch is told to write all the words of the LORD by the mouth of Jeremiah in a book. Baruch was told to go and preach all the things written therein before all the people in the house of the LORD. The words spoken by Baruch draw the attention of the leadership and eventually the king of Judah, Johoiakim who casts the roll of the book into the fire. It is therefore because of these events Baruch is downtrodden, saying "Woe is me now! For the LORD hath added grief to my sorrow; I fainted in my sighing and I find no rest." (3).

The LORD's response to Baruch is by words of encouragement. Baruch is told not to seek things for himself; in other words, don't worry about your personal aspirations for I'm going to destroy this place. The LORD however will see to it that Baruch's life is spared (4-5).

OVERVIEW
CHAPTERS FORTY-SIX THROUGH FIFTY-ONE
The Judgment on the Gentile

What follows in chapters 46 through 51 is the judgment by our LORD of the Gentiles that have been instrumental in persecuting God's people, Israel: Jeremiah 46:1 is the key verse to this section:
> **The word of the LORD which came to Jeremiah the prophet against the Gentiles; (Jeremiah 46:1)**

Thus, what will follow is the word of the LORD against the Gentiles mentioned in these chapters. The reader should take note that there are ten nations mentioned. When Israel first came into the Promised Land they faced 10 nations, three of which were put down before they crossed the Jordan. Therefore, Joshua faced 7 nations as he entered the land of Canaan. The book of Daniel tells of 10 Gentile kings that will be around before the coming of the Messiah and the establishment of His Kingdom. Psalm 83 tells of a ten nation confederacy that will exist in the last days. Also, the book of Revelation mentions 10 Gentile kings that will be involved in the last days before the LORD's return. So then once again we see judgment on 10 Gentiles listed in these chapters. They are as follows:

    Chapter 46   Judgment on Egypt
    Chapter 47   Judgment on the Philistines
    Chapter 48   Judgment on Moab
    Chapter 49:1-6   Judgment on the Ammonites
    Chapter 49:7-22   Judgment on Edom
    Chapter 49:23-27 Judgment on Damascus
    Chapter 49:28-33 Judgment on Kedar and Hazor
    Chapter 49:34-39 Judgment on Elam
    Chapter 50 & 51 Judgment on Babylon

As to the judgment of these Gentiles, historically all of these mentioned have experienced judgment in one form or another. Historically, there are prophecies concerning events that have transpired and we will make note of these as we go through these chapters. However, none of these Gentile people groups or nations are buying for world dominance today. So, while historically these all have had a judgment upon them, these passages are looking beyond to a time in which the LORD will come and judge these nations for their part in persecuting God's people:

For this is the day of the Lord GOD of hosts, a day of vengeance, that he may avenge him of his adversaries: and the sword shall devour, and it shall be satiate and made drunk with their blood: for the Lord GOD of hosts hath a sacrifice in the north country by the river Euphrates. (Jeremiah 46:10)

CHAPTER FORTY-SIX
Egypt

The word of the LORD which came to Jeremiah the prophet against the Gentiles; Against Egypt, against the army of Pharaohnecho king of Egypt, which was by the river Euphrates in Carchemish, which Nebuchadrezzar king of Babylon smote in the fourth year of Jehoiakim the son of Josiah king of Judah. Order ye the buckler and shield, and draw near to battle. Harness the horses; and get up, ye horsemen, and stand forth with your helmets; furbish the spears, and put on the brigandines. Wherefore have I seen them dismayed and turned away back? and their mighty ones are beaten down, and are fled apace, and look not back: for fear was round about, saith the LORD. Let not the swift flee away, nor the mighty man escape; they shall stumble, and fall toward the north by the river Euphrates. Who is this that cometh up as a flood, whose waters are moved as the rivers? Egypt riseth up like a flood, and his waters are moved like the rivers; and he saith, I will go up, and will cover the earth; I will destroy the city and the inhabitants thereof. Come up, ye horses; and rage, ye chariots; and let the mighty men come forth; the Ethiopians and the Libyans, that handle the shield; and the Lydians, that handle and bend the bow. For this is the day of the Lord GOD of hosts, a day of vengeance, that he may avenge him of his adversaries: and the sword shall devour, and it shall be satiate and made drunk with their blood: for the Lord GOD of hosts hath a sacrifice in the north country by the river Euphrates. Go up into Gilead, and take balm, O virgin, the daughter of Egypt: in vain shalt thou use many medicines; for thou shalt not be cured. The nations have heard of thy shame, and thy cry hath filled the land: for the mighty man hath stumbled against the mighty, and they are fallen both together. (Jeremiah 46:1-12)

Judgment on Pharaohnecho King of Egypt (1-12): Historically this judgment is against Pharaohnecho by the hand of Nebuchadnezzar, during the reign of Josiah king of Judah (2). Throughout the reigns of the final five kings of Judah, there was a constant power struggle between Egypt and Babylon, with Jerusalem playing the fence. In this power struggle both Babylon and Pharaohnecho placed kings on the throne of Jerusalem, with the intention of having them be subservient to their control. Pharaohnecho came and placed Jehoahaz in bands at Riblah, and put Eliakim on the throne, whose name he turned to Jehoahaz. Pharaohnecho then made Jehoahaz pay taxes (2 Kings 23:31-35). The battle briefly mentioned here is the battle of Carchemish (2). Under the leadership of Pharoah-necho Egypt lost this battle, marking the rise of the Babylonian Empire. The "sacrifice in the north country" (10) is the battle in Carchemish, a city by the upper Euphrates River (2). Pharaohnecho is warned by Jeremiah not to go up to Carchemiah to battle, for the LORD is against him (10), for they shall not be cured (11).

The word that the LORD spake to Jeremiah the prophet, how Nebuchadrezzar king of Babylon should come and smite the land of Egypt. Declare ye in Egypt, and publish in Migdol, and publish in Noph and in Tahpanhes: say ye, Stand fast, and prepare thee; for the sword shall devour round about thee. Why are thy valiant men swept away? they stood not, because the LORD did drive them. He made many to fall, yea, one fell upon another: and they said, Arise, and let us go again to our own people, and to the land of our nativity, from the oppressing sword. They did cry there, Pharaoh king of Egypt is but a noise; he hath passed the time appointed. As I live, saith the King, whose name is the LORD of hosts, Surely as Tabor is among the mountains, and as Carmel by the sea, so shall he come. O thou daughter dwelling in Egypt, furnish thyself to go into captivity: for Noph shall be waste and desolate without an inhabitant. Egypt is like a very fair heifer, but destruction cometh; it cometh out of the north. Also her hired men are in the midst

of her like fatted bullocks; for they also are turned back, and are fled away together: they did not stand, because the day of their calamity was come upon them, and the time of their visitation. The voice thereof shall go like a serpent; for they shall march with an army, and come against her with axes, as hewers of wood. They shall cut down her forest, saith the LORD, though it cannot be searched; because they are more than the grasshoppers, and are innumerable. The daughter of Egypt shall be confounded; she shall be delivered into the hand of the people of the north. The LORD of hosts, the God of Israel, saith; Behold, I will punish the multitude of No, and Pharaoh, and Egypt, with their gods, and their kings; even Pharaoh, and all them that trust in him: And I will deliver them into the hand of those that seek their lives, and into the hand of Nebuchadrezzar king of Babylon, and into the hand of his servants: and afterward it shall be inhabited, as in the days of old, saith the LORD. (Jeremiah 46:13-26)

Into the Hand of Nebuchadrezzar (13-26): This prophecy is dealing with a time when Babylon comes to smite the land of Egypt (13). Thus, another prophecy regarding a time when Babylonian forces invade Egypt (see Ezekiel 29:12). Throughout this chapter places in Egypt are mentioned, telling us that this prophecy is no longer dealing with the destruction of the city of Carchemish, but rather the punishment of the land of Egypt itself (14, 19 and 25).

But fear not thou, O my servant Jacob, and be not dismayed, O Israel: for, behold, I will save thee from afar off, and thy seed from the land of their captivity; and Jacob shall return, and be in rest and at ease, and none shall make him afraid. Fear thou not, O Jacob my servant, saith the LORD: for I am with thee; for I will make a full end of all the nations whither I have driven thee: but I will not make a full end of thee, but correct thee in measure; yet will I not leave thee wholly unpunished. (Jeremiah 46:27-28)

The LORD's Eternal Purpose with Jacob (27-28): The LORD has an eternal purpose with Jacob (the 12 tribes of Israel). Here once again, we see the eternal purpose of God for His people. Israel will be the head over all nations one day; the LORD will see to it (Deut. 28:13).

CHAPTER FORTY-SEVEN
The Philistines

The word of the LORD that came to Jeremiah the prophet against the Philistines, before that Pharaoh smote Gaza. Thus saith the LORD; Behold, waters rise up out of the north, and shall be an overflowing flood, and shall overflow the land, and all that is therein; the city, and them that dwell therein: then the men shall cry, and all the inhabitants of the land shall howl. At the noise of the stamping of the hoofs of his strong horses, at the rushing of his chariots, and at the rumbling of his wheels, the fathers shall not look back to their children for feebleness of hands; Because of the day that cometh to spoil all the Philistines, and to cut off from Tyrus and Zidon every helper that remaineth: for the LORD will spoil the Philistines, the remnant of the country of Caphtor. Baldness is come upon Gaza; Ashkelon is cut off with the remnant of their valley: how long wilt thou cut thyself? O thou sword of the LORD, how long will it be ere thou be quiet? put up thyself into thy scabbard, rest, and be still. How can it be quiet, seeing the LORD hath given it a charge against Ashkelon, and against the sea shore? there hath he appointed it. (Jeremiah 47:1-7)

Judgment on the Philistines (1-7): This prophecy is against the Philistines and some of their allies, Tyre and Sidon. The time of this prophecy is given in verse one, "before that Pharaoh smote Gaza" which would make it about the time of chapter 46:1-12. It would seem that Nebuchadnezzar is the force that brings destruction on the Philistines. The Philistines have a long biblical history of being an enemy of the people of God. The time of this judgment would seem to have transpired when Nebuchadnezzar came to battle the Egyptians at the battle of Carchemish. Metaphors are employed to depict the Babylonian advancing armies coming upon the Philistines as a flood (2).

CHAPTER FORTY-EIGHT
Moab

Against Moab thus saith the LORD of hosts, the God of Israel; Woe unto Nebo! for it is spoiled: Kiriathaim is confounded and taken: Misgab is confounded and dismayed. There shall be no more praise of Moab: in Heshbon they have devised evil against it; come, and let us cut it off from being a nation. Also thou shalt be cut down, O Madmen; the sword shall pursue thee. A voice of crying shall be from Horonaim, spoiling and great destruction. Moab is destroyed; her little ones have caused a cry to be heard. For in the going up of Luhith continual weeping shall go up; for in the going down of Horonaim the enemies have heard a cry of destruction. Flee, save your lives, and be like the heath in the wilderness. (Jeremiah 48:1-6)

No More Praise of Moab (1-6): The Moabites are the decedents of the first born daughter of Lot, a result of her laying with her father (Gen. 19:37). They allied themselves with Nebuchadnezzar against Israel (2 Kings 24:2; Jeremiah 12:7-13). Though historically

they would seem to be an enemy of God's people, Ruth was a Moabite who marries Boaz; the grandparents of David. These opening verses in this section depict the coming judgment on Moab:
- "Woe onto Nebo! For it is spoiled" (1). Nebo is a mountain in Moab where Moses saw the Promised Land.
- "Kiriathaim is confounded and taken" (1). Kiriathaim is a city in the upper part of Moab.
- "Misgab is confounded and dismayed" (1). Misgab is a town of Moab.
- "In Heshbon they have devised evil against it" (2). Heshbon is the capital city of Sihon King of Ammon. Notice what Ammon says of Moab, "let us cut them off from being a nation" (cf. Psalm 83).
- "A voice of crying shall be heard from Horonaim, spoiling and great destruction" (3 cf. vs 5). Horonaim is a city of Moab.
- "Moab is destroyed her little ones have caused a cry to be heard" (4).
- "For in the going up of Luhith continual weeping shall go up" (5). Luhith is a place in Moab.

The heath of verse 6 is a desert shrub found in uncultivated desert lands. This term would be used for "heathen" an uncivilized people who live out in the "heath". Later the term "heathen" took on religious overtones meaning those who lived in a religious wasteland. Thus, Moab is called upon to flee like the heath that is blown about the desert floor.

For because thou hast trusted in thy works and in thy treasures, thou shalt also be taken: and Chemosh shall go forth into captivity with his priests and his princes together. And the spoiler shall come upon every city, and no city shall escape: the valley also shall perish, and the plain shall be destroyed, as the LORD hath spoken. Give wings unto Moab, that it may flee and get away: for the cities thereof shall be desolate, without any to dwell therein. Cursed be he that doeth the work of the LORD deceitfully, and cursed be he that keepeth back his sword from blood. (Jeremiah 48:7-10)

Judgment on Chemosh (7-10): The works of the hands of the Moabites were the idols they worshiped. They trusted in them to their own demise. Chemosh is the god of the Moabites. Jeremiah pronounces that they and their false gods whom they trusted will go into captivity (7). The land will be laid waste by their enemies (8-9) and those enemies of Moab that turn back their sword from blood will be cursed (10).

Moab hath been at ease from his youth, and he hath settled on his lees, and hath not been emptied from vessel to vessel, neither hath he gone into captivity: therefore his taste remained in him, and his scent is

not changed. Therefore, behold, the days come, saith the LORD, that I will send unto him wanderers, that shall cause him to wander, and shall empty his vessels, and break their bottles. And Moab shall be ashamed of Chemosh, as the house of Israel was ashamed of Bethel their confidence. (Jeremiah 48:11-13)

Moab Has Been at Ease (11-13): The symbolism being used in these verses to depict the ease that Moab has been experiencing is that of wine. Lees is the dead yeast that settles to the bottom of wine during the fermenting process. Moab has been at ease so long that that they like the lees of wine are settled. They have not been stirred up from bottle to bottle and therefore their taste and scent remains (11). However, the day is coming when wanderers will come and break the bottles of wine, thus the LORD will send those who will come and break Moab and their idols (12-13). At that time Moab will be ashamed of Chemosh (their false god they worshiped) just as Israel was ashamed when they set up false worship at Bethel (13 cf. 2 Kings 29:10).

How say ye, We are mighty and strong men for the war? Moab is spoiled, and gone up out of her cities, and his chosen young men are gone down to the slaughter, saith the King, whose name is the LORD of hosts. The calamity of Moab is near to come, and his affliction hasteth fast. All ye that are about him, bemoan him; and all ye that know his name, say, How is the strong staff broken, and the beautiful rod! Thou daughter that dost inhabit Dibon, come down from thy glory, and sit in thirst; for the spoiler of Moab shall come upon thee, and he shall destroy thy strong holds. O inhabitant of Aroer, stand by the way, and espy; ask him that fleeth, and her that escapeth, and say, What is done? Moab is confounded; for it is broken down: howl and cry; tell ye it in Arnon, that Moab is spoiled, And judgment is come upon the plain country; upon Holon, and upon Jahazah, and upon Mephaath, And upon Dibon, and upon Nebo, and upon Bethdiblathaim, And upon Kiriathaim, and upon Bethgamul, and upon Bethmeon, And upon Kerioth, and upon Bozrah, and upon all the cities of the land of Moab, far or near. The horn of Moab is cut off, and his arm is broken, saith the LORD. (Jeremiah 48:14-25)

The Spoiler of Moab is Come (14-25): These verses depict all the cities of the region of Moab that will experience the judgment of the LORD. "The horn of Moab is cut off," depicts the strength and power of Moab being cut off; they will be rendered powerless.

Make ye him drunken: for he magnified himself against the LORD: Moab also shall wallow in his vomit, and he also shall be in derision. For was not Israel a derision unto thee? was he found among

thieves? for since thou spakest of him, thou skippedst for joy. O ye that dwell in Moab, leave the cities, and dwell in the rock, and be like the dove that maketh her nest in the sides of the hole's mouth. We have heard the pride of Moab, (he is exceeding proud) his loftiness, and his arrogancy, and his pride, and the haughtiness of his heart. I know his wrath, saith the LORD; but it shall not be so; his lies shall not so effect it. Therefore will I howl for Moab, and I will cry out for all Moab; mine heart shall mourn for the men of Kirheres. O vine of Sibmah, I will weep for thee with the weeping of Jazer: thy plants are gone over the sea, they reach even to the sea of Jazer: the spoiler is fallen upon thy summer fruits and upon thy vintage. And joy and gladness is taken from the plentiful field, and from the land of Moab; and I have caused wine to fail from the winepresses: none shall tread with shouting; their shouting shall be no shouting. From the cry of Heshbon even unto Elealeh, and even unto Jahaz, have they uttered their voice, from Zoar even unto Horonaim, as an heifer of three years old: for the waters also of Nimrim shall be desolate. Moreover I will cause to cease in Moab, saith the LORD, him that offereth in the high places, and him that burneth incense to his gods. Therefore mine heart shall sound for Moab like pipes, and mine heart shall sound like pipes for the men of Kirheres: because the riches that he hath gotten are perished. For every head shall be bald, and every beard clipped: upon all the hands shall be cuttings, and upon the loins sackcloth. There shall be lamentation generally upon all the housetops of Moab, and in the streets thereof: for I have broken Moab like a vessel wherein is no pleasure, saith the LORD. They shall howl, saying, How is it broken down! how hath Moab turned the back with shame! so shall Moab be a derision and a dismaying to all them about him. For thus saith the LORD; Behold, he shall fly as an eagle, and shall spread his wings over Moab. Kerioth is taken, and the strong holds are surprised, and the mighty men's hearts in Moab at that day shall be as the heart of a woman in her pangs. And Moab shall be destroyed from being a people, because he hath magnified himself against the LORD. Fear, and the pit, and the snare, shall be upon thee, O inhabitant of Moab, saith the LORD. He that fleeth from the fear shall fall into the pit; and he that getteth up out of the pit shall be taken in the snare: for I will bring upon it, even upon Moab, the year of their visitation, saith the LORD. They that fled stood under the shadow of Heshbon because of the force: but a fire shall come forth out of Heshbon, and a flame from the midst of Sihon, and shall devour the corner of Moab, and the crown of the head of the tumultuous ones. Woe be unto thee, O Moab! the people of Chemosh perisheth: for thy sons are taken captives, and thy daughters captives. (Jeremiah 48:26-46)

The Pride of Moab (26-46): The LORD hates pride (26, 29, 42 cf. Prov. 8:13), pride always leads to destruction (Prov. 16:18). Here Moab is drunk with pride and therefore he will be as a drunken man that wallows in his vomit (26). Moab was a land of plenty, Sibmah was known for its vines which the enemies of Moab cut down (32-34 cf. Isaiah 16:8). Thus, weeping is heard from the land of Moab (the cry of Heshbon even unto Elealeh vs. 34). All these various judgments against the land of Moab are a result of their pride and idolatrous practices (35). The results of these invading armies into the land of Moab are seen in the wording: "For every head shall be bald and every beard clipped: upon the hands shall be cuttings" (37); "There shall be lamentation generally upon all the housetops of Moab" (38); "They shall howl..." (39); this is due to the fact their enemies shall fly over them like and eagle (40), so that all Moab is destroyed (41-42). None shall escape the invasion of Moab (43-46).

Yet will I bring again the captivity of Moab in the latter days, saith the LORD. Thus far is the judgment of Moab. (Jeremiah 48:47)

Moab and the Latter Days (47): This verse tells us that Moab will be a world player in the "latter days" which the seen in Psalm 83! They will be part of the uniting of the Muslim nations against Israel.

CHAPTER FORTY-NINE
Ammonites, Edom, Damascus, Kedar and Hazor, Elam

Concerning the Ammonites, thus saith the LORD; Hath Israel no sons? hath he no heir? why then doth their king inherit Gad, and his people dwell in his cities? Therefore, behold, the days come, saith the LORD, that I will cause an alarm of war to be heard in Rabbah of the Ammonites; and it shall be a desolate heap, and her daughters shall be burned with fire: then shall Israel be heir unto them that were his heirs, saith the LORD. Howl, O Heshbon, for Ai is spoiled: cry, ye daughters of Rabbah, gird you with sackcloth; lament, and run to and fro by the hedges; for their king shall go into captivity, and his priests and his princes together. Wherefore gloriest thou in the valleys, thy flowing valley, O backsliding daughter? that trusted in her treasures, saying, Who shall come unto me? Behold, I will bring a fear upon thee, saith the Lord GOD of hosts, from all those that be about thee; and ye shall be driven out every man right forth; and none shall gather up him that wandereth. And afterward I will bring again the captivity of the children of Ammon, saith the LORD. (Jeremiah 49:1-6)

Judgment on the Ammonites (1-6): Like the Moabites, the Ammonites are the product of the incestuous relationship between Lot and his younger daughter (Gen. 19:20-38). The howling of Heshbon for the spoil of Ai, from the daughters of Rabbah are all references to the invasion that Ammon experienced when the Assyrians came to take the Northern Tribes captive (2-3). Heshbon is the capital city of Sihon, king of the Ammonites. Ai is a city in Ammonite territory and Rabbah is the city royal of the sons of Ammon (2 Samuel 12:26). This judgment results from their pride (4), and as he did to Moab, the LORD promises them to return (6); a reference I believe to Psalm 83.

Concerning Edom, thus saith the LORD of hosts; Is wisdom no more in Teman? is counsel perished from the prudent? is their wisdom vanished? Flee ye, turn back, dwell deep, O inhabitants of Dedan; for I will bring the calamity of Esau upon him, the time that I will visit him. If grapegatherers come to thee, would they not leave some gleaning grapes? if thieves by night, they will destroy till they have enough. But I have made Esau bare, I have uncovered his secret places, and he shall not be able to hide himself: his seed is spoiled, and his brethren, and his neighbours, and he is not. Leave thy fatherless children, I will preserve them alive; and let thy widows trust in me. For thus saith the LORD; Behold, they whose judgment was not to drink of the cup have assuredly drunken; and art thou he that shall altogether go unpunished? thou shalt not go unpunished, but thou shalt surely drink of it. For I have sworn by myself, saith the LORD, that Bozrah shall become a desolation, a reproach, a waste, and a curse; and all the cities thereof shall be perpetual wastes. I have heard a rumour from the LORD, and an ambassador is sent unto the heathen, saying, Gather ye together, and come against her, and rise up to the battle. For, lo, I will make thee small among the heathen, and despised among men. Thy terribleness hath deceived thee, and the pride of thine heart, O thou that dwellest in the clefts of the rock, that holdest the height of the hill: though thou shouldest make thy nest as high as the eagle, I will bring thee down from thence, saith the LORD. Also Edom shall be a desolation: every one that goeth by it shall be astonished, and shall hiss at all the plagues thereof. As in the overthrow of Sodom and Gomorrah and the neighbour cities thereof, saith the LORD, no man shall abide there, neither shall a son of man dwell in it. Behold, he shall come up like a lion from the swelling of Jordan against the habitation of the strong: but I will suddenly make him run away from her: and who is a chosen man, that I may appoint over her? for who is like me? and who will appoint me the time? and who is that shepherd that will stand before me? Therefore hear the counsel of the LORD, that he hath taken against Edom; and his purposes, that he hath purposed against the inhabitants of Teman: Surely the least of the flock shall draw them out: surely he shall make their habitations desolate with them. The earth is moved at the noise of their fall, at the cry the noise thereof was heard in the Red sea. Behold, he shall come up and fly as the eagle, and spread his wings over Bozrah: and at that day shall the heart of the mighty men of Edom be as the heart of a woman in her pangs. (Jeremiah 49:7-22)

Judgment on Edom (7-22): The people of Edom are the decedents of Esau. Esau was the child that sold his birthright for pottage (Genesis 25:30-34 cf. Hebrews 12:16). Thus, Edom is often referred to as Esau. The prophet Obadiah deals exclusively with Edom and its judgments. Pride is mentioned as one of the reasons for the judgments against Edom (16 cf. Obadiah 3-4), as is their decision to come up against Israel in battle (Obadiah 12-14). Therefore judgments appear throughout the word of God concerning the Edomites, both historically and prophetically (Amos 1:11-12; Joel 3:19; Obadiah). Isaiah, prophesying of the coming Day of the LORD, sees the LORD coming in garments stained with blood from Bozrah, the capital city of Edom (Isaiah 63:1-3 cf. Jeremiah 49:13). Edom is also one of the world players in the coming confederacy against Israel (Psalm 83).

Edomites are rebuked for their unwise counsel (7). Teman was the son of Eliphaz, Esau's eldest son (7). Historically, Edom did become "bare" (10), yet they are reserved for a future day of judgment (11-13). The historical desolation and the prophetical judgment of Edom are running together in these verses. Historically, Nebuchadnezzar would come upon them like a lion (19) and like an eagle, spreading its wings over them in judgment (22). However, this event also echoes out into the future when the LORD will come against Edom from the city of Bozrah (vss. 13, 22 cf. Isaiah 63), whose destruction will be like Sodom and Gomorrah (18).

Concerning Damascus. Hamath is confounded, and Arpad: for they have heard evil tidings: they are fainthearted; there is sorrow on the sea; it cannot be quiet. Damascus is waxed feeble, and turneth herself to flee, and fear hath seized on her: anguish and sorrows have taken her, as a woman in travail. How is the city of praise not left, the city of my joy! Therefore her young men shall fall in her streets, and all the men of war shall be cut off in that day, saith the LORD of hosts. And I will kindle a fire in the wall of Damascus, and it shall consume the palaces of Benhadad. (Jeremiah 49:23-27)

Judgment on Damascus (23-27): Damascus is the capital city of Syria. The judgment on Damascus is also mentioned in detail in Isaiah 17. Once again historical and prophetic events are mingled together throughout this passage. Isaiah 17 deals primarily with the prophetic destruction of Damascus.

Concerning Kedar, and concerning the kingdoms of Hazor, which Nebuchadrezzar king of Babylon shall smite, thus saith the LORD; Arise ye, go up to Kedar, and spoil the men of the east. Their tents and their flocks shall they take away: they shall take to themselves their curtains, and all their vessels, and their camels; and they shall cry unto them, Fear is on every side. Flee, get you far off, dwell deep, O ye inhabitants of Hazor, saith the LORD; for Nebuchadrezzar king of Babylon hath taken counsel against you, and hath conceived a purpose against you. Arise, get you up unto the wealthy nation, that dwelleth without care, saith the LORD, which have neither gates nor bars, which dwell alone. And their camels shall be a booty, and the multitude of their cattle a spoil: and I will scatter into all winds them that are in the utmost corners; and I will bring their calamity from all sides thereof, saith the LORD. And Hazor shall be a dwelling for dragons, and a desolation for ever: there shall no man abide there, nor any son of man dwell in it. (Jeremiah 49:28-33)

Judgment on Kedar and Hazor (28-33): Kedar and Hazor are cities in Arabia. These verses are fulfilled prophecy concerning the conquering of both Kedar

(28) and Hazor (30) by Nebuchadnezzar. Pride is hinted at here: "... wealthy nation that dwelleth without care..." (31).

The word of the LORD that came to Jeremiah the prophet against Elam in the beginning of the reign of Zedekiah king of Judah, saying, Thus saith the LORD of hosts; Behold, I will break the bow of Elam, the chief of their might. And upon Elam will I bring the four winds from the four quarters of heaven, and will scatter them toward all those winds; and there shall be no nation whither the outcasts of Elam shall not come. For I will cause Elam to be dismayed before their enemies, and before them that seek their life: and I will bring evil upon them, even my fierce anger, saith the LORD; and I will send the sword after them, till I have consumed them: And I will set my throne in Elam, and will destroy from thence the king and the princes, saith the LORD. But it shall come to pass in the latter days, that I will bring again the captivity of Elam, saith the LORD. (Jeremiah 49:34-39)

The Judgment on Elam (34-39): This prophecy is given during the reign of Zedekiah (34). Elam was the son of Shem (Gen. 10:22). The king of Elam during the time of Abraham was Chedorlaomer (Gen. 14:1-17). The doom of Elam is prophesied (Ezek. 32:16, 24; Jer. 25:25). Known for their archery, the LORD promises to break their bow (35), and scatter them in every direction (36). Elam will be gathered again in the "latter days" (39), showing us that their influence will be around as the end times unfold.

CHAPTER FIFTY AND FIFTY-ONE
Judgment on Babylon

The word that the LORD spake against Babylon and against the land of the Chaldeans by Jeremiah the prophet. Declare ye among the nations, and publish, and set up a standard; publish, and conceal not: say, Babylon is taken, Bel is confounded, Merodach is broken in pieces; her idols are confounded, her images are broken in pieces. For out of the north there cometh up a nation against her, which shall make her land desolate, and none shall dwell therein: they shall remove, they shall depart, both man and beast. (Jeremiah 50:1-3)

The Word of the LORD Against Babylon (1-3): Nine Gentile nations have been mentioned, only one remains; Babylon, the land of the Chaldeans, is the tenth and final kingdom in these passages of judgment. The judgment of Babylon is epic and is surrounded by infamy throughout the Scriptures. The LORD dedicates two chapters to its destruction. As with many of the chapters dealing with these

Gentile nations, there are prophetic pronouncements that have already transpired historically, and there are prophetic announcements that have yet to find their fulfillment. The bulk of what is given here is the captivity of Judah, a major event both historically and prophetically. I have often said that the LORD replays world events; nothing exemplifies this more than what transpires historically between Babylon and Israel.

The LORD allows Judah to be taken and Jerusalem to be destroyed for their idolatrous practices, as He had allowed the Assyrians to come and take away Israel years earlier. However, now it's the Babylonians turn to feel the judgment of God upon their idols: "Bel is confounded, Merodach is broken in pieces, her idols are confounded, her images are broken in pieces" (3). The nation the LORD will use to judge Babylon will be Persia, and it is the king of the Persian Empire, Cyrus, that will make the decree for the return of the Jewish people to return to their homeland (vss. 4-8).

In those days, and in that time, saith the LORD, the children of Israel shall come, they and the children of Judah together, going and weeping: they shall go, and seek the LORD their God. They shall ask the way to Zion with their faces thitherward, saying, Come, and let us join ourselves to the LORD in a perpetual covenant that shall not be forgotten. My people hath been lost sheep: their shepherds have

caused them to go astray, they have turned them away on the mountains: they have gone from mountain to hill, they have forgotten their restingplace. All that found them have devoured them: and their adversaries said, we offend not, because they have sinned against the LORD, the habitation of justice, even the LORD, the hope of their fathers. Remove out of the midst of Babylon, and go forth out of the land of the Chaldeans, and be as the he goats before the flocks. (Jeremiah 50:4-8)

The Return of a Remnant (4-8): Historically this is dealing with the return of the Jewish people to their homeland. Babylon falls in a night and the Persian Empire gains control, and therefore world dominance. Under Cyrus, the Jewish people return to their land under the leadership of Zerubbabel, the governor, and Joshua, the high priest. It is that generation that "seek the LORD their God" and "ask the way to Zion" (4-5). The remnant of Jews desire to return to the LORD according their "perpetual covenant" (5). The Jewish people had become "lost sheep" because of their leadership (6). When the Jews return to the land, they never truly gain any footing, as far as being God's covenant people is concerned. It is during the times of the Maccabees that the religious leaders known as the Sadducees and Pharisees gain control over the nation, so that when our LORD comes to His own, He comes to the "lost sheep of the house of Israel" (Matt. 15:24). Their leadership had not had a change of heart, and was still leading them away from the LORD they claimed to serve (Matt. 23). Thus, these passages echo out to a future time in which the children of Israel and the children of Judah (4) once again will be called out of Babylon and brought into their "restingplace" (vs. 6, 8; Micah 4:10; Rev. 18:4).

For, lo, I will raise and cause to come up against Babylon an assembly of great nations from the north country: and they shall set themselves in array against her; from thence she shall be taken: their arrows shall be as of a mighty expert man; none shall return in vain. And Chaldea shall be a spoil: all that spoil her shall be satisfied, saith the LORD. Because ye were glad, because ye rejoiced, O ye destroyers of mine heritage, because ye are grown fat as the heifer at grass, and bellow as bulls; Your mother shall be sore confounded; she that bare you shall be ashamed: behold, the hindermost of the nations shall be a wilderness, a dry land, and a desert. Because of the wrath of the LORD it shall not be inhabited, but it shall be wholly desolate: every one that goeth by Babylon shall be astonished, and hiss at all her plagues. Put yourselves in array against Babylon round about: all ye that bend the bow, shoot at her, spare no arrows: for she hath sinned against the LORD. Shout against her round about: she hath given her hand: her foundations are fallen, her walls are thrown down: for it is the vengeance of the LORD: take vengeance upon her; as she hath done, do unto her. Cut off the sower from Babylon, and him that handleth the sickle in the time of harvest: for fear of the oppressing sword they shall turn every one to his people, and they shall flee every one to his own land. (Jeremiah 50:9-16)

Destruction of Babylon (9-16): Historically, the Medes and the Persians, and later the Greeks under Alexander, will bring the utter destruction of Babylon. However, Babylon has not seen its last days. Passages like these, and others throughout the prophets and especially Revelation, speak of a day in which Babylon will be destroyed, never to rise again. Revelation chapter 18 deals with the great financial influence that Babylon will have on the world's economy in the future, as well as its coming destruction. Isaiah 13:19-22 tells us that its destruction shall be like the day the LORD destroyed Sodom and Gomorrah, never to be inhabited, it shall be a desolation (13), a place for all the unclean animals of the land. Notice the reference to "plagues" in verse 13, an obvious reference to the future destruction of Babylon (Rev. 18:4, 8).

Israel is a scattered sheep; the lions have driven him away: first the king of Assyria hath devoured him; and last this Nebuchadrezzar king of Babylon hath

broken his bones. Therefore thus saith the LORD of hosts, the God of Israel; Behold, I will punish the king of Babylon and his land, as I have punished the king of Assyria. And I will bring Israel again to his habitation, and he shall feed on Carmel and Bashan, and his soul shall be satisfied upon mount Ephraim and Gilead. In those days, and in that time, saith the LORD, the iniquity of Israel shall be sought for, and there shall be none; and the sins of Judah, and they shall not be found: for I will pardon them whom I reserve. (Jeremiah 50:17-20)

Judgment and Blessings (17-20): These passages truly show how history and prophecy are mingled together. Assyria came and took the Northern Tribes captive around 600 B.C.; over a hundred years later the LORD raised up the Babylonians to "punish" the king of Assyria, Babylon being the next world power. Babylon will be punished as well with the rise of the Persian Empire, and the Greeks to follow. These verses transpired historically. However, the time in which the LORD will "seek for the sins of Israel and Judah, but they shall not be found" is a reference to the institution of the New Covenant, and the establishment of the coming Kingdom (Jer. vs. 20 cf. 31:31-34; 36:24-28).

Go up against the land of Merathaim, even against it, and against the inhabitants of Pekod: waste and utterly destroy after them, saith the LORD, and do according to all that I have commanded thee. A sound of battle is in the land, and of great destruction. How is the hammer of the whole earth cut asunder and broken! how is Babylon become a desolation among the nations! I have laid a snare for thee, and thou art also taken, O Babylon, and thou wast not aware: thou art found, and also caught, because thou hast striven against the LORD. The LORD hath opened his armoury, and hath brought forth the weapons of his indignation: for this is the work of the Lord GOD of hosts in the land of the Chaldeans. Come against her from the utmost border, open her storehouses: cast her up as heaps, and destroy her utterly: let nothing of her be left. Slay all her bullocks; let them go down to the slaughter: woe unto them! for their day is come, the time of their visitation. The voice of them that flee and escape out of the land of Babylon, to declare in Zion the vengeance of the LORD our God, the vengeance of his temple. Call together the archers against Babylon: all ye that bend the bow, camp against it round about; let none thereof escape: recompense her according to her work; according to all that she hath done, do unto her: for she hath been proud against the LORD, against the Holy One of Israel. Therefore shall her young men fall in the streets, and all her men of war shall be cut off in that day, saith the LORD. Behold, I am against thee, O thou most proud, saith the Lord GOD of hosts: for thy day is come, the time that I will visit thee. And the most proud shall stumble and fall, and none shall raise him up: and I will kindle a fire in his cities, and it shall devour all round about him. (Jeremiah 50:21-32)

The Pride of Babylon (21-32): The land of Merathaim and the inhabitants of Pekod are suburbs of Babylon. Once again, the destruction of Babylon historically is the subject of the passage. However, the emphasis is now placed on the pride of Babylon, that will lead to its ultimate fall in the day of the LORD's visitation (29, 31, and 32).

Thus saith the LORD of hosts; The children of Israel and the children of Judah were oppressed together: and all that took them captives held them fast; they refused to let them go. Their Redeemer is strong; the LORD of hosts is his name: he shall throughly plead their cause, that he may give rest to the land, and disquiet the inhabitants of Babylon. (Jeremiah 50:33-34)

The Redeemer of Israel (33-34): The LORD is the deliverer of His people from not only the nations that hold them captive, but from the hand of the mighty, the grasp of Satan himself (Isaiah 49:24-26).

A sword is upon the Chaldeans, saith the LORD, and upon the inhabitants of Babylon, and upon her princes, and upon her wise men. A sword is upon

the liars; and they shall dote: a sword is upon her mighty men; and they shall be dismayed. A sword is upon their horses, and upon their chariots, and upon all the mingled people that are in the midst of her; and they shall become as women: a sword is upon her treasures; and they shall be robbed. A drought is upon her waters; and they shall be dried up: for it is the land of graven images, and they are mad upon their idols. Therefore the wild beasts of the desert with the wild beasts of the islands shall dwell there, and the owls shall dwell therein: and it shall be no more inhabited for ever; neither shall it be dwelt in from generation to generation. As God overthrew Sodom and Gomorrah and the neighbour cities thereof, saith the LORD; so shall no man abide there, neither shall any son of man dwell therein. Behold, a people shall come from the north, and a great nation, and many kings shall be raised up from the coasts of the earth. They shall hold the bow and the lance: they are cruel, and will not shew mercy: their voice shall roar like the sea, and they shall ride upon horses, every one put in array, like a man to the battle, against thee, O daughter of Babylon. The king of Babylon hath heard the report of them, and his hands waxed feeble: anguish took hold of him, and pangs as of a woman in travail. Behold, he shall come up like a lion from the swelling of Jordan unto the habitation of the strong: but I will make them suddenly run away from her: and who is a chosen man, that I may appoint over her? for who is like me? and who will appoint me the time? and who is that shepherd that will stand before me? Therefore hear ye the counsel of the LORD, that he hath taken against Babylon; and his purposes, that he hath purposed against the land of the Chaldeans: Surely the least of the flock shall draw them out: surely he shall make their habitation desolate with them. At the noise of the taking of Babylon the earth is moved, and the cry is heard among the nations. (Jeremiah 50:35-46)

The Sword of the LORD (35-46): The LORD will bring His sword against Babylon:
- A Sword is upon the Chaldeans, the inhabitants of Babylon and upon her princes and wise men (35)
- A Sword is upon liars, mighty men (36)
- A Sword is upon their horses, chariots and upon all the mingled people (37)
- A Sword is upon her treasures (37)

The LORD will see to it that Babylon is destroyed, never to rise again (39 -40 cf. Isaiah 13:21). The remainder of these verses point to the historical fall of Babylon to the Persians, and then to the Greeks under Alexander. Notice the king of Babylon's response to hearing of the enemies of the north is similar to that of Belshazzar (vs. 43 cf. Daniel 5:6; Isaiah 45:1).

Thus saith the LORD; Behold, I will raise up against Babylon, and against them that dwell in the midst

of them that rise up against me, a destroying wind; And will send unto Babylon fanners, that shall fan her, and shall empty her land: for in the day of trouble they shall be against her round about. Against him that bendeth let the archer bend his bow, and against him that lifteth himself up in his brigandine: and spare ye not her young men; destroy ye utterly all her host. Thus the slain shall fall in the land of the Chaldeans, and they that are thrust through in her streets. For Israel hath not been forsaken, nor Judah of his God, of the LORD of hosts; though their land was filled with sin against the Holy One of Israel. Flee out of the midst of Babylon, and deliver every man his soul: be not cut off in her iniquity; for this is the time of the LORD'S vengeance; he will render unto her a recompence. Babylon hath been a golden cup in the LORD'S hand, that made all the earth drunken: the nations have drunken of her wine; therefore the nations are mad. Babylon is suddenly fallen and destroyed: howl for her; take balm for her pain, if so be she may be healed. We would have healed Babylon, but she is not healed: forsake her, and let us go every one into his own country: for her judgment reacheth unto heaven, and is lifted up even to the skies. The LORD hath brought forth our righteousness: come, and let us declare in Zion the work of the LORD our God. (Jeremiah 51:1-10)

Flee Out of Babylon (1-10): I know the statement seems redundant, but understanding that the LORD blends prophecy and history together throughout his Word is something all students of Scripture need to have a clear understanding of. When the LORD records prophecy, He has it written in the portion of His Word that is dealing with a historically similar situation. In this case the Jewish people are beginning their 70 years of Babylonian captivity. Following this 70 year captivity, they will come out of Babylon and begin to rebuild the Temple. These historical events are similar to what the LORD will do with His people in the future. Therefore, the LORD has the prophecies concerning this future time recorded in this portion of Scripture, a time that parallels it historically. So then, while the text is historical, it is also very prophetical, especially verses 6-8.

In context, the LORD will call His people out of Babylon; this is the "time of the LORD's vengeance" (6). It is the time in which the LORD will avenge His cause on the earth, and bring destruction to Babylon. The details concerning the prophetic fall of Babylon are recorded in verse eight and Revelation 17 & 18, as is Babylon's making all the nations of the earth drunk with the wine of her fornication (vs. 7 cf. Rev. 17:2, 18:3).

Make bright the arrows; gather the shields: the LORD hath raised up the spirit of the kings of the Medes: for his device is against Babylon, to destroy it; because it is the vengeance of the LORD, the

vengeance of his temple. Set up the standard upon the walls of Babylon, make the watch strong, set up the watchmen, prepare the ambushes: for the LORD hath both devised and done that which he spake against the inhabitants of Babylon. (Jeremiah 51:11-12)

The Historical Destruction of Babylon (11-12): Once again, the historical and prophetical passages of Scripture are mixed together. This is obviously dealing with the historical fall of Babylon by the Medes (and the Persian) Empires (11).

O thou that dwellest upon many waters, abundant in treasures, thine end is come, and the measure of thy covetousness. The LORD of hosts hath sworn by himself, saying, Surely I will fill thee with men, as with caterpillers; and they shall lift up a shout against thee. He hath made the earth by his power, he hath established the world by his wisdom, and hath stretched out the heaven by his understanding. When he uttereth his voice, there is a multitude of waters in the heavens; and he causeth the vapours to ascend from the ends of the earth: he maketh lightnings with rain, and bringeth forth the wind out of his treasures. Every man is brutish by his knowledge; every founder is confounded by the graven image: for his molten image is falsehood, and there is no breath in them. They are vanity, the work of errors: in the time of their visitation they shall perish. (Jeremiah 51:13-18)

The Wisdom of God (13-18): Here Jeremiah compares the "wisdom" and "understanding" of the LORD with the "knowledge" of men. By wisdom the LORD has made the heaven and earth (see Psalm 104; Job 38). The wisdom of the LORD is seen in His creation (Psalm 19), whereas man's knowledge leads him to worshipping idols (17).

The portion of Jacob is not like them; for he is the former of all things: and Israel is the rod of his inheritance: the LORD of hosts is his name. Thou art my battle axe and weapons of war: for with thee will I break in pieces the nations, and with thee will I destroy kingdoms; And with thee will I break in pieces the horse and his rider; and with thee will I break in pieces the chariot and his rider; With thee also will I break in pieces man and woman; and with thee will I break in pieces old and young; and with thee will I break in pieces the young man and the maid; I will also break in pieces with thee the shepherd and his flock; and with thee will I break in pieces the husbandman and his yoke of oxen; and with thee will I break in pieces captains and rulers. And I will render unto Babylon and to all the inhabitants of Chaldea all their evil that they have done in Zion in your sight, saith the LORD. Behold, I am against thee, O destroying mountain, saith the

LORD, which destroyest all the earth: and I will stretch out mine hand upon thee, and roll thee down from the rocks, and will make thee a burnt mountain. And they shall not take of thee a stone for a corner, nor a stone for foundations; but thou shalt be desolate for ever, saith the LORD. (Jeremiah 51:19-26)

The Predicted Desolation of Babylon, the Land of the Chaldeans (19-26): The LORD's judgment upon Babylon is vividly described here:
- I will break in pieces the nations and kingdoms (20)
- I will break in pieces the horse and his rider (21)
- I will break in pieces the chariot and his rider (21)
- I will break in pieces man and woman (22)
- I will break in pieces old and young (22)
- I will break in pieces the young man and maiden (22)
- I will break in pieces the shepherd (23)
- I will break in pieces the husband and the yoke of the oxen (23)
- I will break in pieces captains and rulers (23)

Set ye up a standard in the land, blow the trumpet among the nations, prepare the nations against her, call together against her the kingdoms of Ararat,

Minni, and Ashchenaz; appoint a captain against her; cause the horses to come up as the rough caterpillers. Prepare against her the nations with the kings of the Medes, the captains thereof, and all the rulers thereof, and all the land of his dominion. And the land shall tremble and sorrow: for every purpose of the LORD shall be performed against Babylon, to make the land of Babylon a desolation without an inhabitant. The mighty men of Babylon have forborn to fight, they have remained in their holds: their might hath failed; they became as women: they have burned her dwellingplaces; her bars are broken. One post shall run to meet another, and one messenger to meet another, to shew the king of Babylon that his city is taken at one end, And that the passages are stopped, and the reeds they have burned with fire, and the men of war are affrighted. For thus saith the LORD of hosts, the God of Israel; The daughter of Babylon is like a threshingfloor, it is time to thresh her: yet a little while, and the time of her harvest shall come. (Jeremiah 51:27-33)

Preparing Nations Against Babylon (27-33): The LORD takes nations and moves them at His will. In this case the LORD is moving nations against Babylon to judge them: "Prepare nations against her..." (27), "Prepare against her nations with the kings of the Medes..." (28). Babylon is taken over by the Medes and the Persian Empires.

Nebuchadrezzar the king of Babylon hath devoured me, he hath crushed me, he hath made me an empty vessel, he hath swallowed me up like a dragon, he hath filled his belly with my delicates, he hath cast me out. The violence done to me and to my flesh be upon Babylon, shall the inhabitant of Zion say; and my blood upon the inhabitants of Chaldea, shall Jerusalem say. Therefore thus saith the LORD; Behold, I will plead thy cause, and take vengeance for thee; and I will dry up her sea, and make her springs dry. And Babylon shall become heaps, a dwellingplace for dragons, an astonishment, and an hissing, without an inhabitant. They shall roar together like lions: they shall yell as lions' whelps. In their heat I will make their feasts, and I will make them drunken, that they may rejoice, and sleep a perpetual sleep, and not wake, saith the LORD. I will bring them down like lambs to the slaughter, like rams with he goats. How is Sheshach taken! and how is the praise of the whole earth surprised! how is Babylon become an astonishment among the nations! The sea is come up upon Babylon: she is covered with the multitude of the waves thereof. Her cities are a desolation, a dry land, and a wilderness, a land wherein no man dwelleth, neither doth any son of man pass thereby. And I will punish Bel in Babylon, and I will bring forth out of his mouth that which he hath swallowed up: and the nations shall not flow together any more unto him: yea, the wall of Babylon shall fall. (Jeremiah 51:34-44)

The Future Desolation of Babylon (34-44): Again, these verses are prophetic utterances of the future destruction of Babylon. Babylon will be destroyed and become a "dwellingplace for dragons, an astonishment, and a hissing, without an inhabitant" (37 cf. Isa. 13:19-22 cf. Rev. 18:2). The fall of Babylon will be an epic event: "How is Babylon become an astonishment among the nations!" (41 cf. Rev. 18). The LORD will bring against Babylon the 10 kingdoms under the control of the Antichrist, leaving it to utter destruction (17:15-18). The armies that come against Babylon in the last days are likened to a great flood (42 cf. Rev. 17:1, 15). The final destruction of Babylon will leave only unclean animals in the land (37 cf. Isa. 13:19-24). The fall of Babylon is an astonishment among the nations (41 cf. Rev. 18:1-3), astonishment at how such a mighty nation could be destroyed in one hour (Rev. 18:17-19). Just as Babylon was responsible for the fall of Jerusalem's walls, so now the LORD will see to it that their walls fall[49] (44 cf. 58).

My people, go ye out of the midst of her, and deliver ye every man his soul from the fierce anger of the LORD. And lest your heart faint, and ye fear for the rumour that shall be heard in the land; a rumour

---

[49] The outer walls of Babylon were 25 feet thick, towering 320 feet over the city. The top of the walls of Babylon were so thick chariots would race six wide.

shall both come one year, and after that in another year shall come a rumour, and violence in the land, ruler against ruler. Therefore, behold, the days come, that I will do judgment upon the graven images of Babylon: and her whole land shall be confounded, and all her slain shall fall in the midst of her. Then the heaven and the earth, and all that is therein, shall sing for Babylon: for the spoilers shall come unto her from the north, saith the LORD. As Babylon hath caused the slain of Israel to fall, so at Babylon shall fall the slain of all the earth. Ye that have escaped the sword, go away, stand not still: remember the LORD afar off, and let Jerusalem come into your mind. We are confounded, because we have heard reproach: shame hath covered our faces: for strangers are come into the sanctuaries of the LORD'S house. Wherefore, behold, the days come, saith the LORD, that I will do judgment upon her graven images: and through all her land the wounded shall groan. Though Babylon should mount up to heaven, and though she should fortify the height of her strength, yet from me shall spoilers come unto her, saith the LORD. A sound of a cry cometh from Babylon, and great destruction from the land of the Chaldeans: Because the LORD hath spoiled Babylon, and destroyed out of her the great voice; when her waves do roar like great waters, a noise of their voice is uttered: Because the spoiler is come upon her, even upon Babylon, and her mighty men are taken, every one of their bows is broken: for the LORD God of recompences shall surely requite. And I will make drunk her princes, and her wise men, her captains, and her rulers, and her mighty men: and they shall sleep a perpetual sleep, and not wake, saith the King, whose name is the LORD of hosts. Thus saith the LORD of hosts; The broad walls of Babylon shall be utterly broken, and her high gates shall be burned with fire; and the people shall labour in vain, and the folk in the fire, and they shall be weary. (Jeremiah 51:45-58)

The Recompense of Babylon (45-58): The LORD will bring upon Babylon all they have done to the Jewish people when taking Jerusalem: "As Babylon hath caused the slain of Israel to fall, so at Babylon shall fall the slain of all the earth" (49 cf. 56). The LORD will call out those that escaped the destruction of Jerusalem and went into Babylonian captivity, prior to the city being judged (51-53). And as the spoiler came upon Jerusalem, so the LORD will see to it that the spoiler of Babylon will come and recompense upon them all they have done to Jerusalem (54-56); their gates will fuel the fires of the city (58). A prophetic glimpse at the final destruction of Babylon is hinted at in verse 57.

The word which Jeremiah the prophet commanded Seraiah the son of Neriah, the son of Maaseiah, when he went with Zedekiah the king of Judah into Babylon in the fourth year of his reign. And this Seraiah was a quiet prince. So Jeremiah wrote in a

book all the evil that should come upon Babylon, even all these words that are written against Babylon. And Jeremiah said to Seraiah, When thou comest to Babylon, and shalt see, and shalt read all these words; Then shalt thou say, O LORD, thou hast spoken against this place, to cut it off, that none shall remain in it, neither man nor beast, but that it shall be desolate for ever. And it shall be, when thou hast made an end of reading this book, that thou shalt bind a stone to it, and cast it into the midst of Euphrates: And thou shalt say, Thus shall Babylon sink, and shall not rise from the evil that I will bring upon her: and they shall be weary. Thus far are the words of Jeremiah. (Jeremiah 51:59-64)

The Final Words of Jeremiah (59-64): The book of Jeremiah basically concludes with this chapter; chapter 52 is a historical account of the final siege of the city and capture of Zedekiah. Jeremiah wrote in a book about all the evil that is recorded in these chapters concerning Babylon. He then gave the book to Seraiah, the messenger of Zedekiah, and commanded Seraiah to read all the words concerning Babylon's fate in Babylon. Then Jeremiah commanded Seraiah to take the book and bind it to a stone, and cast it into the midst of the Euphrates, and say, "Thus, shall Babylon sink, and shall not rise from the evil that I will bring upon her: and they shall be weary" (61-64). The words of this prophecy look to the final day when Babylon falls, never to rise again:

And there followed another angel, saying, Babylon is fallen, is fallen, that great city, because she made all nations drink of the wine of the wrath of her fornication. **(Revelation 14:8)**

CHAPTER FIFTY-TWO
Historical fall of Jerusalem

Zedekiah was one and twenty years old when he began to reign, and he reigned eleven years in Jerusalem. And his mother's name was Hamutal the daughter of Jeremiah of Libnah. And he did that which was evil in the eyes of the LORD, according to all that Jehoiakim had done. For through the anger of the LORD it came to pass in Jerusalem and Judah, till he had cast them out from his presence, that Zedekiah rebelled against the king of Babylon. (Jeremiah 52:1-3)

The Rebellion of Zedekiah (1-3): This last chapter of Jeremiah is a historical account of the events surrounding the fall of Jerusalem. These events are also recorded in 2 Kings 24:18-30 -25:30. All of Jeremiah's preaching has been leading to this historical event. The fall of Jerusalem is not only a historical climax for the Jewish people, but it also marks a very important time, prophetically speaking. It is the event that marks the "times of the Gentiles."

The Babylonian captivity and the destruction of Jerusalem mark the beginning of a time of Gentile power, when those nations will rule over God's people, until the "times of the Gentiles be fulfilled." Once this time is fulfilled, the God of heaven will establish His Kingdom, displacing all Gentile rule and authority (Dan. 2:31-45). This remaining portion of Jeremiah is a detailed account of the events surrounding this climax: the fall of Jerusalem and ensuing Babylonian captivity.

Zedekiah was an evil ruler, he did that which was evil in the eyes of the LORD (2). Zedekiah, not willing to obey the prophesying of Jeremiah and other prophets, refused to submit to the authority of the king of Babylon. Zedekiah tried playing the fence between loyalty to Egypt and Babylon. He made a promise before the LORD to be submissive to Nebuchadnezzar, but turned away and sought alliance with Egypt. God holds him accountable for this, and as a result, brings in the final destruction of Jerusalem (2 Chron. 36:11-13 cf. Jer. 21 cf. 2 Kings 24:20).

And it came to pass in the ninth year of his reign, in the tenth month, in the tenth day of the month, that Nebuchadrezzar king of Babylon came, he and all his army, against Jerusalem, and pitched against it, and built forts against it round about. So the city was besieged unto the eleventh year of king

Zedekiah. And in the fourth month, in the ninth day of the month, the famine was sore in the city, so that there was no bread for the people of the land. Then the city was broken up, and all the men of war fled, and went forth out of the city by night by the way of the gate between the two walls, which was by the king's garden; (now the Chaldeans were by the city round about:) and they went by the way of the plain. (Jeremiah 52:4-7)

The Walls Are Breached (4-7): The invasion of the Babylonians armies is recorded in 2 Kings 25; 2 Chronicles 36:11-21; and Jeremiah 39:1-14, 52:1-34. The famine experienced by those who refused to surrender to the Babylonians was horrific. The people had resorted to cannibalism (6 cf. Lamentations).

But the army of the Chaldeans pursued after the king, and overtook Zedekiah in the plains of Jericho; and all his army was scattered from him. Then they took the king, and carried him up unto the king of Babylon to Riblah in the land of Hamath; where he gave judgment upon him. And the king of Babylon slew the sons of Zedekiah before his eyes: he slew also all the princes of Judah in Riblah. Then he put out the eyes of Zedekiah; and the king of Babylon bound him in chains, and carried him to Babylon, and put him in prison till the day of his death. (Jeremiah 52:8-11)

The Death of the Sons of Zedekiah and His Deportation to Babylon (8-11): These events have been commented on extensively in chapter 39 of Jeremiah. Basically, taking out Zedekiah's eyes at Riblah once he beholds Nebuchadnezzar, and his deportation to Babylon, fulfills both Jeremiah's and Ezekiel's prophecies (Ezek. 12:13 cf. Jer. 32:1-5 cf. Jer. 39:4-7).

Now in the fifth month, in the tenth day of the month, which was the nineteenth year of Nebuchadrezzar king of Babylon, came Nebuzaradan, captain of the guard, which served the king of Babylon, into Jerusalem, And burned the house of the LORD, and the king's house; and all the houses of Jerusalem, and all the houses of the great men, burned he with fire: And all the army of the Chaldeans, that were with the captain of the guard, brake down all the walls of Jerusalem round about. Then Nebuzaradan the captain of the guard carried away captive certain of the poor of the people, and the residue of the people that remained in the city, and those that fell away, that fell to the king of Babylon, and the rest of the multitude. But Nebuzaradan the captain of the guard left certain of the poor of the land for vinedressers and for husbandmen. Also the pillars of brass that were in the house of the LORD, and the bases, and the brasen sea that was in the house of the LORD, the Chaldeans brake, and carried all the brass of them to Babylon. The caldrons also, and the shovels, and the snuffers, and the bowls, and the spoons, and all the vessels of brass wherewith they ministered, took they away. And the basons, and the firepans, and the bowls, and the caldrons, and the candlesticks, and the spoons, and the cups; that which was of gold in gold, and that which was of silver in silver, took the captain of the guard away. The two pillars, one sea, and twelve brasen bulls that were under the bases, which king Solomon had made in the house of the LORD: the brass of all these vessels was without weight. And concerning the pillars, the height of one pillar was eighteen cubits; and a fillet of twelve cubits did compass it; and the thickness thereof was four fingers: it was hollow. And a chapiter of brass was upon it; and the height of one chapiter was five cubits, with network and pomegranates upon the chapiters round about, all of brass. The second pillar also and the pomegranates were like unto these. And there were ninety and six pomegranates on a side; and all the pomegranates upon the network were an hundred round about. (Jeremiah 52:12-23)

The Spoils of War (12-23): The plundering of the wealth of the city is recorded here. Any items of value were deported to Babylon. The Ark of the Covenant is not listed among the items taken, which leads to all the mystery surrounding its whereabouts. Nebuchadnezzar's armies leave the poor and unskilled in the land as vinedressers and husbandman (16). These will make up the people group known as the Samaritans of the New Testament.

And the captain of the guard took Seraiah the chief priest, and Zephaniah the second priest, and the three keepers of the door: He took also out of the city an eunuch, which had the charge of the men of war; and seven men of them that were near the king's person, which were found in the city; and the principal scribe of the host, who mustered the people of the land; and threescore men of the people of the land, that were found in the midst of the city. So Nebuzaradan the captain of the guard took them, and brought them to the king of Babylon to Riblah. And the king of Babylon smote them, and put them to death in Riblah in the land of Hamath. Thus Judah was carried away captive out of his own land. This is the people whom Nebuchadrezzar carried away captive: in the seventh year three thousand Jews and three and twenty: In the eighteenth year of Nebuchadrezzar he carried away captive from Jerusalem eight hundred thirty and two persons: In the three and twentieth year of Nebuchadrezzar Nebuzaradan the captain of the guard carried away captive of the Jews seven hundred forty and five persons: all the persons were four thousand and six hundred. (Jeremiah 52:24-30)

Death and Deportation of the People (24-30): The leadership which led the people and king astray are put to death before Nebuchadnezzar at Riblah (25-27). Verses 28-30 are a list of the three deportations of the people:
- In the 7th year- 3,023 Jewish captives (28)
- In the 8th year- 832 Jewish captives (29)
- In the 23rd year- 745 Jewish captives (30)

And it came to pass in the seven and thirtieth year of the captivity of Jehoiachin king of Judah, in the twelfth month, in the five and twentieth day of the month, that Evilmerodach king of Babylon in the first year of his reign lifted up the head of Jehoiachin king of Judah, and brought him forth out of prison, And spake kindly unto him, and set his throne above the throne of the kings that were with him in Babylon, And changed his prison garments: and he did continually eat bread before him all the days of his life. And for his diet, there was a continual diet given him of the king of Babylon, every day a portion until the day of his death, all the days of his life. (Jeremiah 52:31-34)

Jehoiachin (31-34): Jehoiachin, king of Judah, was taken captive by Nebuchadnezzar and replaced with Zedekiah, prior to the final siege of Jerusalem. He was in prison in Babylon throughout the destruction of Jerusalem. After 37 years in prison, Evil-merodach, the current Babylonian king releases him and gives him a distinguished place of leadership (2 Kings 25:27). His reign and life were cut short by a conspiracy, headed by Neriglissar, his sister's husband, who succeeded him.

CONCLUSION

The book of Jeremiah is the history of Judah during the reign of its last five kings (Josiah, Jehoahaz, Jehoiakim, Jehoiachin and Zedekiah). Jeremiah is prophesying within the walls of Jerusalem during all three sieges of the city. He was an eye witness to what war does to a people. He had seen the horrific famine, and the impact it had on him earned him the title "the weeping prophet."

Jeremiah's ministry was to proclaim to the kings of Judah the people to submit and surrender to the coming Babylonians if they wanted to survive; showing to them the way of life and the way of death. If they surrendered they would live; if they resisted they would die. The people chose death. The LORD had promised to preserve Jeremiah's life, and for him to survive three different sieges shows that the LORD was faithful in doing so.

The value of the book of Jeremiah is similar to other pre-exile prophets in that they record the events surrounding one of the most historically important events in all the scriptures, the fall of Jerusalem. This event marks the beginning of the "times of the

Gentiles" (Luke 21:24). It is the fall of Jerusalem that starts the prophetic calendar in motion, until the establishment of the LORD's Kingdom (Jer. 29:10 cf. Daniel 2). So while portions of this book seem gloomy and dismal, Jeremiah points to a time when the LORD will come and avenge Israel of her enemies and remove their sins, cleanse the land, and establish His Kingdom forever:

> *Behold, the days come, saith the LORD, that I will make a new covenant with the house of Israel, and with the house of Judah: Not according to the covenant that I made with their fathers in the day that I took them by the hand to bring them out of the land of Egypt; which my covenant they brake, although I was an husband unto them, saith the LORD: But this shall be the covenant that I will make with the house of Israel; After those days, saith the LORD, I will put my law in their inward parts, and write it in their hearts; and will be their God, and they shall be my people. And they shall teach no more every man his neighbour, and every man his brother, saying, Know the LORD: for they shall all know me, from the least of them unto the greatest of them, saith the LORD: for I will forgive their iniquity, and I will remember their sin no more.* (Jeremiah 31:31-34)

Bibliography

Wiersbe, Warren W. The Bible Exposition Commentary, Prophets. Colorado Springs: Cook Communications Ministries, 2002.

Josephus, Flavius. The Works of Flavius Josephus, Volume III. Grand Rapids: Baker Book House, 1974.

Keller, Werner. The Bible As History. New York: Bantam, 1982.

Jeremiah & Lamentations: An Expositional Commentary. CD-ROM, 2000. Dr. Chuck Missler

www.ingramcontent.com/pod-product-compliance
Lightning Source LLC
Chambersburg PA
CBHW071300110426
42743CB00042B/1118